KING OF THE FRENCH

Louis Philippe

King of the French

A PORTRAIT OF LOUIS PHILIPPE

1773–1850

by

Agnes de Stoeckl

JOHN MURRAY
FIFTY ALBEMARLE STREET
LONDON

First published 1957

Printed in Great Britain by
Butler & Tanner Ltd., Frome and London
and published by John Murray (Publishers) Ltd.

I DEDICATE THIS BOOK
WITH HIS PERMISSION TO MY KIND FRIEND
SIR JOHN MURRAY
K.C.V.O., D.S.O.

He was a Prince, I made him a man.
He was dull, I made him clever.
He was insipid, I brought him to life.
He was a coward, I made him brave.
He was mean, I never succeeded in making him generous.
Munificent certainly, generous—No!

FELICITÉ DE GENLIS

Contents

CONTENTS

Illustrations

* *In the Musée Condé, Chantilly. By permission of E.N.A.*

† *By permission of Marceau Carrière, Niort.*

Acknowledgments

I would like to express my most grateful thanks to Mrs. Elizabeth Hollings-Bap, who for over two years, almost daily, has worked with me on this book. Being a Frenchwoman, her love of France is as great as mine, and it has been a joy for us to recapture the nature and the era of Louis Philippe, King of the French.

I also wish to thank Mr. Wilfrid Edwards for his kindness in revising this book, and M. Jean Bap for his bibliographical research at the Bibliothèque Nationale in Paris.

Thirdly, I wish to thank myself for having lived long enough to end *King of the French* at the age of eighty-three.

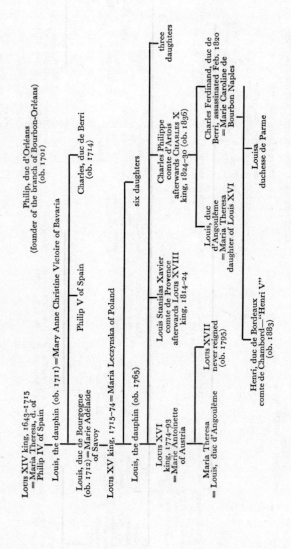

LOUIS XIV king, 1643–1715
= Maria Theresa, d. of
Philip IV of Spain

Philip, duc d'Orléans
(founder of the branch of Bourbon-Orléans)
(ob. 1701)

Louis, the dauphin (ob. 1711) = Mary Anne Christine Victoire of Bavaria

Louis, duc de Bourgogne
(ob. 1712) = Marie Adélaide
of Savoy

Philip V of Spain

Charles, duc de Berri
(ob. 1714)

LOUIS XV king, 1715–74 = Maria Leczynska of Poland

Louis, the dauphin (ob. 1765)

six daughters

LOUIS XVI
king, 1774–93
= Marie Antoinette
of Austria

Louis Stanislas Xavier
comte de Provence
afterwards LOUIS XVIII
king, 1814–24

Charles Philippe
comte d'Artois
afterwards CHARLES X
king, 1824–30 (ob. 1836)

three
daughters

Maria Theresa
= Louis, duc d'Angoulême

LOUIS XVII
never reigned
(ob. 1795)

Louis, duc
d'Angoulême
= Maria Theresa
daughter of Louis XVI

Charles Ferdinand, duc de
Berri, assassinated Feb. 1820
= Marie Caroline de
Bourbon Naples

Henri, duc de Bordeaux
comte de Chambord—"Henri V"
(ob. 1883)

Louisa
duchesse de Parme

Philippe, duc d'Orléans, younger son of king Louis XIII (ob. 1701)
=1. Henrietta Maria, d. of Charles I of England
=2. Charlotte Elizabeth, d. of Charles, elector palatine

1. Maria Louisa
=Charles II, king of Spain

2. Philippe, duc d'Orléans, regent of France (ob. 1723)

Philippe Louis (ob. 1752)

Louis Philippe (ob. 1785)
=Louisa Henrietta, d. of Armand, prince de Conti

Louis Philippe, duc d'Orléans ("Egalité") (b. 1747; ob. 1793)
=Louise Marie Adélaïde of Bourbon, d. of duc de Penthièvre

Louis Philippe, duc d'Orléans
king of the French, 1830–48
(b. 6 Oct. 1773; ob. 26 Aug. 1850)
=Marie Amélie, d. of
Ferdinand IV of Naples
(b. 26 April 1782)

Antoine, duc de Montpensier
(ob. 1807)

Adélaïde, Mademoiselle d'Orléans

Alphonse, comte de Beaujolais
(ob. 1808)

Ferdinand
duc d'Orléans
(b. 1810; ob. 1842)
=Hélène Louise,
duchess of
Mecklemburg
Schwerin

Louise Marie
Thérèse
queen of the
Belgians
(b. 1812; ob. 1850)

Louis Charles
duc de Nemours
(b. 1814; ob. 1859)
=Victoire
princess of
Saxe-Coburg

Marie-Christine
(b. 1813; ob. 1839)
=Prince Frederick
of Würtemberg

Marie-Clementine
(b. 1817; ob. 1907)
=Augustus
prince of Saxe-
Coburg-Gotha

François
prince de Joinville
(b. 1818; ob. 1906)
=Françoise
princess of
Braganza

Henri
duc d'Aumale
(b. 1822; ob. 1897)
=Caroline
princess
of Naples

Antoine, duc de
Montpensier
(b. 1824; ob. 1890)
=Maria Luisa
Infanta of Spain

1. Ferdinand
(b. 30 May 1859)
2. Four daughters

Louis Philippe
comte de Paris
(b. 24 Aug. 1838)

Robert
duc de Chartres
(b. 9 Nov. 1840)

Louis
comte d'Eu
(b. 28 April 1842)

Ferdinand
duc d'Alençon
(b. 12 July 1844)

two
daughters

1. Pierre
duc de Penthièvre
(b. 4 Nov. 1845)
2. A daughter

Louis Philippe
prince de Condé
(b. 15 Nov. 1845)

François
duc de Guise
(b. 5 Jan. 1854)

Prologue

There is a strange story—could it be true?—that the son of an Italian gaoler sat on the throne of France.

This is the story:

In the last weeks of the year 1772, a travelling coach drew up outside the inn of the small mountain town of Modigliani in Tuscany. From it stepped a man of about twenty-five, and a young woman whose pale features, dark-rimmed eyes, and heavy gait denoted a state of pregnancy. They announced their intention of remaining at the inn for several weeks, and gave their names as the Comte and Comtesse de Joinville. Neither the landlord, nor indeed any of those who were to take part in this extraordinary story, would ever know that the man was in reality Louis Philippe Joseph, Duc de Chartres, eldest son and heir of the powerful Duc d'Orléans, cousin of the King Louis XV, and Prince of the Royal Blood of France. He was travelling with his wife, Marie Adélaïde de Penthièvre, a great grand-daughter of Louis XIV and his famous mistress, the Marquise de Montespan.

They had been married for four years, and the Duc, who was deeply ambitious and not overburdened with scruples, was determined to have a male heir. Already at that time he was looking to the future. His aim was to become a power in France, which would impose its will upon the Kingdom and even upon the King. He intended to hoist himself to this position on the shoulders of the lower classes, by allowing them to believe that he wished to become their equal.

Soon he became friendly with the villagers of Modigliani and, in particular, with the gaoler, whose name was Lorenzo Chiappini. This man's wife was in the same state of pregnancy as the Duchesse, and the story goes that the Duc connived with him that, should the Duchesse give birth to a girl, and the gaoler's wife to a boy, an exchange would be made.

The woman Chiappini was won over to the plan when she heard that it would bring them a large sum of money—but how

1

was the Duchesse brought to consent to this deed? That will never be known. The story only relates that on the night of 17th April 1773, a new-born baby girl was carried to the prison, and a boy was brought back to the inn. This boy was taken to Paris and kept hidden until the day of his "official" birth, 6th October 1773. He was given the name Louis Philippe.

The little princess, ignorant of her royal parentage, grew up in the prison quarters of Modigliani under the name of Maria Stella Petronilla Chiappini. Already at a very early age she felt isolated. She wondered what it was which kept her apart from the intimacy of that family. The other children despised her for her small feet and delicate skin. The mother hated her. She knew that the great difference between Maria Stella and her other children was a cause of gossip in the village, and that a rumour was going around that the virtue of La Signora Chiappini was not beyond suspicion.

One day, Lord Newborough, a wealthy English nobleman, passing through the village, stopped at the Chiappini's door to ask the way. Maria Stella appeared, and he was so struck by her beauty that he asked her to marry him.

At first she refused; his manner, his dress, his large equipage, even the haughty coachman, frightened her. He, however, announced that he would delay his journey until he could take her with him as his bride.

That night, in the bed which she shared with two of her sisters, she lay awake, thinking. If she accepted, it would mean leaving all this unhappiness. The next morning she told Lord Newborough that she would be his wife.

So he brought her to England, where, from being a small unwanted girl, she became a great lady. Some years later, after her husband's death, she married a Russian, Baron Ungern-Sternberg, who took her to St. Petersburg. There again she lived lavishly, but ever conscious of her humble birth. It was known that she was the daughter of a gaoler in a small Italian village, and although the world in which she moved now appeared to have forgotten this, yet in her heart she knew that Society never forgets.

Then she heard of Chiappini's death. She received the news with only a momentary regret. The old man had not been unkind to her, but he had been a part of the life which she hated. Yet that life had not finished with Maria Stella. One morning a letter was handed to her, and with a shock she recognized his handwriting:

Miladi,

I have come to the end of my days, without having revealed to a living soul a secret which concerns only you and myself.

The day you were born, of a person whom I cannot name, and who has already passed to another world, a son was born to me.

I was asked to exchange the children and, considering my fortune at the time, I consented to the proposition. It was then that I adopted you as my daughter, and in the same manner my son was adopted by the other party.

I see that Heaven has condoned my sin, as you are now in a better position and condition than your true father, although he was almost of the same rank; and this is what helps to make the end of my life a little peaceful.

Keep this to yourself, so that I shall not be thought totally guilty. Yes, in asking your pardon for my fault, I ask you to keep it hidden, to prevent the world from talking over an affair without cure.

This letter will be sent to you after my death.

LORENZO CHIAPPINI

That letter ruined Maria Stella's life. In her obsession to find the key to her history, she abandoned her husband, her home, her friends, to set out on an endless quest.

By dint of questioning and knocking at every door, she finally obtained the certainty that she was the daughter of the Comte de Joinville, a French nobleman, but about whom she had no further details.

This gave her the courage to go on, and in the year 1823 she left for France. She went straight to Joinville, certain that there in her father's country, she would find the truth.

She discovered the estate to have been an ancient "appanage" of the Royal House of Orléans, and that the late Duc ("Egalité"), executed during the Revolution, had used this title when travelling abroad.

Maria Stella went to Paris and tried by every means to contact the boy born in Modigliani who was by then Louis Philippe, Duc d'Orléans and head of the family. Finally she announced in the newspapers that the Baronne de Sternberg desired to make a most important communication to the heirs of the Comte de Joinville.

Soon this paragraph reached Louis Philippe who, although so far he had ignored Maria Stella, wondered whether there might be in this some advantage to himself. He sent for the old Abbé de St. Phare, an illegitimate uncle, and asked him to interview the Baroness. The Duc and his emissary soon discovered that Maria Stella's disclosure meant not receiving but giving; and then the doors of his palace were closed more rigorously to her than ever.

Frustrated, she returned to Italy in search of further proofs, and obtained a judgment by the Tribunal of Faenza on 29th May 1824, establishing her claim to be the daughter of the Comte de Joinville.

In 1830, when Louis Philippe mounted the throne as King of the French, she was ordered to leave France, but the British Ambassador intervened several times on her behalf.

Tribunals refused to listen to her, and finally it was given out that she was insane. She used to feed a great number of birds, and they would fly to her windows from every tree in the neighbouring Tuileries. This gave some semblance of truth to the rumours, but the very opposite is recorded by many who knew her well.

She was a clever and brilliant woman. She never abandoned her rights, and always signed as La Baronne de Sternberg *née* Joinville. She died in 1843, having maintained her claim to the end; her name is mentioned in the British Peerage as "presumed daughter of the Duc d'Orléans".

Perhaps I have given too much importance to this improbable tale, but it created much talk at the time, and a good deal of discussion in diplomatic circles.

For the King it was a source of anxiety, and it must have been a relief to many when poor Maria Stella, after endless struggles and disappointments, at last lay at peace.

Note. L. Michaud's *Biographie de Louis Philippe* consulted for Prologue.

The Boy Prince and his Father's Mistress

Louis Philippe, according to the Almanach Royal, was born on 6th October 1773. The old king Louis XV still sat on the throne, though worn out by a life of pleasure and self-indulgence: his grandson, the future Louis XVI, had just married the beautiful Austrian Archduchess, Marie Antoinette.

Numberless courtiers still filled Versailles, dressed in gorgeous brocades and velvet, and the ladies preened in their monumental headdresses, their gold and silver, their laces and feathers. Over all hovered an aura of scented powder and of whispered intrigue, in the enchanting surroundings where Madame du Barri exercised her magic power.

But in a few brief months the scene would change, the King would be dead, and his celebrated mistress would have passed into oblivion, to re-emerge only once more, twenty years later, on her way to the guillotine.

The philosophers, encyclopaedists and economists had already begun to awaken the political ambition of the middle class. Disaffection was abroad, the bitter tongue of Voltaire had reached the oppressed peasants, and amongst the needy and destitute of the cities the first murmurs of discontent could be heard.

The small prince knew nothing of all this as he lay in his cradle.

He was given the name of Louis Philippe.

On the day of his birth the infant was merely "ondoyé" (a temporary baptism in the Catholic Church) very privately, by the chaplain of the royal household, in the presence of the vicar of the parish and two valets. The official christening took place twelve years later at Versailles. As far as is known, none of the usual protocol or ceremonies which accompany the birth of a royal prince were carried out on this occasion. This unusual omission later added much strength to the tale of Maria Stella.

Whether Louis Philippe was the son of a gaoler or of the Duc de Chartres, he was brought up with the care and honour due to his presumed rank of heir to all the power of the House of Orléans.

When he was four years old, a very great event took place in his life, although he could hardly have realized it at the time. The birth of his sister Adélaïde, the mentor of his future existence.

*   *   *

It was the day of the Feast of St. Louis, and the sun had parched the early dew as the people awoke to the sound of the bells of the innumerable churches, calling to one another in deep booming tones, and answering in clear rapid scales of sound, cascading in wild confusion, sending forth a message of faith and joy.

To the good people of Paris this was a religious festival, and also a great popular holiday. In the narrow streets, dressed up in their finest clothes, they thronged towards the places which had been thrown open for their enjoyment. The great attraction was the Château des Tuileries, where the gardens had been opened to the public.

The women in their pretty muslin caps and bonnets "en marmotte", or "à la finette", walked about with their children, small girls so fresh and healthy in their little white fichus, and simple frocks showing frilled petticoats.

The humbler mothers gazed with envy at the fashionable ladies, their ample panniered gowns allowing a glimpse of small buckled shoes made of the finest leather of different colours, the high heels encrusted with a line of emeralds, a style which was named "Come and See".

These aristocratic ladies would be accompanied by their families, the girls in a camisole of Indian taffeta, with hooped dresses, and on their heads a bonnet with double frills; the young lords strutting about in their coats of summer quilt

6

ornamented with bands of painted linen, playing the gallant with a toque surmounted by a pouf decorated with feathers and a large bunch of flowers in the middle.

Pedlars were trying to sell combs, scissors, laces; trade was brisk, too, for the herb-water man, carrying on his back a large barrel covered in calico, shaded by a dais of feathers; he was quickly surrounded as he turned a tap, shaped like the neck of a swan, and poured his rather tepid drink into four or five glasses which hung from his neck on little steel chains. The heat was overwhelming, but the fun went on.[1]

Inside the Palais Royal, the residence of the Orléans family, the scene was different. There also the crowds were filling the gardens, shouting, singing and ravaging her lawns and lovely flower-beds. In a room with windows tightly shut to muffle the noise, the Duchesse de Chartres was giving birth to twin daughters, the Princesses Adélaïde and Louise. But the noise could not be muffled; the populace intended to amuse themselves. The household had hoped that, when dusk fell, the people would disperse and make their way to the fireworks, but a few old men with their violins mingled with the crowd and started playing dance tunes. At once the fireworks were forgotten and hundreds of feet began to thump in the garden and yard in wild dances.

The Duchesse's labour had been difficult; the twin princesses were born with bruised and crushed feet. This caused great distress to the Duchesse, but in a few weeks all trace of this had disappeared.

A year later, when Louis Philippe was five years old, he was taken out of the hands of his nurses and given a tutor, the Chevalier Bonnard, poet and libertine, who certainly could not have taken much trouble with an infant of that age, or enriched the child's nature with moral sense. He remained three years with his pupil, and finally left, having displeased the Comtesse de Genlis, one of the Duchesse's ladies, who in a very short time, had become the supreme authority in the Chartres household.

Felicité de Genlis was extremely attractive, pretty, clever, witty and, above all, ambitious.

[1] *Adélaïde d'Orléans*, by Raoul Arnaud. Librairie Académique Perrin.

She was the daughter of the Marquis de St. Aubin. The family was not wealthy, but of noble descent. When she was about twelve years old, they moved to Paris where the Marquise hoped to gain a footing in Society, and eventually to be received at Court—perhaps to be noticed by the King. She did not concern herself much about her daughter, yet even at that early age Felicité craved for celebrity.

Since the age of eight, she had read anything that fell her way, but now she determined to educate herself thoroughly. Her great wish had always been to instruct others and, even before they left their château, the child used to stand on the terrace, gather all the children of the village around her, and teach or preach to them.

Her parents never interfered in her choice of books. Once a friend approached her father to warn him about the literature his daughter was devouring. The Marquis answered, "Why not? A young girl must know life, or else how can she defend herself from the sensuality of the courtiers?"

Felicité loved music. She observed that the harp was played by all the great ladies whom she hoped to emulate, so she chose that instrument and decided to outshine them all. In a short time she showed such talent, that it was not uncommon to see this small girl playing her harp in some of the select salons of Paris, impressing even the most cynical of the guests.

When she was about sixteen, suitors appeared, but never seemed to persist. It may have been the lack of a dowry, or her mother's frivolous mode of life.

At last, one day, she was able to infatuate the Comte de Genlis, a young officer. His family were wealthy but, being a younger son, he could not afford to marry a girl who had even less fortune than himself. Knowing that their union would not be allowed, they eloped.

Later they were forgiven, and the Comte's rich uncle, the Marquis de Puissieux, was so enthralled by Felicité's charm that he presented her at Versailles. Immediately she became a success, and was soon appointed lady-in-waiting to the Duchesse de Chartres, mother to the young Louis Philippe.

Etiquette, at that time, was so important that it almost paralysed life. Some of the great families objected to entering the Court of the Duchesse de Chartres as she was "not of the royal family" but only the daughter of the Duc de Penthièvre, an illegitimate grandson of Louis XIV. So when pretty Madame de Genlis appeared, Madame de Montesson, her aunt, had no difficulty in getting her accepted in the Chartres household. She played her part well, and in a short time made herself indispensable to the Duchesse.

Soon her personality entranced the Duc, and she became his mistress. The Duchesse was blind to this for a long time, and personally implored her to undertake the education of her daughter, Princess Adélaïde. Madame de Genlis tells us in her memoirs that one evening the Duc de Chartres, who was sitting with her, confided in her that he was in despair at the manner in which his two elder sons were being brought up. That very day, he said, Louis Philippe had flown into his room shouting, "Oh, Papa, Montpensier est un cochon!" and Montpensier, his brother, had replied, "Moi, je m'en f . . ."

She adds, "I laughed but he, with tears in his eyes, said 'No, ma chère amie, it is too sad. You must find me a tutor.' He objected to all the names I mentioned, so I said in jest, 'Well, why not I?'

"To my astonishment, he jumped at it, and said, 'Of course, you are the ONE . . . but you cannot be governess to the Princes of France; you will become their Governor.' "

A few days later, when the Duc sought permission of Louis XVI for this appointment, the King, shocked that the education of children of the royal blood should be put into such hands, answered, "Governess or Governor, you may do as you please; fortunately, I have children, and so has my brother the Comte d'Artois" (the future Charles X). With this contemptuous permission, Madame de Genlis was created Governor to the children of the Duc de Chartres.

Immediately, the scheming brain of the new Governor set to work, as she sat in the lovely drawing-room which the Duc, in his infatuation, had furnished for her with priceless works of art. She realized that her hold over her lover was now complete, but she had not the position in the eyes of the world that goes with power. What was lacking?

At that moment, there was a gentle tap on the door. Still

thinking deeply, she rose and called out "Entrez", and the Duchesse walked in with outstretched hands. "Chère amie," she said, "I have come to thank you for all you are doing for my children."

At that moment the Governor knew the answer to her riddle —the mother of her pupils must go, and she reign alone.

*   *   *

The Duchesse de Chartres, to prove her affection and admiration for Madame de Genlis, gave a large dinner party at the Palais Royal in her honour. It was to be a public acknowledgment of her gratitude for the so-called devotion of Madame de Genlis in giving up her life to the royal children.

The Dinner took place in the great oval dining-room. Thirty guests were invited. The fashion for large centre pieces had passed; so had the later one of plastering the tablecloth with clay and sticking flowers in it. Now a more refined, if quaint and costly mode, prevailed. The sandman, a special artist, traced on the table a most complicated and ingenious design with multi-coloured powdered marble, crushed glass and breadcrumbs.

The dishes were sparse; the guests were supposed just to taste the food. It was not considered seemly to be hungry. The great thing was to hasten to leave the table to prove one's lack of appetite.

In the great white and gold salon, to which, after dinner, the guests repaired, it was not etiquette to sit on the sofas spread invitingly in different corners, or on the heavy gilt armchairs, but one sat on low upholstered stools.

Women, powdered, almost weighed down by elaborate headdresses, their ample gowns trimmed with bunches of flowers, frills, garlands, and cascades of pearls and precious stones, sat round a large table covered with a green cloth. They "parfilaient" or sewed small objects in gold and silver thread, while the men stood behind them, wearing dark "fracs" in the English fashion, carrying two watches and many rings.

The conversation was gay and witty. The society of the

Palais Royal blended the tone of the ancient Court with the new manner which was creeping in, of light laughter, mockery and frivolity, with a disdain for austerity.[1]

At that time the Palais Royal was the fashionable rendezvous of all Paris. Built in the year 1629 by the celebrated architect Lemercier for Cardinal de Richelieu, it was called the "Palais Cardinal", but in 1636 it became the property of the State, and the name changed to "Palais Royal".

During the next two centuries it was considerably enlarged. The famous glass-fronted gallery, the Galerie d'Orléans, was added in 1820, replacing an old wooden structure, which was supposed to be infested with rats.

When it was known that the old gallery was to be destroyed, thousands of people turned up, some from as far as St. Germain, with baskets of food, children and sewing; some even settled down in front of the gallery the night before the event, so as to have the best view—all to witness the deluge of panic-stricken rats. People were a little apprehensive, and yet as excited as if about to witness a royal procession.

As the old structure came crashing down, the women clutched their babies in their arms in expectant terror; there was an awful hush. Not a rat was to be seen. The disappointment was such that cries of anger and frustration were heard, and there was an uproar, which had to be quelled by the royal guards.

Soon gamblers and "apaches" met in the new gallery and created a den of scandal, but although known for its bad repute, no one dared to interfere, until at last it became a centre for dangerous intrigue. It was finally closed in 1834.

The Palais retained its old-world charm, with its different galleries lined with renowned shops—jewellers, milliners, dressmakers and restaurants—encircling the immense courtyard and gardens.

There, in the afternoons and evenings, all the "monde" and "demi-monde" of Paris would mix; some strolling, some sitting to listen to the music. Even the scum of the city found their way there. But when all these had retired, in the early morning, it became a refuge for humble citizens. Work girls would sit on the

---

[1] *Adélaïde d'Orléans*, by Raoul Arnaud.

empty seats to eat their breakfast before starting their daily
sewing at one of the big dressmakers. Birds, unafraid, picked
up the crumbs thrown to them; it almost looked like a monastery
garden in its shadowy silence. Later, when the shops opened their
shutters, the noise and bustle drove the sparrows further afield.
Then the gay crowd returned once more. How often the
Orléans children must have wondered at the ever-changing
scene, set in that lovely garden, as they gazed out of their long,
heavily-curtained windows.

*   *   *

Louis Philippe was eight years old when Madame de Genlis
became Governor of the children. She tells us in her memoirs
that "Louis Philippe was completely ignorant and had no
intention of remedying this defect."

The first day she commenced her tuition by reading aloud
from a history book; he did not take the trouble to listen, but
lay down on the sofa upon which they were sitting and,
stretching his legs so as to rest his feet on the table, he yawned
loudly!

She lost no time in standing him in the corner of the room.
He was surprised, but realized that he had met a stronger will
than his own and from that moment he became passionately
attached to her. No one counted in his life for many years
except Felicité de Genlis, his "tendre mère". In later years he
told Victor Hugo that she was the only woman with whom he
had really been in love.

As soon as she undertook the education of the royal children,
everything was altered. She insisted that all ancient languages
give way to modern ones. Their French servants were removed
and foreign ones installed in their place. Louis Philippe and
his brothers, the Duc de Montpensier and the Comte de
Beaujolais, Princess Adélaïde and her twin sister Louise who
died in childhood, were really brought up in a Spartan manner.

They rose at six o'clock, winter and summer, they worked
most of the day, except when they took walks, and then leaden
soles were attached to their boots to make their legs strong.
They had only one hour for recreation, and even during that
time Madame de Genlis read them books she had written for

PRINCESSE ADÉLAÏDE D'ORLEANS
From the painting by Cogniet

their instruction. They spoke a different foreign language at each meal. They slept in cold rooms, with only one blanket, were permitted no outside friends, never ate any cakes or sweets.

The Duc, and even the Duchesse, did not question the authority of the Governor. Gradually she seized more and more power. She persuaded the parents that the atmosphere of the Palais Royal was too worldly, and that it prevented her pupils from attaining the degree of education she desired, so the Duc consented to buy Bellechasse in the suburbs of Paris where she betook herself with her charges. In reality, those secluded surroundings were admirably suited to her secret meetings with the Duc.

From that moment the Duchesse began to perceive the Governor's true aim—to detach the children from every home influence, and to make them utterly her tools.

Such was the woman who was destined to dominate the first twenty years of the life of Louis Philippe, future King of the French. Later, his sister Adélaïde took over this task. His whole life was ruled by two wilful women.

2

Versailles, Bellechasse, and a Lonely Duchesse

It was during this period that, early one morning in 1785, at Versailles, Louis Philippe, now twelve years old, stood being dressed by several valets under the supervision of the Comtesse de Genlis. One by one they helped him into his white satin breeches, his white velvet coat lightly embroidered in gold, his jabot of the finest lawn, his white silk stockings and buckled shoes. On his head was placed a small tightly-curled wig.

While all this was going on, the Abbé Guyot was endeavouring to impart some religious tuition, as that afternoon the prince was to be christened: Louis XVI and Marie Antoinette were his godparents. It was difficult for the child to attend seriously to the admonitions of the good Abbé, as Madame de Genlis kept on interrupting with instructions as to the way he was to conduct himself during the ceremony, reminding him of the etiquette to be observed towards their Majesties, his parents, and the high dignitaries of the Court.

When all was finished and the valets had withdrawn, he stood in full view; his beauty seemed overwhelming, an angelic picture.

Versailles, with all its pomp and ceremony, was very brilliant that day, as equipage after equipage drove up to the palace. The chapel was ablaze with innumerable candles, the glow from which seemed to transform the walls and altar into molten gold. The gilt chairs were occupied by the royal family, behind whom stood the whole Court—women in gorgeous gowns covered with jewels, small and lovely powdered heads made enormous by coiffures of feathers, birds and flowers; men in uniform, officials in Court dress; the Cardinal at the altar in his robes and mitre, holding his golden crosier, surrounded by priests and acolytes.

14

All awaited the entrance of the King and Queen and their young godson. Suddenly the fanfare of trumpets heralded their arrival. All stood as their Majesties, holding the small prince by the hand, entered, the King very solemn and thoughtful, the Queen tall and slim, a vision of grace and beauty, her dress covered with jewels, on her high powdered coiffure a cascade of diamonds and pearls. They walked slowly to the font, and there the ceremony began.

At the end, the young Duc walked up to his parents, kissed their hands, then, going to the altar, stood facing the throng and bowed right and left with elegance and grace.

When all was accomplished and the *Te Deum* ended, the procession reformed and walked to the banqueting hall where the newly-christened prince sat between the King and Queen.

During this same year Louis Philippe's grandfather, Louis "le Gros" Duc d'Orléans, died.

By his death Louis Philippe became Duc de Chartres, and his father, now head of their House, took the title Duc d'Orléans.

*   *   *

During the years that Madame de Genlis lived at Bellechasse with her royal charges, existence was not dull. Although she appeared to have given herself up entirely to their education, her private life was far from being monastic. She used to entertain all that Paris counted of outstanding men—she had few women friends. To the objection of the Duchesse d'Orléans that she was supposed to have chosen Bellechasse as a retreat, so that the princes should not be disturbed in their studies, her answer was: "They must be taught to receive polite society, to listen to, and take part in, intellectual conversation, to learn the art of holding a salon."

But in reality she must have intended thus to break for herself the monotony of teaching, and to enable her to keep in touch with the Revolutionary ideas which more and more were dominating the mind of the Duc, and which she, for her own ends, was fostering in her pupils. The Duc often went to Bellechasse, officially to discuss the studies of his children, but the true motive of those visits, which often lasted until the early hours of the morning, was no secret.

The Duchesse, abandoned by all for whom she cared, remained in the Palais Royal. She carried in her heart a burden of deep melancholy which nothing could lighten. She realized only too well that Madame de Genlis had stolen her children from her and possessed them entirely—their hearts, their souls, and their minds. Sometimes the Duchesse's lips smiled, but she never laughed; her eyes only came to life to weep.

She had long ceased to plead her cause in speech, but often she would pass her nights writing long imploring letters, begging her husband to return the children to her care once more.

If the Duc answered these appeals, it was ever the same reply: neither he nor his children could manage without their "mentor".

*   *   *

For three years, outwardly at least, events continued in more or less the same manner. The Court shone with its fêtes at Versailles, Trianon, or Fontainebleau. The Duchesse d'Orléans in the Palais Royal lamented the absence of her children and the loss of their affection. The Duc drove continually to Bellechasse, where in secret his mistress aided him to compose ignoble pamphlets aimed against the Queen. Madame de Genlis continued to instil into her charges a hatred of the monarchy; whilst secretly in taverns, in cellars and in backrooms, men were preparing to change the face of the world.

3

The Bastille is Ablaze!

14th July 1789. The Revolution had begun; the first shots had been fired; many hearts were cold with fear, many hearts were acclaiming the age of liberty.

That same day, the luncheon had just ended in the Château de St. Leu, one of the country places of the Duc d'Orléans, near Paris.

The Comtesse de Genlis and her pupils were acting charades in the shade of the great trees. The young Louis Philippe was masquerading as a Greek God and the other children, in costumes of the same period, were busily going through their parts. Madame de Genlis was directing the scene, criticizing here and there, in her usual masterly fashion.

Suddenly, a messenger rushed from the house: the mob had attacked the Bastille, and shooting had begun. All present seemed galvanized at the news. Madame de Genlis gave orders. The children were to change their clothes, carriages must be ready. No time must be lost as they were to start for Paris immediately. All the guests wanted to see what was happening; some of them did not even take the trouble to change their clothes before they crammed into the numerous vehicles. The Comtesse seemed exuberant, and urged her enthusiasm on her pupils.

Paris was in a state of commotion; notwithstanding this, they drove right through the heart of the inferno to the house of Monsieur Beaumarchais, a friend of Madame de Genlis, which was close to the Bastille. There, they scrambled to the roof, whence they could watch the incredible scene—the fortress burning, guns pounding, people dying, the screams, the terror, the exultation.

So the children watched.

*   *   *

After the storming of the Bastille by the mob of Paris, the young princes remained at the Palais Royal. The contempt and hatred for Louis XVI, which until then had only been insinuated to them, was now the daily talk around them. They were learning that each step towards the destruction of the King meant a step towards the rise of the House of Orléans.

One day, the Duc de Chartres and his brother, the Duc de Montpensier, were sent to attend a sitting of the National Assembly at Versailles. From then on, they went there regularly, and later even took part in some of the most important discussions.

On 5th October 1789, during a sitting of the Assembly, it was announced that a mob composed of the dregs of the Paris slums had arrived at Versailles, determined to take Louis XVI and Marie Antoinette together with the two royal children, the Dauphin and Madame Royale, back to the city. Mirabeau [1] rose, and in the vilest language denounced this unfortunate family. The Orléanists joined in, cries of "Blood" were heard. The husband of Madame de Genlis (who had now inherited the estate and title of Sillery), Mirabeau and Alexandre de Lamet cried, "We must provide victims for the Nation." The Duc d'Orléans, "Egalité" as he was now beginning to be called, and his sons, the Ducs de Chartres and Montpensier, seemed intoxicated by this lust for blood, and the young Duc de Chartres was loudly applauded when he shouted, "Yes! The Nation demands blood!"

When one realizes that the boy who uttered these words was barely sixteen, one cannot doubt that he was already well aware of his father's criminal intentions.

The royal family passed a last tragic night at Versailles. At dawn the following day, the King was obliged to consent to an immediate return to Paris and to the gloomy Château des Tuileries. Louis Philippe was attending a sitting of the Assembly when a messenger brought him a note. After reading it he quickly left his place with his brother, and both drove as fast as they could to Passy, a suburb of Paris. There they joined their father, who had preceded them, at the house of Monsieur de Boulainvilliers, the windows of which overlooked the road from Versailles to the city.

[1] An orator of great authority at the start of the Revolution, 1749–91.

18

PHILIPPE, DUC D'ORLÉANS ("EGALITE ")

Ecole Française

Their "tendre mère", Madame de Genlis, was awaiting them. She, anxious lest they should miss any detail of the procession, took them to a terrace nearer the scene, whence they saw passing close below them, a horde of drunken women walking arm-in-arm with the disarmed soldiers; in their midst marched men carrying on pikes the severed heads of the Gardes Suisses whom they had murdered on the steps of Versailles, whilst the victims were trying to defend the royal family. They dragged with them sixty waggons loaded with flour, pillaged from some store, to create the belief that the Court had been hoarding provisions with the idea of starving the people.

General de Lafayette, with some Gardes Nationaux [1] carrying drawn swords, escorted the large carriage in which sat the King, his brother, the Comte d'Artois, his sister, Madame Elizabeth; in another coach were the Queen and the two royal children with their governess, Madame de Tourzel. A deputation of a hundred members of the Assembly followed. Again and again the cortège was forced to a standstill by the howling mob, who trampled on one another as they thronged around the carriage. Curses and shouts of "à la lanterne!" mingled with cries of welcome.

Monsieur de Clermont-Gallerand, who happened to be near the Orléans children, relates in his memoirs published in 1825, that he was shocked to see them, casual and unmoved, watching the scene with nothing more than a detached curiosity.

At the age of eighteen, Louis Philippe became a member of the Jacobin Club. He wrote in his diary, "Yesterday, 1st November 1791, I was received as a member of the Jacobin Club. Monsieur de Sillery presented me; I was loudly applauded."

The noviciate was not easy; at first the prince had to perform menial tasks as porter and announcer, fetching and carrying for the members, but such was his zeal for the cause that nothing seemed too humiliating for him.

A few months later, he became a full member of the Club.

Humbled and broken-hearted, the Duchesse d'Orléans had

---

[1] The Garde Nationale was a militia of citizens formed for the internal defence of the country. Later, it played a very important role in the rise and fall of Louis Philippe.

left the Palais Royal, but she still attempted to retain some influence over her children; to her, the admission of Louis Philippe to the Jacobin Club was an insult to herself, to her faith, and to her loyalty to the King. She demanded once again that Madame de Genlis be sent away; thus for a short time the fatal hold of the Governor over her charges was relaxed.

This separation seemed to bring a change in Louis Philippe. He became moody, restless. In reality, Madame de Genlis was the only woman who had lived close to him, and her absence had awoken in him the first stirrings of desire. Not knowing where to turn for advice and sympathy, he wrote to his mother:

> My morals are, I dare say, as pure in every respect as they can be, they are intact. . . . I would not hide from you that I have not preserved my purity without a struggle, without suffering; sometimes even my physical well-being is affected . . . nevertheless I would sooner die than fail in what I owe to my faith. . . .[1]

This confidential mood between mother and son was to be short-lived, for soon Princesse Adélaïde fell ill, and clamoured for her "tendre mère", vowing that she would die if Madame de Genlis did not return to her. So the woman was reinstated in the household, and for the next few months Louis Philippe's diary reveals a strange elation. In February 1790 he wrote, "I left Bellechasse [where Madame de Genlis was residing with Adélaïde] the happiest of men". Then again, on New Year's Day 1791, "I dined yesterday at Bellechasse. . . . After dinner I went to my friend, and remained with her until the early hours. . . . None could make me happier. I do not know what I should become without her." [2]

Can we surmise that Madame de Genlis had used the supreme method to dominate him? She did not hold him for long as, after a few months, he had to join his regiment.

*   *   *

At his birth Louis Philippe had been given the rank of Colonel, as was then the custom, so, accompanied by an A.D.C.,

[1] *Louis Philippe*, by J. Lucas-Dubreton. Librairie Arthème Fayard.
[2] *Ibid.*

he arrived at the garrison town of Vendôme where his regiment of dragoons was quartered. His first step was to attend the local branch of the Jacobin Club, and to make a speech; this took place three days after the National Assembly had issued a decree abolishing all title and distinctions.

"I hope you, my comrades, believe me when I tell you with pride, that I applauded the new decree, and it is with happiness that I have given up all titles and privileges, which are but worthless baubles, and in future I shall only value those which belong to personal courage and patriotism."

4

From Spring Sunshine to Guillotine

In 1792—it was spring in Paris—life was bursting forth again, leaves were opening everywhere, and among them the birds were busy looking for a safe place to build their nests. Joy and happiness seemed ready to offer their fruits, and yet, in the midst of all this rebirth, in the interior of the Tuileries, consternation reigned.

In his private writing-room, Louis XVI was pacing up and down in utter confusion and bewilderment. A few minutes earlier, he had been forced to receive a deputation from the National Assembly, who had insisted that he should immediately declare war on Austria: they said that Austria was allowing the French émigrés there to organize troops against the government of the Revolution, and this must be stopped. The members of the delegation were not even civil, but with many threatening words ordered the King to do their will.

After their departure, a side door opened and Marie Antoinette walked in; she was very pale and almost trembling with anger; she had been listening outside.

For a few seconds she stood facing her husband unnaturally quiet, then she asked him whether he intended to obey his subjects. When he remarked helplessly that he didn't have much choice in the matter, she suddenly lost control and almost shrieked, her voice becoming hard and strident.

"This has ever been your attitude—there is no choice! There is a choice—my choice! We must write at once to beg Austria and Prussia for help.

"I have here a letter I have already written to my brother, Joseph of Austria: it is for you to write to Prussia at once."

That was why the King paced his study in confusion and

bewilderment. What he finally did is well known—he did both. He obeyed the National Assembly *and* Marie Antoinette.

The appeals and the declarations of war went forth, and on 10th August 1792, Austria and Prussia invaded France.

* * *

Louis Philippe, his training completed, made his way to Valenciennes full of Jacobin fervour, having been posted to the army of Kellermann on whose staff was the Duc de Biron.

Biron had been a friend of General Dumouriez, the Commander-in-Chief, ever since they had fought together in the Corsican campaign of 1768. They were totally different in character; Biron, better known as Duc de Lauzun, had broken many hearts and had gone through life heedless of aught but his own amusement.

A rather diverting incident took place whilst Biron was in Valenciennes, waiting to begin operations against the Austrians.

One day there arrived at the camp an elegant phaeton drawn by three high-stepping horses, and driven by a pretty woman dressed in an extraordinary costume—blue riding habit, round her waist a large tricolor sash, a beaver hat tilted coquettishly on her head.

The excitement was instantaneous. The whole camp ran to look at her. Things were rather dull at the time, so the lovely intruder caused a sensation. When asked whom she wanted, her reply was, "The Duc de Biron."

Her name was Suzanne Giroux; she was the daughter of rich business people who lived in Paris. When very young, she married a lawyer from Soissons named Guillet, and afterwards had a liaison with the President of the Convention, Hérault de Séchelles. She was romantic and utterly feather-brained, and although she had never seen Biron, his notorious escapades had filled her with curiosity; so she set out for Valenciennes, but thinking her name, Guillet, was too common, she called herself Madame de Morency.

Biron, only too pleased at the prospect of such a break in the monotony of camp life, received with all his accustomed charm and gallantry, this unexpected visitor. She was so truly enchanting, with her mass of chestnut hair, her eyes sparkling

23

with youth, her small mouth inviting and sensual; she made such an impression on the general that he could hardly tear himself from her side.

Alas, their romance was short-lived. She loved riding, and careered wildly through the countryside, disregarding the proximity of the invaders. One day she went too far and fell into the hands of a party of Uhlans, who carried her off to the Austrian camp where her beauty attracted a good deal of attention.

The officers had a Tyrolean hussar uniform made for her: it was of light blue with canary-coloured revers; the hat with a blue and yellow tuft.

All this delighted her vanity, but as the Austrian army was very virtuous (by command) during the campaign, she was bored by their chastity and, at the first opportunity, she escaped to the French lines.

Biron was no longer there, so she moved on to Lille where, after numerous adventures, she became the mistress of Dumouriez, the Commander-in-Chief. Later she wrote novels.

Despite the scandals and gallant adventures with which his path was strewn, Biron was renowned for his bravery and audacity under fire.

Louis Philippe was next transferred to the staff of General Dumouriez, who was destined to play an important part in his life. He was a courageous general who might have become a great man, had he not been an incurable double-faced schemer who sought only his own advancement; he saw in the young and easily influenced prince a most promising tool which he could use for his own ends.

It was in this year, 1792, while serving under Dumouriez, that Louis Philippe took part in the two famous victories of the Revolutionary army: Valmy against the Prussians and Jemappes against the Austrians. During these two battles, Louis Philippe first displayed the tenacity which later made him break through all the vicissitudes which blocked his way, to reach his one goal, the throne of France. Many years after, Madame de Genlis said of him: "He was a coward, I made him brave." At Valmy and Jemappes he first showed how well he had learned his lesson.

Both victories were decisive, and they made possible the occupation of Belgium by the French army. Paris went wild with joy, despite the severe losses sustained by the French; Louis Philippe was a hero.

It was at this moment that the young prince heard that his King, Louis XVI, had been brought to trial before the Convention, to which the Assembly had delegated supreme power on 20th September 1792.

By January 1793, the Revolution had passed beyond the control of those who had started it on its headlong path, at the end of which loomed the guillotine, a bloody symbol of the authority of the mob.

Since 11th December 1792, the King had daily appeared before his self-constituted judges, being mocked and insulted. The Orléans family publicly vaunted their loyalty to the new order of things. The Duc d'Orléans—now known as "Egalité" —flattered the leaders and worked assiduously against the monarchy and all for which it stood. His sons were fighting under the orders of the Convention.

During all these terrible days, in which the name Orléans stank in the nostrils of every royalist, a woman was praying and fearing for him, Mrs. Elliott.

She had been in love with him for years, although she realized that he had often been unfaithful to her, and that his present mistress, the Comtesse de Buffon, was ruling the Palais Egalité, as the Palais Royal was now termed. Hers was a curious story: when young she had married Mr. Dalrymple-Elliott, a man much older than herself. She was very lovely, and when they came to live in Paris she met the Duc d'Orléans, and they both fell in love.

It was an infatuation that lasted for years, for him to take and leave, but it never left her. During one of her visits to London, the Prince Regent, afterwards George IV, heard of her beauty, and she made another conquest.

The outbreak of the Revolution found her in Paris. The Prince Regent sent her a message, asking her to keep a diary of all she saw and heard. She did so, and years later is was published as her memoirs.

On the evening of 15th January 1793, in her lovely house in the rue Miromesnil, quite near the village of Monceau, where the Duc's small country residence was situated, Mrs. Elliott was sitting alone anxiously waiting for news, when her friend the Duc de Biron was announced. He seemed very agitated, and indeed the news he brought was gloomy. On the 20th, the final verdict for or against the King would be pronounced.

As she stood facing him, Biron saw her suddenly turn pale. All the horror of the present and fear of the future flooded into her mind. She looked at her calendar. There were only five more days left. She thought of Egalité, and she could not speak. Biron waited too; he appeared crushed by the awful suspense.

"What will the Duc do?" she cried at length.

"I know nothing," answered Biron. "I have not seen him since Tuesday; if I could only speak to him!"

"He is coming here this evening; please remain."

They both knew only too well how low he had sunk, loathed by the Royalists and despised as a turncoat by the Jacobins who knew that now he was entirely in their power. He seemed to have lost all moral sense and self-respect; but at that moment Mrs. Elliott's only thought was to stop him on his fatal course.

Biron tried to take her mind off her anguish. He drew up a table, took up a pack of cards, and continued.

"My dear, tell me my fortune, as you have done so often before."

She shook her head and rang the bell to order hot punch.

"No! I cannot concentrate tonight. You will take wine with me while we wait for the Duc."

They sat by the fire holding the warm glasses in both hands. They spoke little; there was so much in the balance.

They heard the door bell ring, and a few moments later Philippe d'Orléans, Egalité, walked in. As they rose to greet him, they experienced a shock. Was it possible to change so much in a few days? One of the handsomest men in France had suddenly become old! He mumbled a few words of greeting and, taking a glass from Mrs. Elliott's hand, he let himself drop heavily on to a couch.

Biron could scarcely recognize his old friend. Only a few days before, on his arrival from the Army of the Rhine, he had

called at the Palais Egalité to see the Duc and Madame de
Buffon, who had so easily replaced Madame de Genlis. Then,
the Duc had seemed his old self, and did not even mention the
tragedy that was taking place, and only spoke of the bravery
of his two sons, Chartres and Montpensier. Now he seemed a
doomed man.

Mrs. Elliott broke the silence.

"I hope, Monseigneur, that you will not attend the Convention, and sit next Saturday with that infamous gang."

The Duc looked up. "My position as a member obliges me
to do so."

"Is it possible," almost shouted the young woman, "that you
could countenance your King being dragged publicly to judgment before this miserable crowd who have been outraging
him daily with interrogations? I almost wish I could be there:
I should pull off both my shoes and throw them at the head of
the President and Santerre, who dare to insult their King and
Master."

Then, controlling her temper, "I hope, Monseigneur, that
you will vote for the King's liberty."

"Certainly," he retorted sarcastically, "and for my own
death!"

By now the Duc was furious, and Biron tried to appease him.
Turning to Mrs. Elliott he whispered, "Calm yourself or you
will achieve nothing." Then, in a louder tone, so as to be heard
by the Duc, "How could he vote against his cousin? Of course,
Monseigneur has many grievances, but next Saturday he can
easily plead illness and remain at home."

"Then I feel sure that you will not attend the Convention
on Saturday," said Mrs. Elliott.

Orléans seemed suddenly to have regained his composure.
"I never intended to do so," and Mrs. Elliott pursued:

"Will Monseigneur swear on oath to his two old friends that,
although he may feel that Louis XVI has not carried out his
promises to his people, nothing in the world could make him
vote against the King?"

The Duc d'Orléans rose and, lifting his glass, said, "I swear."

With this solemn oath the atmosphere seemed to clear, but
after a short time he left, still looking morose and perturbed.

On Saturday morning, 20th January 1793, Biron sent a note to Mrs. Elliott, asking her to come to spend the evening with him at his hôtel St. Marc, rue St. Marc. In that manner she would hear the news and, he added, "whatever the future may hold."

All that day the tension grew. Never had such extremities of feeling been seen in Paris. While some marched aggressively about the streets, shouting slogans or singing the "Carmagnole," others went tensely about their business, hardly daring to raise their eyes for fear of revealing their feelings to passers-by.

The churches were thronged all day long with people incessantly coming in and going out. There was a universal feeling of helplessness, and a certainty that the fate of the King lay in the hands of a few half-demented fanatics, many of low extraction, utterly intoxicated with their lust for power.

As Mrs. Elliott entered the hôtel, she sensed at once a state of unrest; people were hurrying across the hall with worried, tragic faces; there was much whispering and many silent gestures.

The Duc de Biron came to meet her and led her to his apartments. In the salon were his A.D.C. Rutaut, and General Dumouriez, the latter confident of the King's acquittal and triumph. It was a sad vigil. Every half-hour a report of the latest speeches for and against the King was brought in. The reports were not very reassuring, but Dumouriez persisted in his opinion. Surely they would not dare to condemn the Sovereign.

Soon, however, all illusions were dispelled. The voting was almost unanimous for the monarch's condemnation.

Mrs. Elliott asked, "Can nothing be done to save him?"

"There is one hope," answered Biron. "Remember the Duc d'Orléans will not be present and this may prove a great factor. They may fear to pronounce a final verdict in the face of his disapproval."

At that moment, a note was handed to Biron. Slowly he unfolded it, and in silence he passed it to the others. It read, "At eight o'clock the Duc d'Orléans entered the Convention."

The vigil continued.

At ten o'clock another note was brought. Once more Biron

28

unfolded the message. Slowly he rose, and said, "The Duc d'Orléans has voted, and Louis XVI is condemned to death."

*   *   *

After the execution of the King, the floodgates of the Terror were opened in all its audacity and ruthlessness. Fear was in every heart, the mob feared the Royalists, the Royalists feared the mob even more—the mob in whose hands the power now lay. The story of those months is too well known to be described here, but one curious and interesting scene which took place is worth relating.

Like all who had expressed sympathy for the late King, Mrs. Elliott stood in danger. The strain of those critical weeks had been so great that she was physically worn out; for a month she lay ill at her country home in Meudon. During these weeks, an obsession formed in her mind: Escape! But how could she obtain a passport, since none were being issued? Only one person could help her, Philippe Egalité: but she had a horror of approaching him! At last, she asked him to receive her. I have often wondered if there was still something left of that strange, almost mystical, worship which once reigned in her mind.

She reached the Palais Egalité with dread in her soul. The old porter recognized her and pressed her hand. "Oh, Madame," he muttered, "God have mercy upon us all!"

The hall was full of soldiers in different uniforms, some still trying to look smart, others in tattered clothes, officers, generals, privates, a curious medley of washed and unwashed faces.

She was taken to the Duc's study, a room she knew so well. He came forward to meet her. He was dressed in deep mourning and looked embarrassed. She felt faint; perceiving it, he made her sit down, handing her a glass of water.

"You look ill," he said. Suddenly, the horrible situation flashed upon her.

"I suppose, Monseigneur, that you are, as I am, in mourning for the King."

He smiled a forced smile, and answered, "Oh! No, I am in mourning for my father-in-law, the Duc de Penthièvre."

Then, rising, she said, "I suppose the King's death hastened his end; or perhaps that horrible trial and your vote for death

29

broke his heart, as it has broken mine. But believe me, you, Monseigneur, will also die, like your King, on the scaffold."

He turned pale, and said quickly, "Tell me what you require, and try to believe me when I say that I have little power left. But for your sake I will risk all."

As she turned to leave, having made her request, she looked back, and suddenly a wave of pity overcame her contempt for him. He stood there, with a look of utter loneliness and despair. Then an awful thought came to her: that is the man for whom a short time ago I would have given my life.

She never saw him again.

* * *

A very few weeks after this, the young Louis Philippe left the army and fled from France. The Convention had issued a decree that all members of the Bourbon family were to be instantly arrested, and Egalité and his family were in no way to be spared.

When the news reached him, Egalité was at table, alone with one of his intimates, a man of wit and pleasure.

"Good God!" cried the Duc, striking his forehead, "is this possible, after all the proofs of patriotism I have given, after all the sacrifices I have made, to bring such a disgrace upon me! What do you say, Monville?"

"It is disastrous, Monseigneur," answered Monville, without disturbing himself, and continuing to squeeze the juice of a lemon upon the sole he was preparing to eat, "but what will you; they have had all they wanted from your Highness, so they are doing what I am going to do when I have pressed all the juice out of this lemon." And Monville threw the fruit into the fire, saying coolly that the sole must be eaten hot.

On 4th November 1793, the Duc d'Orléans was brought to Paris from Marseilles, where he had been in prison with his wife and younger sons Montpensier and Beaujolais ever since their arrest. The Duc was tried, condemned, and executed in the space of a few hours.

He showed great dignity and courage. After the sentence, he was taken back to his cell, a priest was brought to him, and he made a confession of his whole life.

Three other victims were to die at the same time. Two were members of the Convention, the third, Nicolas Laroque, an old soldier. As they waited to be taken in the tumbrils, the Duc d'Orléans was led in, and Laroque, seeing him, cried out in a loud voice: "I do not now regret having to leave this world, as one who betrayed my country is to receive the punishment for his crime; but what humiliates me is to be obliged to die under the same knife as he."

From the Conciergerie to the Place de la Révolution is a long distance. At first nobody realized, as the cortège passed, that the Duc d'Orléans was amongst those condemned; those carts jogging along, surrounded by soldiers, had become an almost hourly occurrence, and the passers-by scarcely troubled to cast a glance at the victims.

The Duc had taken great care that nobody could accuse him of cowardice. His hair was powdered and, although his hands were tied, he stood erect and haughty. His gaolers had thrown his coat about his shoulders; it was made of grey cloth and had a black cape.

As the cart passed the Palais Egalité, an order was given to stop, and for about ten minutes it stood there. It was thought that by letting the Duc linger thus before the Palais where he had been so powerful, his agony would be intensified, and his last moments embittered.

By now the crowd had learnt the name of the principal victim, and no insults or threats were spared him. But the Duc d'Orléans remained unmoved. He carried himself nobly and looked down on the crowd for whom he had sacrificed himself by becoming one of them. Now, he must have thought, it had all been in vain, but no quiver of emotion showed upon his face.

At last the procession arrived; when he perceived the guillotine, he turned slightly pale, but did not flinch. He walked up the ladder and helped the executioner to untie his cravat. He looked once more upon the surging mass of upturned faces, and made no gesture. So he died. His head was lifted high above the populace.

Thus ended Philippe Egalité, Duc d'Orléans. He had plotted, he had betrayed the monarchy, he had grovelled to the revolutionaries, and it had availed him nothing.

For all his astuteness, he had been too blind to see that once Louis XVI was dead, the Jacobins had no further use for him, and he paid the same price as all those who created the Revolution—whether idealists or opportunists—death.

Louis Philippe was now Duc d'Orléans.

5

Exile. Court Dinners for Three Shillings

During the early part of the year 1793, even before the issue
of the decree against the Bourbon family, General Dumouriez
had realized the growing danger. Even the strongest supporters
of the Revolution were now being discarded, without any
apparent reason.

He therefore consulted Louis Philippe, and they decided that,
before it was too late, General Dumouriez should present himself before the Convention and offer his resignation.

To their astonishment it was refused. Dumouriez felt that,
although he was no longer trusted, he was still useful as a
general, so he returned once more to his headquarters to plan
the invasion of Holland. He soon found that he was only a
figurehead; orders came to him from Paris, dictating absurd
and unrealistic plans of campaign which led to the defeat at
Neerwinden on 18th March 1793.

Convinced that they would be the scapegoats and shortly
arrested, the general and Louis Philippe decided on a risky
plan; it might succeed—if all went well.   The plan was to turn
their troops against the Government of the Revolution, with the
help of the Austrian army; but no time must be lost if this was
to be organized.

So on 21st March, Colonel Montjoie was sent to contact the
Chief of Staff of the Austrian army, General Mack, to arrange a
truce. On the 27th, Dumouriez and Louis Philippe met Mack
in great secrecy, and an agreement was concluded: General
Dumouriez was to march on Paris with his forces, and if they
proved inadequate to overthrow the Revolution, the Austrians
agreed to reinforce them.

Dumouriez did not act quickly enough; as he had foreseen,
the defeat of Neerwinden had enraged Paris, and four Com-

missioners were sent to arrest the general and his satellite, Louis Philippe. But instead, Dumouriez arrested the envoys.

At this juncture the troops became suspicious and threatening; Dumouriez and Louis Philippe realized that their only safety lay in flight.

So abandoning all their grand ideals, they fled to Tournay, in Belgium, where Princesse Adélaïde was staying with Madame de Genlis. The latter tells us in her memoirs that, as Tournay seemed no longer safe, she determined to leave the princess with her brother, and flee alone to Switzerland. It is a sad revelation, and one cannot help thinking that it would have been better for her to have left the painful scene out of her diary.

This is how she tells her story:

"On a cold, grey April morning, I crept out of the house. I had not awakened my young charge, fearing the shock the child would experience on feeling herself abandoned by her 'tendre mère'. The carriage stood in the rue St. Amand. I entered it, and the postilions were already cracking their whips."

Louis Philippe, who had guessed what Madame de Genlis intended to do, snatched his sister from her bed in her nightgown and, not even waiting to put a wrap around her, carried her out into the street, pushed her into the carriage amongst the bandboxes, and so the child and her Governor went on their way to Switzerland.

It was a dangerous journey, overshadowed by the fear of the conflicting armies, the perils of the road infested by marauders and brigands, barely enough money to enable them to reach their destination, and but little hope, once there, of being able to subsist.

It is a curious fact that, from that moment, Louis Philippe changed; previously his love for Madame de Genlis had blinded him to her faults. Now her true character was revealed to him; her selfishness in wanting to abandon his sister, when the order for her arrest, as well as his own, had been given, turned his love into contempt and disgust.

In a very short time, the Convention decided to put a price on the heads of the fugitive Bourbons, and Louis Philippe had to leave Tournay in search of a safer refuge. He travelled through Germany in a small dogcart under several assumed names, and at length reached Switzerland, where he met his sister and Madame de Genlis; but the odium which surrounded the name of Orléans had fallen on them also, and they were being chased from place to place; no canton would grant them asylum for more than a few days.

At last General de Montesquiou Fésensac, a deputy of the nobility of 1789, found a refuge in a convent for the two women: to Louis Philippe he said, "Your only hope is to roam about the mountains, and avoid being recognized."

So the future King of the French began a vagabond life, constantly on foot, with his faithful valet, Beaudoin, as his only companion, existing on thirty sous a day, often cold and hungry, sleeping in fields or under hedges.

At last, he had only thirty francs left in the world: in despair he got in touch once more with General de Montesquiou, who managed to obtain for him a post as teacher of mathematics at the College of Reichenau in the Grisons, where nobody guessed that the somewhat shabby Monsieur Chabaud-Latour was the *ci-devant* Duc d'Orléans.

I must now introduce Marianne Banzori, cook at the College of Reichenau. Imagine her, a plump little woman with a placid face. Unaffected in her backwater by the turmoil raging in Europe, she must have been a very soothing presence to the wandering Bourbon. For her, having hitherto divided her time between the kitchen and the attentions of her *amant*, the local carpenter, the arrival of this Frenchman was a stirring event. His appearance was not very remarkable, but he had travelled and was a brilliant talker, and when she saw him pacing the grounds with Mr. Jost, the Headmaster, talking so fluently of high politics, she was very proud of his interest in her.

The idyll prospered until Marianne announced to Mr. Jost that she was pregnant as the result of Mr. Chabaud's attentions. The suspected father emphatically denied his responsibility, and left Reichenau with some precipitation, while poor Marianne, now a subject of gossip for the whole neighbourhood, went to Milan to give birth to her child. The royal bastard was placed in a home for abandoned children, and there ends his brief role in history.

35

Remorse, perhaps, inspired the love letters which Louis Philippe wrote to the unhappy Marianne: "When I had torn myself so hastily from your beloved arms, I wanted to return to you, my darling. Death was in my soul when I embarked. The boatman remarked that you were a charming little thing, and that pleased me. You see that I am not the only one to find you pretty. If we should meet again. . . . Oh, my dear little one, how happy your Chabosli will be."

And again later on . . . "I find your letters easier to read, my beloved treasure, and I see that you are trying to write more legibly . . . you do well not to write very often, busy as you are with so much cooking throughout the week. You are always before my eyes, and your Chabosli will never forget his little treasure."

He soon forgot the banal episode, but the little cook of Reichenau never did.[1]

*   *   *

As Louis Philippe landed from the small ferry which had borne him away from Reichenau, he remembered the day he had arrived, forlorn, a fugitive, not knowing what awaited him. It was different now, he had a little money and could sit down and think. First of all, he must get to England. He knew that there lay the only part of his father's fortune which had not been confiscated. So his next step was to get to Hamburg and sail from there. Once in England, he could regain his position as a Prince of the House of France. But whilst in Hamburg waiting for a passport, he received a letter from his mother, the Duchesse d'Orléans, imploring him to leave for America where she and her two younger sons could join him, there to live peacefully, away from all the horror of France.

The Directoire, which had now replaced the Convention, had agreed to release the Duc de Montpensier and his brother the Comte de Beaujolais, on condition they all left for the New World; Louis Philippe had to accept, and the three princes set off on a sight-seeing tour of the United States, but without their mother, who was still held captive in the Luxembourg prison.

[1] This episode was brought to light by Monsieur Recouly in *Louis Philippe, Roi des Français*. Editions de Paris, 1936.

They visited the whole country from the Niagara Falls to New Orleans.[1] At Mount Vernon, they were received by the hero of all Jacobins, George Washington, who let Louis Philippe do all the talking.

One day, as they were travelling through a forest, Louis Philippe stopped at an Indian village to ask the way. The interpreter begged him to visit the chief, who was very sick. He hesitated; it was growing late and he was in a hurry. He looked beyond the clearing at the gathering gloom in the forest, and then at the circle of dark, intent faces around him.

He said weakly: "I am no doctor." But they would not be put off; he was a white man and he knew things. So he went into the hut of the chief, and there performed a bleeding as Madame de Genlis had taught him.

When he re-emerged, he was overwhelmed by the gratitude of the people and, a rare honour, invited by his patient to spend the night on a straw mat between the latter's grandmother and great aunt.

In Cuba, the Spanish Government arrested the brothers, apparently because they had fought under the Republican flag. Late in 1799 they were expelled from the colony and, only after a good deal of negotiation, obtained permission to enter England.

How strange London must have seemed to the young men. There was no one to whom they could turn. Although the English capital was overflowing with French émigrés, none would deign to approach the sons of Egalité the regicide. They had very little money, and their Court consisted of one gentleman, Monsieur de Montjoie.

A house in London was prohibitive as the rents were beyond their means. At last an acquaintance told them that the country would be less expensive, so they set out to seek a decent but modest abode.

In Twickenham they found a mansion, not too large, with a beautiful garden undulating down to the Thames. The furniture was simple, but comfortable. It was destined to be the home of the Orléans family for many years.

[1] General de Montesquiou and the Comtesse de Flahaut had financed them.

Gradually it was whispered that three charming Orléans princes were living in Twickenham, lonely and sad. English society, ever romantic, and delighted with anything a little "exotic", visited them; invitations were sent and accepted.

Louis Philippe posed at first as a sad refugee, and was slightly diffident. Soon he forgot all his revolutionary creed, and wore the title of Duc d'Orléans with all the prestige it carried.

*   *   *

Much had happened in Europe since the Orléans brothers left for the United States.

France had suddenly emerged from the chaos of ten years into a terrifying military nation. A young general named Bonaparte had just seized power as First Consul, and wherever he led his armies, he seemed to gain a shattering victory. He had already risen to such summits, and yet he was still only in the foothills of his career. How incredible that in his house at Twickenham, with his one-man Court, Louis Philippe should still have dreamed of calling him rival.

General Dumouriez had also reached England, and was soon active in rebuilding the Orléans cause. Seeing the abyss which existed between Louis Philippe's actual circumstances and his vaulting ambition, it was he who first suggested a reconciliation with the elder Bourbons, explaining that it would strengthen the Orléans position. As things were, Louis Philippe stood alone, an émigré with a tainted name. If he could rejoin the royal family of France, his name would carry a certain prestige. To achieve this, Louis Philippe did not flinch from humiliation. He was quite prepared to bow down and grovel. He knew that an elaborate *mea culpa* would be demanded. After all, mere words need not fetter his future actions.

The Comte de Provence, heir to the French throne, who now styled himself Louis XVIII, was living in Mittau under the precarious protection of the Czar Paul I. His brother, the Comte d'Artois (the future Charles X), was in London, at 46 Baker Street, surrounded by an ill-assorted Court of aristocrats and parasites: to him Louis Philippe decided to appeal.

It was not easy, as the Comte d'Artois, like all the Bourbons, loathed the very name of Orléans, but, notwithstanding this,

Louis Philippe wrote to him, in the most humble terms, begging for an audience.

The letter expressed sorrow for his past life, and pleaded as an excuse, "the folly of youth". Now, "in the full flush of manly reason", he repented and, although unworthy of approaching his Majesty, wished to make his submission to Louis XVIII.

At last the Comte d'Artois received him, and it required all Louis Philippe's powers of flattery and persuasion to blind the suspicious prince to his deceit. He consented to forward the following letter to the King:

> Sire,
>
> I declare and am convinced that the great majority of the French people share the sentiments which animate me. I reaffirm, in the name of my loyal compatriots as well as in my own, the sacred oath which we swore on our swords to the King, to live and die faithful to our honour, and to our legitimate Sovereign. If the unlawful use of force succeeds, which God forbid, in placing on the throne of France any other than our legitimate King, we shall follow the voice of honour which bids us appeal in his name, with our last breath, to God, Frenchmen, and our Sword.

The King received this letter at Mittau and, whether he believed it or not, he acted as one deeply touched. At once an answer was sent, giving full recognition to the Princes d'Orléans and their sister, Madame Adélaïde, and asking foreign Courts to grant them the rights and privileges accorded to Princes of the Royal House of France.

For a time, Louis Philippe hoped that his reconciliation with Louis XVIII would improve his relations with the French émigrés: but it really made no difference; they still regarded him with hostility and suspicion. Once or twice he attended the receptions of the Comte d'Artois where a medley of people assembled.

It was a strange scene; duchesses and ne'er-do-wells, bishops and adventurers, all the real and the sham trying to re-create Versailles in Baker Street. Even in this oddly assorted crowd, Louis Philippe was made to feel that his father was Egalité. On one occasion, an émigrée lady came up to him and said:

"Monseigneur, you seem solitary without your Jacobin friends."
These were the only words that were addressed to him that
night.

The visits to Baker Street became as rare as he dared to
make them, and he fell back on English Society which was
more sympathetic to him and received him with all the flattering honour in which he revelled. The Comtesse de Boigne
writes: "The Princes d'Orléans dined out, but always as
Princes. Their manner excluded familiarity. Although their
name was abhorred by the émigrés, they seemed to ignore this;
they behaved with dignity and modesty." [1]

In contrast to them, the Duc de Berri, the second son of the
Comte d'Artois, who also lived in London at this time, led a
wild life, his usual company Creole women. He allowed himself
many liberties with people, and tolerated the same from them.
He lived at this time with a low-class streetwalker, was seen
with her at the races, even drove her in his own carriage, took
her to the opera and sat by her side.

Sometimes he would suddenly realize his undignified position, and take refuge in the box of Madame de Boigne, but as
he left the Opera House, loud cries of "Berri, Berri!!" were
heard; it was his notorious *protégée* calling for him to fetch the
carriage.

He was very quick-tempered, but had a kindly nature and
ever sought to help his compatriots in distress. Witty, amiable
and gay, he was also quite gifted and often, when friends were
assembled at his house, he would act and mimic well-known
personalities in a delightful manner.

*   *   *

When first the Comte d'Artois arrived in Great Britain, he
spent some time at the Palace of Holyrood-house in Edinburgh,
where he was safe from his creditors. His liaison with Madame
de Polastron was so long-established that it had completely
ceased to be a scandal.

At first, he was inundated with requests from Catholic
organizations to attend innumerable religious ceremonies; as he
was not particularly pious, this got on his nerves.

[1] *Mémoires* of the Comtesse de Boigne.   Librairie Plon.

It was the last straw when, for one of the religious feasts, he was obliged to drive twenty miles to spend five or six hours in a draughty chapel.

After this, Madame de Polastron wrote to a friend, asking her "to find a priest, just to say Mass for the household. He must be of the lower class, so that he need not be invited into the drawing-room. Monseigneur intends that he should eat with the valets."

The friend wrote back, "I have found what you require, a humble priest, son of one of my porters. He is young, not bad-looking; I think he has no pretensions, and you will not have to take much notice of him. His name is Abbé Latil." The offer was made, and the young man entered the household.

The Duchesse de Guiche had just arrived from France with a certain Monsieur de Rivière of the "petite noblesse", who was her lover. At length she fell dangerously ill and the Abbé lost no time in gaining her confidence, and ended by converting her and Monsieur de Rivière. She died in great sanctity.

Madame de Polastron, edified by the death of her friend in piety and peace, placed herself and her conscience in the hands of the Abbé. Later, when living in London, she became con-sumptive, and as she grew weaker, the Comte d'Artois spent many hours at her bedside. The houses in Baker Street were not large, so they could not live in the same building, but their houses were almost adjacent. It is touching to think of the Comte staying day by day with his dying mistress.

He would arrive at noon, remain till five o'clock, leave her to dine, returning at seven and staying until nearly midnight.

Towards the end, Madame de Polastron could hardly speak, but liked to hear holy books read aloud, first by the prince, then by the Abbé Latil. The prince, who had scoffed at religion for so long, was now impressed by all he read; she, when she was able, spoke of her faith, and her deep love for him made her the more eloquent. She felt sure that he entered fully into all her sentiments—so sure that, a few moments before her death, she took his hand and placed it in that of the Abbé, saying, "My dear Abbé, here he is, I give him to you; keep him safe, I recommend him to your care." Then, addressing the prince, "Mon ami, follow the Abbé's instructions, that you may be as peaceful as I am now, at the moment when you rejoin me."

Madame de Boigne tells us that, from that hour, the Abbé Latil gained a great influence over the Comte. He led him to the French Church in King Street, where he confessed and took Holy Communion.

The Abbé ceased to eat with the valets and helped the Comte d'Artois to regain his faith. The "petit prêtre" without pretensions, eventually became Cardinal-Duc de Latil, Chaplain to Charles X and a peer of the realm.

The Comte d'Artois was gracious, handsome, a prince to the tips of his fingers. Before the illness of Madame de Polastron, he often went into society, and was frequently seen at the same parties as the Prince of Wales, later George IV, but it was always the French prince who stood out as the "grand seigneur".

*   *   *

Emigration brings with it a train of abnormal ways. Ladies of the higher aristocracy worked for ten hours a day to be able to buy food for their children; at night they brought out their evening dresses, danced, sang and enjoyed themselves until the early hours of the morning. The ugly side of this life lay in the fact that they criticized one another concerning their different occupations, envying with jealousy the one who earned most. It was a mixture of ancient nobility and a daily struggle for existence.

Some still kept up their grand Court manners. Such a one was the Duchesse de Fitz-James, who had established herself in a small house in the suburbs of London. She would invite the "cream" of her aristocratic friends, and would receive as if still at Versailles. But it was understood that, as the guests left, they would drop three shillings into a cup which was placed on the mantelpiece—and woe to him who could afford more, but only gave the minimum. Notwithstanding this, there was a grand air about that humble house.

After receptions, many duchesses or marquises climbed wearily into a hackney carriage, in their evening gowns and arrayed in all the jewels they had so far saved from the pawn shop.

The majority of the émigrés led an irreproachable life, which amazed English Society and completely changed their ideas as to the debauchery of the French nation.

Some of the political notions of the émigrés were ridiculous. One was supposed to be ready to return to France at any moment; in consequence, it was considered bad taste to hire a house or apartment for longer than a month; it was even better to take it by the week. It was disloyal not to expect a counter-revolution at any moment. I must not pass in silence the be-haviour of the Catholic clergy: they were an inspiring example to the English people who, at the beginning of the Revolution, had little use for them. In a short time, wealthy families were glad to have an Abbé in the house to educate their children.[1]

Amongst the women of the émigré Society, Madame de Staël stood out as remarkable. Although not particularly good-look-ing, her eyes were brilliant, her hands and arms, which she used freely, were perfect.

At first she lived in Manchester Street, London, but the strenuous *mise en scène* which she planned around her every word and gesture must have been fatiguing, as she said she needed country air, and rooms were engaged at a Richmond inn, where perhaps she rehearsed some of her famous discourses.

As soon as she entered a room, she would be surrounded by all the men of intellect, the cultured, the curious, and even by those who did not appreciate her wonderful conversation. Every sentence she uttered was caught, repeated and revered.

The first time she appeared after her arrival from France was at the house of Lady Jersey. As she was being led by her hostess to be introduced to Lady Hertford, the favourite of the moment, the latter rose in righteousness, looking with scorn at the Baronne de Staël, determined not to make the acquaintance of this atheistic and immoral woman. Madame de Staël was above such rebuffs, her renown was universal, so, turning aside, she went into another room and chose a high chair where she was

[1] Descriptions of émigré society in London are taken from the *Mémoires* of the Comtesse de Boigne.   Librairie Plon.

well in evidence. In a few seconds, the first drawing-room was left empty, except for Lady Hertford.

Madame de Staël's hatred for Napoleon was proverbial: she described him as "not a man, but a system; he considers women as only useful to produce conscripts for his future wars—otherwise they are a sex which he would like suppressed". Her hatred for him was only equalled by his for her.

6

First Steps on a Tortuous Road

At about this time, Louis Philippe was overwhelmed to receive from Louis XVIII a message asking him to use his influence with the British Government on his behalf.

In his mind the Czar was beginning to play with the idea of a reconciliation with Napoleon, and had decided to turn Louis XVIII out of Russia. The only refuge which the King could think of was England, but he guessed that the British Government would not be over-enthusiastic at receiving him. He also knew that his brother, the Comte d'Artois, was playing a role in London, almost posing as the lawful King, and that any attempt to ask for his aid would be useless. It was then that he stooped to Louis Philippe, the man he despised, but who would not dare to refuse him.

Louis Philippe, elated by this mark of the King's confidence, busily set about his mission—he approached the Government with his most persuasive manner but was met with a refusal; undaunted, Louis Philippe wrote to Louis XVIII:

> I feel assured that should your Majesty arrive unannounced, alone and without a suite, nobody would dare to oppose your Majesty's entry into England; it is certain, Sire, that immediately the King's Ministers would receive you and arrange an abode for your Majesty.[1]

On receiving this, Louis XVIII realized that his young cousin was resourceful, perhaps dangerously so, but, for the time being, worth using. So, one day he disembarked alone at Yarmouth, was received, though without much enthusiasm,

---

[1] *Louis Philippe*, by J. Lucas-Dubreton.

and permitted to take up residence at Hartwell House, near Aylesbury.

It was here that Louis Philippe came to pay his respects. He was graciously welcomed by the King, who found it expedient to show gratitude to his cousin for what he had done.

It was on a Sunday: the Duc d'Orléans arrived rather earlier than was expected, just as the royal family were leaving the Chapel after hearing Mass. Marie Thérèse, Duchesse d'Angoulême (daughter of Louis XVI and Marie Antoinette), was crossing the hall, when she suddenly found herself face to face with Louis Philippe. All the horror of the past stood waiting to bow before her. She became deathly pale, and uttering a sharp cry, collapsed on the floor. Louis Philippe, abashed and mortified, asked the King to allow him to retire; but the King said that it was only a passing *malaise*, to which the Duchesse was subject, and asked him to remain; by the time dinner was served, his niece would have recovered completely.[1]

Still, the feelings of the Duchesse were so obvious that, just as he had learnt to shun the Court of the Comte d'Artois, so Louis Philippe made his visits to Hartwell as rare as possible.

*　　　*　　　*

While the Society of the old France loved, laughed and died amongst themselves, Louis Philippe and his brothers lived on at Twickenham, deeply attached to each other, each following his own pursuits; Louis Philippe seeking to ingratiate himself with the circle of the Prince Regent; Montpensier absorbed in his music; Beaujolais pursuing a life of pleasure.

We are told that, at that time, Louis Philippe was fairly good-looking. He dressed with great care, but had no distinction; his figure and manners were decidedly bourgeois; yet he was clever, and in his conversation one sensed a great depth of knowledge. Madame de Genlis had not been in vain.

The Duc de Montpensier was fascinating, although ugly; he had great charm, was the acme of a "grand seigneur", gracious yet friendly, possessing a deep love of beauty. Was it already the fatal illness enveloping him which kept him away from the whirl of Society in which his eldest brother revelled?

[1] *Mémoires* of the Comtesse de Boigne. Librairie Plon.

Montpensier was the essence of a French nobleman, as contrasted with the English gentleman of that period. The latter though gallant, lacked the subtle *delicatesse* which is so intangible.

Gradually, the cough grew worse. Louis Philippe nursed him to the last. Montpensier wasted slowly. On 18th May 1807 he died, and was buried in Westminster Abbey a few days later. During the ceremony, Louis Philippe looked at Beaujolais and took fright. He was handsome and a great charmer, yet how different from the brother they were mourning.

He loved life; his whole philosophy was that existence was short and must not be frittered away in dull and idle politics. His days were passed in drinking and making love.

Rapidly, consumption gripped him, too. The doctors declared that only a warm climate might save him. His eldest brother took him to Malta, but once there he seemed to grow worse. Louis Philippe, distracted, wrote to King Ferdinand IV of the Two Sicilies for permission to take his dying brother to Sicily, in the hope that the rays of the Italian sun might work a miracle. Alas, before permission was granted, the young prince was dead. He was twenty-eight years old, and lies buried in Malta. Sometimes travellers pass by his grave and ask, "Who was the Comte de Beaujolais?" How few know the answer!

Only two of the children of Egalité were left now—Louis Philippe and the Princesse Adélaïde. Their mother, Egalité's widow, towards the end of a long life of suffering, had retired to Barcelona. She had been humiliated by the numerous and notorious liaisons of her husband, separated from her children by the cruelty of Madame de Genlis, and finally ruined and imprisoned by the Revolution; at the last, her spirit broken, she nursed her bitterness in solitude.

During the Revolution a man named Rouzet had entered her life. Probably on account of her age, he was able to work on her feelings, and gradually gained untold influence over her. He even prevailed on her to obtain for him the title of Comte de Folmont from the King of Spain. After this, he reigned supreme in her household, and gained complete control of her affairs. His arrogance and jealousy of any influence other than his own

47

over the Duchesse were such that all but the most formal con-
tacts between mother and children became impossible.

*   *   *

In the house at Twickenham, some months before he left for
Malta, Louis Philippe had realized that all his social activities
and his efforts to ingratiate himself with the elder Bourbons had
failed to advance his position. He was still only a stray figure
on the canvas of the times.

His one hope, often discussed with Dumouriez (who also had
found refuge in England), lay in an advantageous marriage.
He was getting on, thirty-five years old, and knew only too well
that no decent dynasty was likely to welcome with open arms
the son of Egalité, not to mention his own early association with
the Jacobins. Still his brain worked.

There was a certain Princess of Naples, Marie-Amélie, the
daughter of King Ferdinand IV of the Two Sicilies; her mother,
Maria Caroline, was a daughter of the Empress Maria Theresa
of Austria, and a sister of Marie Antoinette. He had heard much
about the princess, and what he heard was not very attractive.

She was not pretty—tall and thin, with fair hair and very
small blue eyes; her teeth, though not bad, were uneven, but
she carried her head well, had a charming smile and, above all,
was very "grande dame". She spoke several languages and had
been very carefully educated by her governess, Donna Vicenza
Rizzi, widow of the famous lawyer, Signor Ambrosio.

The princess had many suitors, among them the Prince of
the Asturias: even Napoleon had proposed his stepson, Eugène
de Beauharnais, but this had been scornfully refused, for, after
all, her family regarded Napoleon as a *parvenu*.

A few words seem inevitable on the history of the Two Sicilies
and their monarchs, whose descendants Louis Philippe was
soon to meet.

Sicily belonged to the Byzantine Empire until the ninth century, when the Saracens captured it from the Emperor Michael.
In the eleventh century, they were in their turn driven out by
the Normans under Roger Guiscard. The kingdom was then

conquered successively by the Emperor Frederick II (1198) of
the Holy Roman Empire, and later by the Comte d'Anjou
(1265), who established a French tyranny over the Two Sicilies,
until the hideous massacre of the French, known as the Sicilian
Vespers, forced them out of the island.

The kingdom was then divided into two portions, the Counts
of Anjou reigning in Naples, the Kings of Aragon in Sicily.
During the next four hundred years the two Kingdoms were
the subject of incessant disputes between the rival dynasties,
until the Treaty of Vienna in 1735, when it was decided that
the Crowns of Sicily and Spain should never be worn on the
same head, and the Two Sicilies were reunited under a Bourbon
King. Charles, the father of Ferdinand IV, the present King,
had been a well-loved monarch, but in 1759 he gave up the
Crown of the Two Sicilies to reign as Carlos III in Spain, when
his brother, the King of Spain, died childless.

His eldest son was insane, so the second son became heir to
the throne of Spain; the third, Ferdinand, father of Marie
Amélie, received the Crown of Sicily.

Alas, the new King was far from resembling his father. He
was incredibly ignorant, caring only for low company and the
basest of amusements. When he was seventeen, he married,
much against her will, the Archduchess Maria Caroline
Carlotta (at that time fifteen years old), seventh daughter of
the Empress Maria Theresa of Austria, and future mother of
Marie Amélie.

A few weeks after her marriage, which took place at Caserta
in May 1768, she wrote to her governess: "My life is a martyr-
dom, all the worse because one has to appear pleased. If religion had not said to me, 'think of God', I would have killed
myself."

By dint of tact and ability, she soon gained a great influence
over her husband and the whole kingdom. She it was who ruled
with a strong hand that most fickle and turbulent people, the
Neapolitans.

*　　　*　　　*

The bay of Palermo has been described as one of the most
beautiful and enchanting sights in the world; the city shines

like a jewel in a marble setting. By its architecture one can trace all the masters who ruled successively this lovely island, the Byzantine, Saracen, French, Spanish, and finally Bourbon.

Two wide avenues crossed in the Ottangolo Square in the centre of the city. The eye could wander down those broad vistas, bordered by marble palaces and shaded by tall trees, leading to the four great gates which stood as sentinels over the Sicilian capital.

During the day, the heat was so intense that social life only began in the evening. Then, in an exotic garden, filled with the scent of countless flowers, people sat listening to the strains of an orchestra which began as the cathedral bells chimed the midnight hour.

It was in this beautiful island that Louis Philippe arrived one very hot day in 1808. He was in deep mourning for his brother Beaujolais, his whole manner and bearing was that of a man in sorrow, coming to thank the King for the sympathy shown on his brother's death. Secretly, he was watchful, curious, and very anxious to make a good impression. At last his opportunity had come to meet Marie Amélie.

He felt nervous as he made his way to the palace. How would he be received? He had little fear of King Ferdinand; he knew that he was easy-going and too indolent to hate, but what of the Queen, sister of the tragic Marie Antoinette? He almost turned back—but no, it was too late, he must go on.

At length he mounted the steps: there at the top stood the Queen Maria Caroline, awaiting him. As he bent over her hand, her first words revealed her thoughts, "Monsieur, I know why you come; you come for my daughter."

He followed her to a boudoir. There, standing in the recess of a window, she took his head between her hands and gazed at him for a long time without speaking; at last she said:

"I ought to detest you, and yet I feel I like you."

Then she sent for her daughter.

The princess recorded in her diary:

Mamma sent for Isabel and me, and presented the Duc d'Orléans to us. He is of middle height, inclined to be stout;

50

he is neither handsome nor ugly. He has the features of the House of Bourbon, is polite and well educated.[1]

One must remember that Marie Amélie was then twenty-seven, and at that age eligible princes were not easily obtained. It seems strange that Queen Caroline, who was supposed to abhor the very name of Orléans, should show so much affection and friendliness for Louis Philippe at their very first meeting. He himself was astonished, but it proved that any suitor at all possible would be welcome.

That night, when he returned from the palace, after the interview, he weighed in his mind the advantages of the marriage; although far from struck by the looks of the princess, he felt that with her lay perhaps his only chance for the future. On the other hand, what would his old friends and associates think if he became the son-in-law of the autocratic Queen of Sicily, the brother-in-law of both the Empress of Austria and the heir to the throne of Spain? Would his marriage into such a despotic family mar his hopes of one day reigning on the throne of France? All this was a problem!

At last he sat down to write to his sister that he had had an unhoped-for reception, the princess was very *distinguée* and well educated, "elle me plaît".

She pleases me. . . . This short phrase was the *leitmotiv* of his long attachment for her.

So began one of the happiest periods of his life. As guest in an island where he was growing more popular every day, his vanity was deliciously flattered by the attention he received: a frequent visitor to the palace—already it was noticed that Princesse Marie Amélie's eyes were very bright when the Duc d'Orléans was near.

A curious conversation took place one evening between Queen Maria Caroline and Louis Philippe. The King was singing. This was one of his favourite pastimes, which his family and guests had to tolerate, even though he was not always quite in tune.

Louis Philippe was far away in his thoughts, examining

[1] *Journal de Marie Amélie*, edited by S.A.R. Madame la Duchesse de Vendôme. Librairie Plon.

listlessly the ornaments on a small table. Suddenly his attention was arrested as he picked up a miniature of Emma Lady Hamilton. For a long time he gazed at the features of the celebrated woman, then he heard the voice of the Queen beside him:

"She was very beautiful." Then she added, "Come, I will tell you about her," and they walked out into the warm night.

"It must be seventeen years ago that I first met her. She was then a fascinating creature and, like many who have led a questionable life, could be very kind.

When Sir William Hamilton first arrived as British Minister, I was warned against receiving her, her position in his household being a trifle ambiguous. Indeed, later on, no one knew whether she was mistress of Sir William or of Horatio Nelson, or of both. It was a curious combination, this *ménage à trois*; in other circumstances it would not have mattered, but this was different, affecting as it did two prominent men.

I was so intrigued by all I heard that I was tempted to forgo all ceremony and receive her privately, but feared this might cause a scandal. When the news spread that Sir William had married his beautiful *protégée*, I was delighted. I could now receive the woman who had become respectable in the eyes of the world.

I doubt whether that marriage made much difference to her life, but it made a difference in mine.

The first time I saw her was at a reception at the Legation. She was at the height of her loveliness. In reality, she never rose to a high standard of education, but she certainly was gifted, and quickly acquired the knowledge of beauty, which Italy, and the cultured taste of her husband, offered. She studied music, which she blended with her extraordinary personality to create a new and unique art. It was called 'the attitudes of Lady Hamilton'.

At the wish of Sir William, she would put on a simple white gown, a narrow belt encircling her waist, her lovely hair loose upon her shoulders or held in place by a comb. She would avail herself of two or three shawls, an urn, a perfume burner, a lyre and a tambourine.

With these few articles, and in her classical costume, she

would stand in the centre of the drawing-room. First she threw over her head one of the shawls which covered her entirely, even trailing on the floor; thus hidden from view, she draped the others about her. When ready, she would remove the first one, in such a manner that it fell into its place as part of the character she was representing.

The effect was always that of a beautiful statue. She drew her inspiration from ancient sculptures, never copying them exactly, just suggesting them to the poetic Italians by these unbelievably beautiful attitudes." [1]

"I have always heard that she was an extraordinary woman," murmured Louis Philippe.

The Queen's manner changed. "Have you, Monsieur? Perhaps so, but at heart she was vulgar, hard, and not a good friend to me."

MARRIAGE

Daily, Napoleon gained victories. An invincible strength seemed to make him unconquerable. Louis Philippe, as usual, adapted his tempo to fit each era, and now his vaunted hatred of Bonaparte cast a halo around him at the Sicilian Court.

Suddenly, in 1803, the news of the enforced abdication of Carlos IV, the King of Spain, and the abduction of the Spanish Royal Family by the French Commander, acting under the orders of Napoleon, set Sicily in a state of fever.

King Ferdinand determined to act as Regent during his brother's absence. He felt confident of accomplishing this without opposition, as the Spaniards were rising against the invaders.

He decided to send his second son, Prince Leopold, Duke of Salerno, then aged eighteen, to act for him. Louis Philippe saw his opportunity. He realized that, so far, his enforced inactivity had led him nowhere, and that, if he could contrive to accompany the Duke, he himself might gain some prestige.

The first thing was to approach Queen Maria Caroline, to obtain permission by persuading her that he could not remain idle, or allow her son to undertake such a difficult and dangerous

[1] This description is partly taken from the *Mémoires* of the Comtesse de Boigne. Librairie Plon.

task alone. The Queen seemed touched, and consented, though she was too astute not to guess his real motive.

The next step was to prepare the ground in Spain. The English had taken over the conduct of the war, and he wished to go to Spain, not as the mere cicerone of the young prince, but as a personality of importance who could influence the course of the war.

Several trusted negotiators were used in the intrigue: the Chevalier de Broval, a childhood friend of Louis Philippe; Sir William Drummond, the British envoy in Palermo; a Spanish agent, Don Mariano Carnerero; and a Sicilian, Robertoni. Their mission was to obtain from the Junta and from the British a military command for the Duc d'Orléans, befitting his rank.

At this juncture in his career, Louis Philippe expressed opinions which, in the light of subsequent events, sound somewhat discordant. His hatred of Napoleon seemed to develop into a repugnance for the whole French nation.

In his letters, we find him wishing passionately for the destruction of the whole French army, giving advice to the Coalition to this effect, and constantly voicing his longing for military command. He calls himself, "English, both out of need and out of principle", and tells how much pleasure it would give him to join the British Expeditionary Forces.

Another recurring topic in his correspondence was his devotion to Louis XVIII. His letter seeking permission to fight in Spain is a good example:

Sire,
I have asked for the honour of serving in the Spanish armies against Bonaparte and his satellites: their Sicilian Majesties have deigned to grant my request. I feel that I should first have sought Your Majesty's agreement, but I thought that I need have no doubts of this. I flattered myself that my zeal would be my excuse, and that you would feel, Sire, that I could not have waited without letting pass a unique opportunity.

Sire, may I soon have the privilege of fighting your enemies. May I have the even greater privilege of being the means by which they may return to the fatherly government,

54

to the tutelary protection of Your Majesty. . . . We cannot know the decrees of Providence, or the fate which awaits us in Spain, but I see only one alternative: either Spain will succumb, or her triumph will cause the downfall of Bonaparte. I shall be but a Spanish soldier, until circumstances allow me to display with advantage the standard of Your Majesty. We shall not miss the occasion, and if we could persuade the army of Murat or that of Junot to turn against the usurper; if we could cross the Pyrenees and penetrate into France, it will never be but in the name of Your Majesty, proclaimed in the face of the world and in such a way that, whatever our fate may be, our tombs may bear the epitaph: "they perished for their King, and to deliver Europe from all the usurpers by whom she is soiled".

It is my impression that such a letter reveals the true character of the man who was to usurp, in his turn, twenty years later. If his motives were as pure as his exalted protestations suggest, why is it that the British not only refused to allow him to take part in the war, but even denied him admission into Spain?

They were stopped at Gibraltar, where the Duke of Salerno was received with courtesy, but only with the greatest difficulty did Louis Philippe obtain permission to land at all, and even then only as a private person.

After this mortifying experience, the princes, sadly and rather shamefaced, abandoned the adventure. The young Duke went home, but Louis Philippe paid a quick visit to England, perhaps to collect funds. It was in Portsmouth, as he was about to embark to return to Sicily, that he was joined by his sister Adélaïde. They had not met for fifteen years. They were never to part again.

Now there seemed no reason to delay the engagement of Louis Philippe and Princesse Marie Amélie. But Queen Maria Caroline insisted that there should be no marriage unless his mother, the Duchesse d'Orléans, sanctioned it by her presence. This, however, was only an excuse for delay. Around her, people were saying that the Duc d'Orléans was in league with the British, supporting their policy against the House of Naples.

To ascertain the truth of these rumours, she had him followed: it is said that one evening, as Louis Philippe was walking to the Villa Guarnera to pay court to his fiancée, a shot was fired at him. Officially, it was given out that a sentinel had fired by mistake, but many believed that the Queen, not over-scrupulous in her methods, would have been rather relieved to be rid of him.

At last, word came from the Duchesse d'Orléans that she would not give her consent to the marriage. She was urged to this by the Comte de Folmont, who was determined to thwart any reconciliation with her children.

When it seemed that Louis Philippe, with all his tact and wiliness, would have to leave Palermo as he had come, without a bride, the unforeseen happened. Marie Amélie, who had never dared to contradict her mother, appeared before her astonished family and declared that she had made up her mind to enter a convent.

The King and Queen, too dazed to answer back, listened.

"There is one way to prevent this," went on the princess, "that is for you to assemble the Court and officially announce our betrothal: or else tonight I leave the palace, and ask the Abbess to admit me to the Noviciate."

At last the Queen answered, "You may marry on condition Louis Philippe obtains the consent of his Majesty King Louis XVIII, and the Duchesse d'Orléans attends the ceremony."

So Louis Philippe left for Minorca to see his mother. As Louis XVIII sent his formal permission for "the marriage of the Duc d'Orléans, first Prince of the Blood, to Her Royal Highness the Princesse Marie Amélie of the Two Sicilies", the old Duchesse could not refuse, and the preparations began.

The true feelings of Louis Philippe at this time are best understood from letters he wrote to his friends after his engagement.

What an advantage this means to me! What a blow to the prejudice against me; what a benefit is the close union of the House of Austria with mine! It will be a great boon to marry a Bourbon, and probably, at least I hope so, to have children.

I hope that the British Government will realize that I can be of service to them in Sicily; in England, I am quite useless. This uselessness puts a kind of extinguisher on the top of my head, which is no help to them or to me.[1]

From that time on, his policy was to co-operate closely with the British, who then controlled everything that took place in the island.

A few days before the wedding, Queen Caroline, feeling a certain remorse for her suspicions, took him apart, saying, "Mon gendre, is Masso still in your service?" Masso was his Sicilian valet.

"Yes, Madame."

"Well, please dismiss him."

"But, Madame, I am very pleased with him, and shall only dismiss him if your Majesty definitely orders me to do so."

"Then I order it: for I must tell you that this man was placed near you by my police. It would be most unseemly if an informer, known throughout the city, went behind the carriage of my son-in-law." [2]

The people of Palermo rejoiced to hear of the coming festivities; life at the palace had been somewhat austere lately, and business had been correspondingly slack. The British Government allowed the royal family a mere £300,000 for the upkeep of the Court and their own existence.

The Queen was generous; she helped many of the French émigrés who had known her sister Marie Antoinette, and she had still to support several of her children. Money troubles loomed very real before their eyes.

On the evening of 15th November 1809, the marriage contract was signed. The event was celebrated with much ceremony, but what gave it weight for the future bridegroom was the letter of consent from Louis XVIII.

The religious ceremony had to be postponed as King Ferdinand had broken his leg. It finally took place on 25th November, in the King's bedroom.

---

[1] *Louis Philippe*, by J. Lucas-Dubreton.   [2] *Ibid.*

Only in the countries of southern Europe, where religious faith is undimmed, could one behold such scenes as greeted the princess that day. The November sun shone brightly with its silvery golden rays. The room had been transformed into a bower of flowers and lights, and an altar erected, which seemed almost to disappear under the arches of blooms and candles.

As Marie Amélie entered, escorted by her mother, a low murmur of admiration went forth. She looked very regal in the gown of silver thread which the Sicilian women had woven for her. On her head she wore a diamond tiara, and just a few soft feathers nestled among the ringlets of her hair. She looked like one of the Byzantine madonnas of her country. Later they entered the palace chapel, which was one of the finest examples of pure Byzantine architecture known.

There, kneeling side by side before that peerless altar, the bridal couple assisted at Benediction and, with their hearts in joyful harmony, they intoned with the Cardinal the *Te Deum*.

Then began a life of contentment for the Duc d'Orléans; but for his wife, the new Duchesse, it was a period of ecstatic happiness. After a time, this peaceful existence grew too humdrum for Louis Philippe; his mind could never rest, especially as his mentor, Adélaïde, was never very far from him, ever watching, working and urging him on.

They were agreed that Louis Philippe's best chance of furthering his plans lay in Spain. The Spanish people, almost alone among the nations of Europe, had risen with fearless spirit to defend their independence against Napoleon, but the patriot forces were leaderless, since their irresolute King, Carlos IV, had been forced to abdicate by Napoleon.

The royal family having retired to the Isle of Leon, there was nobody in the Peninsula to act as a rallying point and symbol of unity. Louis Philippe felt that no one was better qualified than he to fill this position. His wife was a niece of the dethroned monarch, and he was a cousin.

Dumouriez wrote to Viscount Wellington who commanded the Allied armies in Spain, recommending the Duc d'Orléans as "the only man who could give political sense to the war".

He received no assurances in reply, but he was so certain that he had managed to dispose him favourably towards the Duc that he encouraged the latter to pursue the intrigue from Palermo.

The Spanish minister in Sicily approached the Council of Regency in the Isle of Leon, to persuade them that the Duc d'Orléans could exercise a powerful influence on events in Spain; he even hinted that Louis Philippe might be able to undermine the Imperial régime in France.

In March 1810, King Ferdinand IV of the Two Sicilies received a letter from the Spanish Council of Regency, asking that a Prince of his household should "command the Spanish army with a view to exciting rebellion within France, and wresting a crown, stained with blood, from the brow of the oppressor". Another letter enclosed in this, and addressed to the Duc d'Orléans, offered to him this supreme position.

Delighted, Louis Philippe accepted, without hesitation, without a qualm at the thought of fighting against his fellow-countrymen: he embarked on 21st May 1810 on the ship *Venganza*, and arrived at Tarragona full of high hopes. He felt sure of gaining an easy popularity in a country with which he was so closely connected.

But these high hopes were soon to be dashed. The British had not been consulted over his appointment, and when they heard that the Duc d'Orléans was approaching Spain, knowing his reputation they immediately gave orders that he was not to be allowed to assert himself. So that, after being received in Spain with much honour and homage, Louis Philippe was offered, not an army, but a handful of French deserters.

He refused: he had not come for this. Instead, he went to Cadiz, where Marshal Soult was besieging the British. Here again, nobody wanted him, although he was treated with the utmost respect.

While he was in Cadiz, an amusing episode occurred. One evening a messenger came in great secrecy, bringing a note from Marshal Soult to the Duc, asking for a private interview, in a house on the Cortadura, between the two camps. Louis Philippe, very intrigued and always ready to treat with any party, accepted the rendezvous. Meanwhile, the British Commander, informed by spies, became suspicious. He drove in person to see the Duc, to warn him that he was about to fall into a trap.

Many years later, Louis Philippe, when King of the French, had a conversation with Soult: "Do you know why I did not keep that appointment?" asked the King.

"Sire, I never knew," replied Marshal.

"Because I was informed that you intended making the Duc d'Orléans a sequel to the episode of the Duc d'Enghien, and that your aim was to have me shot as soon as I appeared." The King smiled and continued, "In all honesty, Monsieur le Maréchal, was that your intention?"

Soult hesitated, then a secretive smile broke slowly on the cunning old face. "No, Sire," he answered, "I merely wanted to compromise you." [1]

After a time, Louis Philippe returned to Sicily; his second expedition to Spain had proved as fruitless and frustrating as the first. On his arrival, all sense of humiliation vanished, when Marie Amélie put into his arms his son, the Duc de Chartres, born during his absence.

On the evening of 20th March 1811, all the bells of Paris were ringing, cannons were booming, cheap red wine was distributed to the populace, who were dancing and singing in the streets. The Empress Marie Louise had brought forth a son, the King of Rome. At last the Napoleonic dynasty seemed secure.

When Louis Philippe heard the news a few days later, he must have thought of his own little son, the Duc de Chartres, just one year old. Which of the two would one day reign over France?

It is God's great gift to us that, in all our hopes and anxieties, no voice is near to whisper what the future has in store. In reality, neither of these babies would fulfil their father's dream. The King of Rome was to die of consumption, an exile at Schoenbrünn, in 1832. Ten years after the Duc de Chartres was to fall from a carriage to his death.

On his return from Spain, Louis Philippe was immediately confronted with all his familiar problems. He knew how ruthless Queen Maria Caroline could be, and he determined to

[1] *Louis Philippe*, by J. Lucas-Dubreton.

make every effort to appease
Revolutionary party in the isla
figurehead and, to complicate th
were using him in their struggl
power in Sicily.

King Ferdinand gave the Orl
Palazzo Santa Teresa; it was old
Philippe, for the first time in hi
talents as a builder of palaces; an
lict became the magnificent Pal
Amélie and her husband received
institution hitherto totally unknov

Interesting foreigners, as well a
It became known as the centre of
too, came the disciples of Voltaire,
of Revolution. They came to Lou
his future through them. Side by s
monious existence in the Palazzo d'
ing between the Queen and her sor

Louis Philippe made no secret
Liberal party on the island, and was
the hands of the British Governmen

The Queen Maria Caroline was
bay the dreaded forces which had d
Antoinette; she was now firmly convi
hand way, Louis Philippe was workin
who were daily gaining strength. She
undermining the principles she had i
Prince Royal. She had guessed too la
daughter's husband. She confided to a
will make a good husband to Marie A
in him that his conduct and opinions w
must suffer, as in the depth of her soul
truth. She is not brilliantly clever but
goodness she may gain a certain infl
Adélaïde allows her to. That woman is
only meet an ambitious man and e
Philippe is a man who appears outw
fluenced. Inwardly, he will always seek

It is cu
did give
what ma
In N
Napoleo
parte, h
Napoleo
Joachim
and Sici
throne c
husband
Apar
play th
with he
enrage
retrogr
She
had be
was; th
and Q
Sir W
situatic
was de
Sir
forced
was a
separa
of he
wrote
count
of an
Ev
home
may
she l
H
boy,
of F

...cious how justly the Queen judged her son-in-law. He
...he impression of being hesitant and weak-willed; yet
...followed more consistently the same course!
...ples, Joachim Murat, Grand Duc de Berg, one of
...'s Marshals, and his beautiful wife Caroline Bona-
...d usurped the Bourbon throne. On 18th July 1808,
...had appointed his "well-beloved brother-in-law,
...Murat, Grand Duc de Berg, to the throne of Naples
...y, vacant by the succession of my brother Joseph to the
...Spain", and it was added that if Caroline survived her
...she should succeed to the throne before her sons.
...from her beauty, Caroline Murat was well fitted to
...Queen. The Neapolitans, ever fickle, were all in love
...having quite forgotten their lawful Sovereign. This
...Queen Maria Caroline, and she became even more
...de in her method of ruling the island.
...efused to bow before Sir William Bentinck, who by now
...n made Captain-General of Sicily. What a muddle it
...Murats, King and Queen of Sicily; King Ferdinand IV
...een Maria Caroline, also King and Queen of Sicily; and
...liam Bentinck the actual ruler of the island. The whole
...n was rather like an *opéra comique*, but what sorrows it
...stined to bring in its train.
...Villiam won the battle, and Queen Maria Caroline was
...to leave the country with her youngest son, Leopold. It
...terrible ordeal for Marie Amélie, who had never been
...ted from her mother, but she realized that for the peace
...country, this departure had to be. In her journal she
..."My heart was torn by conflicting emotions—love of my
...y, compassion, justice, honour. I seemed to float in a sea
...uish." [1]
...ntually Maria Caroline made her way to her beloved
...Vienna. Perhaps in those, her last months on earth, she
...ave recaptured the peace of her youth, and realized that
...d fought in vain against the rising tide of liberalism.
...r solace in her hours of desolation was a small, fair-haired
...her great nephew, the Duc de Reichstadt, once the King
...ome. How strange that the son of the man who had

...urnal de Marie Amélie (ed. la Duchesse de Vendôme). Librairie Plon.

QUEEN MARIE AMÉLIE AND HER SON, THE DUC DE CHARTRES

From the painting by David

brought disaster to her and to her family should be her consolation; now his father, Napoleon, was in exile, and for Queen Caroline the struggle and passions of life were over.

The little boy would be led in to her by his mother, Marie Louise, Archduchess of Austria, once Empress of the French; and often Maria Caroline would reproach her.

"Remember, my dear niece, a woman should never abandon her husband; you have done so. When Napoleon was in his glory, you stayed; when he was shorn of it, you left. I tell you this, I who have lost all through him."

One morning in 1814, Queen Maria Caroline of the Two Sicilies, Archduchess of Austria, was found dead, struck down by an attack of apoplexy.

When the Queen departed from Sicily, Louis Philippe sighed with relief; his great opponent had gone, the one person that he feared. She had mistrusted him, the command of the Sicilian army had been taken from him by her order; she had told him that it was the King who had decided it, but Louis Philippe knew who ruled the King. He suspected several times that she would willingly have got rid of him.

Now the air was clear and he knew he was safe. What next? Must he be content to serve the British in a small impoverished island? Or did the news from France permit a ray of hope?

7

The Cobwebs of the Palais Royal are Blown Away

London, 20th April 1814. "Bonaparte has signed his abdication —Bourbons proclaimed—Victor, Ney, Marmont, Abbé Sieyès, etc., etc., have signed. The Emperor has a pension of 200,000 per ann., and a retreat in the Isle of Elba. . . . There are to be immense rejoicings on Monday—white cockades and tremendous illumination. Carlton House to blaze with fleurs de lis, etc. The Royal Yacht is ordered to take the King [Louis XVIII] to France, Admiral of the Fleet the Duke of Clarence to command her—all true, honour bright—I am just come from the Prince." [1]

Europe went wild with relief, as the Sovereigns converged towards the capital of France, filled with all the enthusiasm of victory; but despite the arrogance of the conquerors, none dared to stay at the Tuileries. Was it a superstitious fear of that palace of so many tragedies and bitter tears, of so much misery and heartache?

The Czar chose the Palais de l'Elysée, but only for a short time; later he moved to the rue St. Florentin to stay with the Prince de Talleyrand. The Emperor appreciated the wily prince, although he mistrusted him; Talleyrand amused and interested the Czar.

The King of Prussia went across the Seine to the Hôtel de Villeroi, rue de Lille, and the Emperor of Austria chose the Hôtel Borghese in the Faubourg St. Honoré.[2] Only Louis XVIII, Sovereign of France, was absent.

In England, at Hartwell House near the market town of

[1] *Creevey*, selected and re-edited by John Gore, c.v.o.
[2] Now the British Embassy.

64

Aylesbury, the commotion had been terrific, but now all was in readiness for Louis XVIII to leave for France. The King had been far from well for some days, and the feverish anxieties of all, including his niece the Duchesse d'Angoulême, were centred upon his gouty foot.

But alas, on the fateful morning, the Sovereign was in such pain that even the most sanguine of those around him had to abandon all hope. The only alternative was to send his brother, the Comte d'Artois, to represent him.

The Comte, on arrival in the French capital, attended a Service of Thanksgiving in Nôtre Dame, then hastened to take up residence at the Tuileries.

How strange that he felt no qualms in occupying the very apartments which had been those of his brother, Louis XVI, and which the Empress Marie Louise had vacated only fifteen days before. As soon as he entered the palace, the white flag with the fleurs de lis was broken on the dome of the central pavilion, and so the Bourbons were proclaimed.

On 3rd May 1814, at three o'clock in the afternoon, Louis XVIII made his state entry into the capital. It was a beautiful day, and Paris showed a welcome beneath its sun and blue sky; but how often before it had welcomed and shone for new rulers! The whole city seemed bathed in white—white cockades, white dresses, white wreaths, and white flags. The King's carriage, drawn by its eight horses, swaying white plumes on their heads, passed slowly through the lines of Gardes Nationaux.

The King, ignoring his throbbing toes, smiled, acknowledging the clamour of the delirious crowds. Next to him, stiff and morose, sat the Duchesse d'Angoulême. She seemed almost unable to raise her head. What suffering must have pierced her heart as she passed amidst the same mob, whom she had last heard howling their hatred, and saw again those very places where she had so often walked and laughed with her parents and brother, twenty-two years earlier.

As she entered the Tuileries, the home of her youth, it was almost too much for her. She had come face to face with the memory of that fatal night of 9th August 1792, when she had accompanied her parents to the Temple.

At the Restoration, the royal family consisted of the King, Louis XVIII (his wife, Josephine de Savoie, had died leaving no children), his brother Monsieur, the Comte d'Artois, also a widower but with two sons, the Duc d'Angoulême whose wife was the daughter of Louis XVI, and the Duc de Berri who in 1816 was to marry Princesse Caroline de Bourbon-Naples, niece of Marie Amélie.

After the royal family, the Duc and Duchesse d'Orléans took precedence as first Princes of the Blood, then the old Duchesse d'Orléans, widow of Egalité and her daughter, Princesse Adélaïde; lastly, the aged Prince de Condé, his son the Duc de Bourbon, later known as the Prince de Condé, father of the unfortunate Duc d'Enghien whose tragic death, by order of Napoleon, shocked the world.

*　　*　　*

On the evening of 17th May 1814, Louis Philippe arrived in Paris from Sicily: he was alone, weary and dusty. After an absence of twenty-two years, he stood once more in the garden of the Palais Royal. No one noticed him as he followed the galleries and crossed the Cour des Colonnes, and at last entered his home.

A Garde Suisse stopped him and in an arrogant voice called out: "Where are you going?"

The Duc muttered an almost inaudible reply and, pushing him aside, knelt down reverently to kiss the lowest step of the Grand Staircase.

As he rose and slowly mounted the Grand Staircase, a feeling of forlornness assailed him. All that he remembered and had cherished during the long years of exile had vanished. Instead, desolation and the smell of decay filled the empty rooms. The gilded walls were tarnished, holes gaped where once the splendid mirrors hung, cobwebs fell in festoons and swayed in the draught from the broken windows. Was this the grim spectre for which he had fought? Was this the ideal which stood behind the "Marseillaise" and the Tricolor and had moved him to such enthusiasm in his youth?

The Garde Suisse followed him and once more challenged him. He turned round and eyed the man coldly.

"I am the Duc d'Orléans—*je suis ici chez moi!*"

"Chez moi"! Those words seemed to re-echo in his brain as he stood motionless in that great empty hall, listening to the footfall of the guard dying away in the distance. This was another epoch. The Revolution was dead, but its ideals might be used one day to serve a new crown—his crown.

He moved through those silent rooms; every step revealed more abandonment and filth. Could it ever be made worthy of a first Prince of the Blood, as it had been when his father had been alive? His father! whom he could now judge with indulgent contempt, who had worked for precisely the same ends as he, but who had blundered so clumsily to his death.

At last he had to leave the Palais Royal. He had a duty to perform, which could be delayed no longer. His heart beat faster at the very thought; he remembered so well his humiliation at Hartwell House, at Baker Street—would the Tuileries be the same? Reluctantly he entered his carriage and drove to see the King.

One of the King's Chamberlains was waiting for him, and preceded him to the King's Cabinet. Louis XVIII was sitting in a wheeled chair; he made a gesture and said: "My cousin, I should like to greet you standing, but—" he pointed to his wrapped foot—"this makes it impossible."

Although large, ungainly, and evidently in pain, a certain kingly charm emanated from him. Across his chest lay the ribbon of the Ordre du Saint Esprit. Notwithstanding his apparent friendly welcome, Louis Philippe felt that it was not genuine. There was a certain stiffness which reacted on Louis Philippe.

Then the King's tone changed—"Monsieur," he said, "twenty-five years ago, you were a Lieutenant-General; it is my pleasure to announce to you that you still hold this rank."

Louis Philippe was suddenly overcome. "Sire, in this rank I shall serve your Majesty to my utmost capacity."

With the Comte d'Artois later, the interview was not so smooth. Louis Philippe was wearing the white cockade. The Comte was in the uniform of a Colonel-General of the Garde Nationale.

As Louis Philippe was crossing the corridor, the Comte

d'Artois came up to him, and with a sneering grin said: "Really, my cousin, you change your cockade too often."

"And you, my dear cousin, change your coat," answered Louis Philippe.

As Louis Philippe walked down the Grand Staircase, he smiled to himself. How disturbed the émigrés would be, those who had shunned and humiliated him, when they found him back in his old rank! Yet that exchange of words with the Comte d'Artois had shown him where he really stood—no nearer to the senior branch of the Bourbons. The Tuileries meant so much; would he ever be the one, not to receive favours, but to bestow?

His reverie was broken as the Garde Suisse cried out, "The carriage of his Highness the Duc d'Orléans waits below."

The immense *appanage* conferred by Louis XIV on the founder of the House of Orléans, was now owned by Louis Philippe. During the Revolution, the Orléans princes were deprived of this fabulous wealth by a decree of the Assemblée Constituante. The restitution by Louis XVIII dated 20th May 1814, three days after the Duc's return, was a curiously worded document, clearly showing the monarch's caution: being a decree signed by the King alone, it was also revocable by him. Nevertheless, the Duc was most grateful, and he renewed his oaths of loyalty and fidelity to the Crown.

Louis Philippe determined to occupy his royal residence as soon as possible, and now, assured of a very large fortune, he sent for all the great artists of the time; Monsieur de Fontaine, who had been architect to Napoleon, was entrusted with the supervision of the work. Soon the Palais Royal regained some of the grandeur of its lost glory.

The right wing was allotted to the Duchesse and to his sister, Madame Adélaïde; his heir, the Duc de Chartres, had the left wing, and his own private apartments were on the first floor overlooking the forecourt.

From now on, he had to consider most carefully his future conduct, as first Prince of the Blood—a junior branch, it is true, but one which might hold very high destinies. He planned, therefore, to maintain polite relations with the Court, yet not to intrude, as he knew only too well the resentful sentiments of those around the King: but he would never allow them to forget that he was a prince.

He returned to Palermo for a few days to bring his wife Marie Amélie and his children to their new home. It was a really sumptuous residence that awaited their coming. Architects, painters, decorators, had performed a rapid and wonderful feat. All was ready. At half past seven in the evening of 22nd September 1814, Marie Amélie saw the Palais Royal for the first time. Bewildered, she stepped from the carriage.

The Palais was brilliantly lit up, people coming from every direction to welcome her; she was rather astonished to see amidst all the grandeur, shops intruding to the very foot of the principal staircase, which was lined by a multitude of servants in the rich Orléans livery. The noise made her head throb, her advanced pregnancy was beginning to tell. As she was led to her room, acknowledging mechanically all the greetings, her one idea was to sleep.

The next morning, Marie Amélie awoke for the first time to the sunshine of Paris. The atmosphere, the very smell of the city, was so different from that of Sicily. As the curtains were drawn back by her faithful maid, Saveria, she asked in the soft Italian language which she always used with her own servants:

"Where is the Prince?"

The maid answered that he had given orders that she was not to be disturbed, and had gone out. Marie Amélie reclined once more on her pillows; then thoughts must have assailed her.

What would their future be in the home of Philippe Egalité, which was now her home? Had his sin brought a curse upon this house; could her prayers ever erase it? She feared for her husband, his restless ambition and the animosity of the Bourbons; above all, what chance had she to restrain him when Adélaïde never ceased to urge him on and to whisper in his ear?

That afternoon, at half past two, Marie Amélie entered the Tuileries for the first time. In her journal she describes the scene.

"Nothing can equal the beauty and magnificence of the Palais des Tuileries. It is truly worthy of sheltering a great monarch." [1] Coming from Marie Amélie, who had known the lovely Sicilian *palazzos* and also those of Austria, this was a great tribute.

The King received her most affectionately, and kissed her tenderly. She was really one of them, in rank and in name; with Louis XVIII such things counted. To prove his welcome, he even kissed Madame Adélaïde, and asked her to sit down; this was a terrific mark of condescension.

Marie Amélie had never before seen the King, and her impression was, "He is small, rather fat, holds himself badly on his legs, has a handsome head, sparkling eyes. He takes snuff incessantly, is rather slovenly in his dress, but one forgets all this in the charm and dignity of his manners. He is witty, and at the same time deep and cultured." [2]

Marie Amélie and he seemed to understand one another, and whatever he felt against the other members of the Orléans family, he never failed to make her feel his affection. After leaving the King, Marie Amélie, followed by Adélaïde, visited the Duchesse d'Angoulême, who at once gave her first cousin a warm welcome. Only between themselves could they speak of their mothers, those two sisters who had loved each other so deeply, Maria Caroline of the Two Sicilies and Marie Antoinette of France. [3]

Thus was formed a friendship which lasted through all the vicissitudes until the end of their lives.

[1], [2], [3] *Journal de Marie Amélie* (ed. la Duchesse de Vendôme). Librairie Plon.

8

The Bees are Removed, the Bees are Replaced

During the first months after the return of the Bourbons, workmen filled the Tuileries, removing Eagles and Bees from every ceiling and corner of the palace. Portraits of Napoleon and his generals seemed to fill every stateroom, corridor and staircase. Monsieur Lenôtre, in his remarkable book on the Tuileries, tells us that it was a difficult problem to decide whether to store them away or destroy them. When all the emblems had been either hidden or sold, one white elephant remained, a colossal statue of Napoleon by Canova. It was a remarkable work, carved from a solid block of marble ten feet high and eight feet broad. Apart from the value of the work, the marble alone cost 66,000 francs. There was an attempt to sell it, but nobody wanted such an effigy.

At last, the British Ambassador, in the name of His Britannic Majesty, offered to pay the required price on condition that the transport and packing was borne by the French Government. So Napoleon was sold to Great Britain. The weight was ten tons; it took two days to haul it to Port St. Nicolas, and four months before it reached London safely.

The pomp and ceremony of the Court had been revived and etiquette was rigorous. The men of the bodyguard were all required to be six foot in height; their duties were to stand on guard in the anteroom, and to accompany "His Majesty's Meats" from the kitchen to the royal table: as the dishes passed, all rose and stood in silence until the last plate had disappeared into the royal apartments.

To a certain extent, Louis Philippe took part in all this, but often he felt a sense of humiliation, as he was only a Serene Highness, while his wife was a Royal Highness. When they entered a stateroom, the double doors were thrown open for

Marie Amélie, then rapidly shut while Louis Philippe and Madame Adélaïde waited; then one of the doors only would be opened to allow them to pass through.

Louis XVIII insisted on the strictest observance of the rigid etiquette of the last reign. Thus, one day, he slipped and fell heavily to the floor; almost helpless, he lay, unable to raise himself. Monsieur de Nogent, one of the officers of the Guard, rushed forward to help the King, but Louis XVIII repulsed him, saying in an angry tone: "Oh, no! Monsieur de Nogent." And he waited patiently until the Captain of the Guard appeared; then he allowed the man of higher rank to assist him to rise.[1]

The return of the Duc d'Orléans to France made little impression, and passed almost unnoticed in the fever and enthusiasm of the new reign. The French nation is ever avid of sensation; scenes may change, but as long as there is some excitement which brings distraction and fermentation, the people cheer. Dull routine usually succeeds these outbursts of novelty —it is then that danger lurks.

Louis XVIII soon discovered that it was an impossible task to satisfy the demands of the returned émigrés on the one side, and those of the Republicans who had rallied to his cause on the other.

The former insisted upon the restitution of their confiscated estates, and the latter refused to surrender the spoils.

Gradually, jealousies and resentment spread as hopes and illusions faded. The benefits of the new policy came to be forgotten, or taken for granted, and only personal grievances seemed to count.

Some of the Orléans supporters saw in this an opportunity, and fostered this spirit of unrest, and very subtly the name of Louis Philippe began to be whispered. One must admit that this prince of the royal blood stood out from amongst the others.

His exquisite politeness, especially to those of lower rank, his remarkable memory—he never forgot the face and history of a person he had once met—the way in which he could hold the attention of many by his interesting conversation, his figure,

[1] *Louis Philippe*, by J. Lucas-Dubreton.

enhanced by the brilliant uniform of a lieutenant-general, all attracted the attention of the people. Added to all this, his early revolutionary tendencies made him in their eyes a prince, half-royal, half-republican, and of a different type from the other Bourbons.

The Prince de Talleyrand was amongst the first to perceive, and to warn the monarch of these dangerous traits.

One day, after Louis Philippe had left for Sicily to fetch his family, this shrewd statesman remarked to the King:

"Does Your Majesty intend that the Duc d'Orléans should return from Palermo?"

"Naturally," answered the King, "His Highness will be back within a month."

"Does Your Majesty think that the climate of France suits His Highness as well as that of the Two Sicilies?"

"My cousin indeed returned last time in very good health, but I do not think that the air of Paris will affect his constitution."

Talleyrand saw that his hint would not be accepted, and said no more. It was the Prince himself who told Louis Philippe of this conversation years later.

The Duc affected to ignore all these undercurrents, and played his somewhat ambiguous role extremely cleverly. The Revolutionary party, which had been crushed and almost annihilated by Napoleon, had revived under the new Constitutional liberties, and they cast their eyes around for a figurehead; they settled, timidly at first, on Louis Philippe. They saw in him all they needed, a prince who had associated with the Jacobin Club of 1791, and a warrior who had fought for the Republic. The Duc himself carefully concealed the fact that only the British Government had prevented him from fighting the French armies in Spain; and he now posed as a Nationalist, the prince who had always refused to fight against his country.

Thus a new Orléanist clique grew up among the Republican party. These men, who included Laffitte, the rich banker, Benjamin Constant, author of *Adolphe*, and Lafayette, hero of both French and American revolutions, wanted a prince who could combine monarchy with Republican ideals. Louis

73

Philippe, with his apparent modesty, seemed best to fit this part, and intrigues sprang up in his favour.

At this time, he was constantly in touch with the opponents, secret and avowed, of the Government; but his instinct warned him that the time was not ripe to match his strength against the hereditary monarchy.

There were still too many people in the country who were so relieved to see the end of war, that they were more than content to be ruled by the legitimate Bourbons. So he affected to lead a life of great retirement, and to devote himself entirely to his home and family.

France seemed to be regaining her serenity. The King was leading the country, the "Charta" had been inaugurated, the Court revived, and nobility, bourgeoisie and peasants were beginning to rejoice in the blue skies of peace. Then, on 5th March 1815, at eleven o'clock at night, the Duc de Blacas, one of the King's Equerries, rushed to the Palais Royal and insisted on seeing the Duc d'Orléans at once.

Shown into Louis Philippe's bedroom, he told him that he had been sent by the King to command the Duc to go at once to the Tuileries. Louis Philippe was startled, and protested:

"I am not dressed. I must ring for my valet to bring me the correct clothes."

"No, sir, put on the coat you have just taken off; there is no time to lose."

On the way to the palace, the Duc de Blacas turned to him and said, "Bonaparte is in France." Louis Philippe gave a cry of surprise and horror.

"The news causes you great disquietude?"

"Yes, great."

"Well," went on the Duc de Blacas, "you will find the King very calm; he sees no danger."

Arrived at the Tuileries, they found a strange scene, which the Duc never forgot. He himself was almost trembling with agitation, but as he entered the room, he saw the King in his wheeled chair, obviously suffering from an acute attack of gout, but outwardly very calm and serene. He said:

"Well, Monsieur, Bonaparte is in France."

74

"Oh, Sire, I am very upset."

"I should prefer him out of the country, but as he is here, we must hope that it will bring on a crisis which, once and for all, will rid us of such a creature."

"I admire the self-possession of your Majesty, and I am happy to see you, Sire, so calm. As for me, I find the crisis rather acute."

"Oh, we shall take measures to deal with the situation."

And the King proceeded to explain his plan of action.

"My brother, Monsieur le Comte d'Artois, will go to Lyons; his sons, the Duc d'Angoulême and the Duc de Berri, will leave for Nîmes and Besançon respectively. You will serve under my brother at Lyons."

"Does your Majesty think it prudent thus to send all the princes without troops?"

"I am sending troops at the same time, but the princes must show themselves, and recall to the population that our dynasty is reigning, and that Bonaparte is now a vagabond."

"But, Sire, would it not be safer to group some of the army at certain important points, to judge their temper and loyalty? If I may be allowed to give my opinion, we must not forget that Napoleon, marching towards the capital, although still far away, is a serious menace. Many of the people of France still have a feeling akin to hero-worship for the ex-Emperor."

Louis XVIII cut the Duc short. "My orders are that you are to leave for Lyons; once there, my brother will give you a command—a division, or a corps; anyhow, something, whatever he chooses. I do not tell you to leave tonight. Grease your boots and come back tomorrow."

"My boots are ever greased in readiness to serve your Majesty."

As Louis Philippe left the presence, the humiliation of serving under the Comte d'Artois assailed him. He also saw the stupidity of the plan. The Comte was not a famous general, and for him to lead soldiers of uncertain loyalty would be a tragedy.

The interview with the King on the next day brought nothing new, and that night the Duc left for Lyons. Directly on his arrival in that city he reported at the Archbishop's Palace, where the Comte d'Artois was staying, and asked for news.

75

"Oh! the news is not cheerful," replied the Comte. "Bonaparte is already at Grenoble, which he entered on the night of the 7th and 8th. He has found over a hundred guns and a huge quantity of ammunition of every kind: but the most alarming sign is that all the troops which were in the Dauphiné have gone over to him. Believe me, he will soon be at the gates of this town. I have made a survey and we have not one gun, not a rifle, not a bullet—and, above all, not a five franc piece. This is how we stand, my dear cousin. In fact, it only remains for us to go and polish the Imperial Eagles, and all will be in order to receive him."

I have sometimes wondered what Louis Philippe felt at this moment. He could not wish for the triumph of Napoleon, and he knew enough of the temper of the country to realize that the people were utterly weary of the Imperial régime, weary of its incessant wars, weary of the Emperor himself. Even if he was carried back to the Tuileries on a wave of momentary enthusiasm, his triumph would be ephemeral, like a bubble which would soon explode into a million colours.

What of the Bourbons? Could they take up again the reins of government, if they left the country now? Would this new crisis bring the Orléans dynasty to power?

That night, at his inn, he could not sleep. He felt peril coming nearer with the tumultuous advance of Napoleon; and with the Comte d'Artois, who was in command, not knowing how to act! First of all, he must be got away, and with him, his suite. They must not be captured by Napoleon. He rose from his bed; it was scarcely dawn. He awoke Marshal Macdonald and asked him to accompany him. They walked through the silent street, their steps re-echoing in the darkness.

"I wonder, Maréchal, if all these snoring citizens care whether Louis XVIII or Bonaparte rules them?"

"Do you, Monseigneur?"

Louis Philippe looked towards him.

"Frankly, Monsieur le Maréchal, I do not know. Time will tell."

"Yes," answered the Marshal, "but one thing is certain; the time will not be long before neither Napoleon nor the Bourbons will be sitting on the throne."

Louis Philippe understood, but made no reply. They were reaching the Archbishop's Palace. Just then a messenger, panting, caught them up.

"They are coming," he gasped, "they are probably in the Faubourg now."

Inside the palace, not a soul stirred; once more the Duc turned to the Marshal.

"Is this heedlessness or stupidity?"

They found a servant, who informed them that the Captain of the Guard held the key to the Comte's bedroom, and that he had gone to rest. At last they came across a valet who held the key of the dressing-room, and Louis Philippe was able to enter. The Comte was fast asleep. The Duc drew aside the bed curtains, awoke the occupant, and instantly informed him of the danger.

"Bonaparte is perhaps this minute entering the Faubourg de la Guillotière on the outskirts of Lyons."

The Comte d'Artois, scarcely awake, turned to the other side of his pillow and did not seem in the least perturbed.

Then the Marshal shouted. "But get up, Sir. This is no joke; there is not a moment to lose."

Reluctantly the prince sat up. "What is all this nonsense?"

Without waiting for more, the Marshal rushed out of the room to order the prince's horses, and to warn his suite that they must leave at once. In his room, the Comte d'Artois kept muttering, "All this is useless; we have plenty of time."

At that moment, the Comte Roger de Damas, one of the Aides de Camp, burst open the door without ceremony and confirmed that the Imperial hussars were actually in the Faubourg. So the Comte gave the order that they must leave Lyons instantly.

When all was ready, Louis Philippe felt free. He had obeyed the King's command; had put himself under the orders of the Comte d'Artois; but now that the prince was leaving, he could carry out his own plans. As he accompanied the prince to his carriage, he said:

"Now that you, Sir, are leaving, I suppose that I am no longer useful. I ask leave to get away from this town."

"Monsieur le Duc, you may leave if it pleases you, but where do you intend to go?"

"I shall travel to Paris and put my family in safety, so as not to allow unnecessary hostages to fall into his hands, should Bonaparte ever reach the capital."

So, without wasting any more time, Louis Philippe returned to Paris. A few hours later, a large travelling coach drove up to the Palais Royal. It had been hired from a coach builder, and bore no arms upon its doors. The Duc dare not use his own carriage lest his coat of arms be recognized.

Into this vehicle stepped Marie Amélie, who was expecting her fifth child, with her four other children, and they drove off, heading for Calais, on their way to England.

In the short time that elapsed between his arrival from Lyons and the departure of his family, the Duchesse Marie Amélie had written an affectionate letter to the King explaining her departure.

As Louis Philippe re-entered the Palais Royal after watching the coach drive away, he wondered if the King would rebuke him for his haste in sending his family to safety. He ordered one of his Aides de Camp to carry the letter to the Tuileries, as he thought that it might smooth matters considerably.

The King seemed perturbed the next time he received his cousin.

"You were in rather a hurry to send your family away; but it does not matter, I forgive you."

In reality, the King had been told rather alarming truths; one of these was that the Duc's retinue had shouted "*vive l'Empereur*" as he had driven into Paris. Could the Duc have ordered this so as to create a sensation?

Monsieur d'André, the Chief of Police, had been told to approach the Duc tactfully but firmly on the question of his leaving Paris.

"Monseigneur, in your own interest, leave Paris. Too much is known."

The Duc turned to face the Chief of Police; his face was bland and he drew out his snuff box with deliberation before he answered.

"But, Monsieur, my only desire is always to serve his Majesty."

He was not deluded by André's apparent concern for his

interests, and he felt certain that if he refused to leave the capital of his own free will, the King would soon find some way of sending him away; which, in fact, actually happened.

A few days later, Louis Philippe, by order of the King, was driving to Lille with Marshal Mortier to inspect the troops in the north. Conflicting feelings must have assailed him, fear of Napoleon, the knowledge that he was certainly no longer *persona grata* at the Tuileries, and anxiety over his own fate. In all his confusion, no star appeared to pierce the gloom. On one point only he felt at ease: he had left the Princesse Adélaïde in Paris to watch over his interests, and to keep him in touch with any developments which might arise. The King had promised to protect her, but in those few days before they all fled, she did not appear at the Tuileries, but spent her time on mysterious and suspicious errands. Even when the Duc de Blacas called at the Palais Royal to bring her 100,000 francs on behalf of the King, "Her Highness is out"! [1]

When Louis Philippe reached Lille, he soon realized that here, as elsewhere, the whole country was in a state of collapse. He met, among the officers, General Drouet-d'Erlon, Colonel Lefevbre-Desnouettes, the Lallemand brothers, and nothing in his attitude revealed his knowledge that these men were secretly preparing a coup d'état in his favour; but all their hopes were ruined as Napoleon's army rumbled nearer.

As they wavered and dithered, wondering whom to rally with the least loss to their cause, Louis XVIII arrived.

He looked tired and unhappy, struggling to conceal his weariness and his gout; and his greeting to Louis Philippe was icy. He had already heard through spies that, whilst dining with a group of officers, Louis Philippe had remarked loudly, "I would willingly don again the tricolor cockade," and had later added that it enraged him to see the Crown which might one day be his, endangered by the folly of the elder branch of the family. The monarch never forgot these remarks.

The whole day passed in deliberations. Where was the King to go? At last, about midnight, his Majesty cut short the discussions with the announcement that he was leaving for Ostend. One by one, his generals took their leave. Macdonald and

[1] *Adélaïde d'Orléans*, by Raoul Arnaud.

Mortier were kindly received and thanked for their loyalty. Louis Philippe was the last; he stood before the King and said:

"Sire, I have come to receive my orders. Where does your Majesty wish me to go?"

Louis XVIII was reading a document. He did not take the trouble to look up.

"Anywhere. I am not interested."

"I intend to leave for England to join my family."

"That is the best thing you can do."

And the King resumed his reading.

9

The Prince Regent Drives to an Hotel

On 25th March 1815, the Duchesse d'Orléans arrived in London with her children, Chartres, Louise, Marie and Nemours, the latter's wet nurse, two ladies' maids, the Comte de Grave who had escorted them from France, and the Duchesse's lady-in-waiting, the Comtesse de Vérac. A whole floor had been reserved for them at the Grillon Hotel in Albemarle Street, and at once the Duchesse was surrounded. Feeling against Napoleon was so strong, that she, as a distinguished refugee, was almost overwhelmed with attention.

The evening after her arrival, Lord Castlereagh, the Foreign Secretary, asked to be received. She wrote of him in her journal, "A man between forty and fifty, tall, thin, serious, cold beyond expression; I feel it would be an impossibility to stir his feelings, or to make him weep." [1]

More and more important people came to visit her. The Duke of Kent, an old friend of Louis Philippe, whom Marie Amélie described as "big, fat, handsome, entirely bald! he has a good open expression, very *sympathique*".[2]

A few days later, the Prince Regent—later George IV—announced his intention of paying a visit. The excitement was terrific. So much depended upon the impression she made on him. Marie Amélie had heard how easily he became bored, and if this happened, he would not return to be bored again.

Saveria, her devoted maid, was ordered to adorn the rather banal hotel drawing-room with flowers. The children were dressed formally, and Marie Amélie herself looked regal in a heavy brocade gown and emerald necklace.

[1,2] *Journal de Marie Amélie* (ed. la Duchesse de Vendôme). Librairie Plon.

The Prince Regent arrived after dinner, and was most courteous. They spoke of France and he especially stressed his anxiety to see the King re-established on the throne.

"France must be a Kingdom; it is indispensable for the peace of Europe," he said.

The visit lasted three hours, and again Marie Amélie describes her visitor: "He is big and fat, like his brother the Duke of Kent. His manners are extremely polite, but slightly affected. He likes to talk, and relate, and describe, and one can discern that he likes above all to be listened to. He must have been very good looking." [1]

All the fashionable world followed suit, and Marie Amélie and her bevy of lovely children were much sought after. But she, a very simple person, accepted all this adulation only on account of her husband. For his sake, she played the role, but in her heart, she longed for a quiet spot where she could relax alone with Louis Philippe and their children, and for a time without Adélaïde!

On the morning of 3rd April, at six o'clock, she was awakened by knocking. She told Saveria to open the door, and to Marie Amélie's delighted surprise, Louis Philippe walked in with his hands outstretched.

Alas! she had only a few hours' tête-à-tête with him, before, at five o'clock, Adélaïde arrived with Madame de Montjoie. So once more Marie Amélie resigned herself to be a third—a rather shadowy third—in this *ménage à trois*.

Certainly, the Prince Regent seemed determined to show his sympathy with the royal refugees: that evening at eight o'clock he came again, accompanied by his brother, the Duke of Clarence. They remained until midnight. The Prince had come to hear the latest developments in France, but again he alone discoursed, with grace and great intelligence. It suited Louis Philippe, who was too cautious to say much.

The Duchesse d'Orléans described in her Journal, edited by the Duchesse de Vendôme, the reception which the Prince Regent offered them at Carlton House:

[1] *Journal de Marie Amélie* (ed. la Duchesse de Vendôme). Librairie Plon.

We drove to Carlton House; we were shown into a room in old Chinese lacquer, magnificently furnished, but dark and heavy. The Regent arrived half-an-hour late; he excused himself and led us into a large drawing-room, the walls covered in black velvet, blue curtains ornamented with fleurs de lis, where we found his mother, the Queen. She is certainly more than seventy years old, small, stout; she has nothing distinguished about her looks, but her manner is agreeable. She has a strong German accent, her life is eminently respectable, and most austere and religious.

The Princesses Elizabeth and Mary were also present. Nobody seemed to mind when the Marchioness of Hertford appeared, the favourite of the moment. She is tall and large, like a statue, about fifty or sixty years of age, and dresses like a young girl of sixteen.

We sat and drank coffee; then, after a time, we went down a small staircase into another apartment comprising several galleries, gorgeously furnished, but to my mind the ceilings were too low. There we found a great many assembled, diplomats with their wives, and members of the highest society, standing in a row along the galleries.

The Queen went first, and spoke to each one; then Princess Elizabeth took me by the arm, and charmingly named each person to me as I made the circle. The Queen then went to the further gallery to play a game of cards. We sat in the nearer one, and talked to the guests. At eleven o'clock the Queen left, after once more shaking hands with each person, and we did the same, very touched by the great kindness of the royal family.

A curious conversation took place that evening between the Prince Regent and Louis Philippe. Taking the latter aside, the prince remarked, half in jest: "My good friend, you appear to be an object of exceptional interest to the King of France." Louis Philippe raised his eyebrows enquiringly. "Indeed, your every movement seems to interest his Majesty," continued the Prince Regent. "Were I in your place, I should find such solicitude a shade—embarrassing?"

Louis Philippe understood the allusion. He merely said: "I thank your Royal Highness," and they parted.

Almost at once Louis Philippe noticed how true the warning was; paid spies surrounded him and his sister. He decided to remove his family to Twickenham, to his old house which had been made ready for them.

But once there, he discovered that many of the servants and even a few gardeners were spying on his every action. For the moment he decided his best policy was to ignore it all.

The arrival of the Duchesse d'Angoulême with her haughty suspicious manner—she too had been sent to watch over them —made Louis Philippe and Princesse Adélaïde extremely cautious. For the present all their activities ceased. When Monsieur de la Châtre, the French Ambassador, was replaced by the Marquis d'Osmond, father of the Comtesse de Boigne, life became easier, as he trusted the Orléans. A more friendly atmosphere reigned between the Embassy and Orléans House.

Even then, one day, an agent of Louis XVIII went to see the Ambassador, saying:

"Your Excellency, at last Monsieur le Duc d'Orléans is unmasked. Seditious proclamations are being printed secretly at Twickenham, and sacks of them are about to be sent to France."

Monsieur d'Osmond replied: "If you bring me, not only a proclamation, but any publication issued from a press at Orléans House, I will pay you a hundred guineas on the spot." He waited in vain.

The following Sunday, the Ambassador and Madame de Boigne visited the Duc, and found the whole family assembled round a small toy press which had been bought to amuse the children, and all were engrossed in printing a poem written years before by the Duc de Montpensier.[1]

The suspicions of Louis XVIII were not entirely unjustified. He had heard on good authority that, during the Congress of Vienna, all the powerful men in Europe had been approached with insinuations that the Crown might go to the Duc d'Orléans. Even the Duke of Wellington had been asked to use his influ-

[1] This episode is described by the Comtesse de Boigne in her *Mémoires*. Librairie Plon.

ence in favour of Louis Philippe, but his answer had been:
"The Duc d'Orléans himself has declared that if he was obliged
to take the Crown, he would only accept it to return it to its
august and legitimate owner."

This was certainly true, but Louis Philippe had also said: "I
will not cause the Crown to fall from the head that wears it, but
if it falls, I will pick it up."

AN EAGLE IS BROKEN

Turmoil and apprehension swept Europe during the terrible
Hundred Days. Regiment by regiment, the French rallied to
their hero Emperor; divisions sent to arrest his progress and
secure his person, fell under the magic of his personality.

On 5th April 1815, the Duke of Wellington arrived in
Brussels to take command of the Allied Armies in Belgium. The
Duc d'Orléans watched closely the events from Twickenham.
Many of the émigrés blamed him for not following Louis XVIII
to Ghent, but it was less compromising to remain in England.

The news from France continued to be disheartening.
Marshal Macdonald, who was trying to rouse some enthusiasm
for Louis XVIII among his troops, found that the aura of
Napoleon was like a magnet. His men told him to go back to
the King and remain faithful to him if he pleased, but that
they would go over to the Emperor.

"None will fail Bonaparte; no one can resist him, all France
seems to belong to him once more."

Creevey recorded:

A short time before the battle of Waterloo—a fortnight
perhaps—I was walking in the park at Brussels, when opposite the Ambassador's house, the Duke of Wellington joined
me. It was the day before the papers had arrived from England, bringing the debates in Parliament, where the question
was War.

"The whole thing is a question of expediency," said the Duke.

"Granted," I replied, "and now, will you let me ask you,
Duke, what do you think you will make of it?"

He stopped, and said, in the most natural manner:

"My God! I think Blücher and myself can do the thing."

"Do you calculate," I asked, "upon any desertion from Bonaparte's army?"

"Not a man," he said, "from the Colonel to the private in a regiment, both inclusive. We may pick up a Marshal or two, perhaps, but not worth a damn."

"Do you reckon," I asked, "upon any support from the French King's troops at Alost?"

"Oh, do not mention such fellows. No! I think Blücher and I can do the business."

Then, seeing a private soldier of one of our infantry regiments entering the park and gaping about at the statues:

"There," he said, "it all depends on that article whether we do the business or not. Give me enough of it and I am sure."[1]

*   *   *

At this moment it is interesting to go over to the French side and note the despair and disillusion of a French officer, General de Rumigny,[2] at the disaster of Waterloo.

The Battle of Waterloo, as seen by General de Rumigny, at that time serving in Napoleon's army

On 18th June 1815, a lively discussion took place in the French lines between Marshal Grouchy and General Gérard.

The General was saying: "Monsieur le Maréchal, it is an axiom of war, that when one hears the cannon, one walks towards the cannon."

The Marshal replied: "General, the orders I give are to be carried out, and not interpreted."

At last, the General went back to his staff and said: "When, after twenty-five years of war, one has to witness such imbecilities, it is the duty of a self-respecting General to get killed." Then, in spite of our protests, he took off his coat and walked towards the Prussian lines.

The bullets were falling thickly, and suddenly one laid the General on the ground. We seized him, carried him to the rear, and left him in the care of Dr. Cuttinger.

[1] *Creevey*, selected and re-edited by John Gore.
[2] General de Rumigny later became A.D.C. and a close friend of Louis Philippe. His *Souvenirs* are published by Emile-Paul Frères.

At eleven o'clock at night, General Gérard called for me. He spoke with difficulty.

"My dear Rumigny, I am probably going to die; my lungs are full of blood. But first I wish to render a last service to the Emperor. Go to Brussels, where he must be by now; tell him I have no hatred or ill-will towards Marshal Grouchy, but that any Army Corps, isolated and left in his hands, is lost to the French Army."

I swore to deliver the message and, weeping, left him, mounted my horse and set off. The Prussians were holding the bridge of Wavre, so I went downstream with a few horsemen until I found a ford. Having crossed it, I was about to head for the forest of Soignies, when I saw some cavalry pursuing one of our trumpeters who, bareheaded, threw himself in our midst.

His first words were, "The Emperor is beaten; go away, *nous sommes foutus*." I had just learnt the horrible disaster of Waterloo.

*   *   *

Once again the Tuileries became the residence of Louis XVIII, and the stream of the émigrés started flocking back to France.

General de Rumigny tells an amusing story which took place on the return of Louis XVIII. He was standing on a balcony to watch the procession. Among the company with him was the beautiful and celebrated actress of the Théatre Français, Mademoiselle Bourgoin.

She was known for her fanatic Royalist leanings, and for her hatred of Napoleon. It went very far—her one idea in life, apart from acting, was to shower insults on the Emperor's name. General de Rumigny relates the origin of this loathing.

It appears that her vanity was very great; she imagined that no one could resist her charms or whims. This had led to several rebuffs from high personages at the Imperial Court, which had caused her extreme annoyance and displeasure. It had come back to her that these same people had ridiculed her. Then Mademoiselle Bourgoin saw red!

So, when Napoleon returned from Elba, he was told that

Mademoiselle Bourgoin had made the most insulting remarks about him. The Minister of Police reported her words; it rather amused him, so he decided to have his little revenge.

One evening, he sent word that he desired to see her. She, very intrigued, and rather flattered, notwithstanding her apparent hatred, arrived at the Tuileries.

She was shown into a lovely room, beautifully furnished, at the top of one of the private staircases. All was prepared, an enormous bed, with the covers opened, was ready. She, knowing the ropes, lay in it, awaiting the Imperial lover. It rather tickled her fancy to think that the man she loathed, yet dreaded, would ask for her love. Time passed. The Emperor continued his punishment, seeming to forget his guest. At about one o'clock in the morning, he arrived in her room, and gazed for a long time at the waiting beauty. Then, shrugging his shoulders, he turned his back on her, saying: "If it is only this, really it is not worth bothering."

The anecdote amused everybody, but for such a woman, accustomed to admiration on every side, it was a terrific offence. She often boasted that at Erfurt, the Czar Alexander I had found her much to his taste, and her rage at being thus flouted by the upstart Emperor from Corsica was indescribable.[1]

* * *

On 26th July 1815, Louis Philippe wrote from Twickenham:

"I have received from Paris a number of letters, all urging me to return as soon as possible. The King has not condescended to invite me. To bring me back to Paris, they have found more peremptory methods; they have omitted to lift the ban imposed on my property by Bonaparte. I am rushing straight to the Palais Royal, if the porter is good enough to let me in."

Then, a month later, "I am back in Twickenham, for, having offered my services to the King, I have been informed that for the moment his Majesty could not employ me." [2]

[1] This episode is described in the *Souvenirs* of General de Rumigny.
[2] *Louis Philippe*, by J. Lucas-Dubreton.

A few weeks after this, both Chambers were summoned to meet. In Paris, people were uneasy and apprehensive, dreading the vengeful mood of the Royalists against those who had rallied to Napoleon. This period was known as the White Terror, and Monsieur Fouché, Minister of Police, was drawing up long lists of those who had defaulted.

The King could hardly do otherwise than summon the Duc d'Orléans to the opening of the Chambers. So, once again, Louis Philippe crossed the Channel, and arrived at the Palais Royal. The next day at the Chambers, emotion ran high when the Address to the Throne was debated.

At the supreme moment, when the famous resolution was being discussed, urging severe penalties for those who had rallied to the Emperor during the Hundred Days, Louis Philippe asked that it should be removed. The uproar, when a Prince of the Blood dared to suggest such a thing, was terrific. The King heard of it, and sent him a message to leave France. By the end of October, he was back in England.

What a curious mixture he was, servile and proud at the same time, accepting any number of rebuffs, affecting contempt, yet rushing back at the least sign from the very people who had insulted him.

*　　*　　*

The Duc d'Orléans had bought Orléans House from a Mr. Pocock, and now he built on to it and beautified it. In later years it was occupied by the Duc d'Aumale, his son.

The house was large and simply furnished; green lawns with shady trees undulated down to the river Thames. Now there is little left; it was mostly pulled down and another erected upon the site. There is, however, one tower standing. I visited it some time ago: it contains a beautiful room with a high dome, the walls painted in grey-blue and ornamented with much gilded panelling. It must have served as the dining-room. On the side, a door leads into a small room containing the dinner lift.

As I sat on one of the tapestry chairs, the whole scene of over a hundred years ago rose before me. Louis Philippe, always elegant, Marie Amélie in her lace cap, surrounded by her sons and daughters. We are told by Madame de Boigne how she would often drive to Orléans House to dine with the royal family at five o'clock in the afternoon—very indifferent food, but the animated conversation of the Duc would keep everybody interested.

Later they would adjourn to the drawing-room, where the Duchesse would sit at a round table with her embroidery, while the small princesses played with toys and romped around the room, and the six-year-old Duc de Chartres, with a gracious bow, retired with his tutor to continue his studies.

The Duc would continue talking; boats passed on the river, the birds sang and the dogs chased each other on the green lawns. It was a happy, quiet life, not very exciting, but pleasant and wholesome. What went on beneath the surface no one knew; outwardly all seemed unruffled as cream in a saucer.

*   *   *

That year the Duchesse, accompanied by Adélaïde, paid her first visit to Princess Charlotte of Wales, the daughter of the Regent. She had her own establishment within the precincts of Carlton House, and no one could visit her without passing through the forecourt of her father's residence, and without his permission. Did he fear her popularity, compared to his unpopularity? Certainly, every movement of hers was reported to him at once.

Princess Charlotte was nineteen at the time of this visit, and the Duchesse found her "handsome, in a flamboyant way, resembling the Prince Regent, fair of complexion, with prominent blue eyes, her hair of a golden tone, but not very abundant, good figure, but too large for her age; she had a boyish manner of walking and bowing which shocked one in a young Princess. She was very outspoken, sincere and most cordial in her welcome, but the whole tone seemed out of place."

They were told that she modelled her behaviour on that of the great Queen Elizabeth. She led a very sad life, seeing no one, going nowhere; she scarcely ever saw her father, and did not dissemble how heavily this slavelike existence weighed upon her heart.[1] She seemed delighted to be able to speak freely at last, and took a great fancy to Marie Amélie.

[1] *Journal de Marie Amélie* (ed. la Duchesse de Vendôme). Librairie Plon.

The extraordinary cruelty meted out to the princess was the result of the fact that she had always stood up for her mother, defying her father's wishes in this matter, and refusing to meet other members of the royal family—even her grandmother—holding them responsible for the way in which her mother was treated.

It was the policy of the Orléans family to maintain good relations with all parties, and especially to avoid giving offence to the Prince Regent. But the princess was important in her role of the future Queen of Great Britain; she had taken Marie Amélie to her heart, and the lovely children delighted her. At this time, the Duc de Chartres was really beautiful, so brilliant, so full of life, that already he charmed—that charm which throughout his short existence fascinated all around him.

Princess Charlotte often paid surprise visits to Orléans House to watch the young princes and their sisters playing on the lawns under the shady trees. They were a charming group, Chartres, Louise, dark-haired Marie, wide-eyed, smiling Nemours, still in babyhood.

The princess would join in their games, happy, carefree. She would tell Marie Amélie, "I feel secure here, no one to spy on me. I can run, sing and laugh."

Princess Charlotte was not always so amiable: the Orléans family saw the best side of her character. When she had to attend one of her father's receptions at Carlton House, she made a point of showing her dislike of those women who surrounded him. At this time Lady Hertford was the favourite and, while the princess spared her no insults, Lady Hertford, sure of her position, showed her disdain to the princess.

All these intrigues made the Orléans' position difficult, but the subtlety of Louis Philippe enabled him to thread his way amidst their susceptibilities.

Once long ago there had been a faint suggestion of a possible union between Louis Philippe and Princess Elizabeth, but the idea of marrying a foreign prince, an exile, and above all a Catholic, was unthinkable. Yet even now Marie Amélie looked upon the princess as a rival.

Heiress to the Throne

During those two long years of exile—or shall we call it enforced absence from France—two important events took place in the British royal family; the marriage of Princess Charlotte, heir presumptive, to Prince Leopold of Saxe-Coburg-Gotha, who in later years became first King of the Belgians; and that of Princess Mary, daughter of George III, to her first cousin, the Duke of Gloucester.

On 2nd May 1816, Princess Charlotte was awakened by the stir of the city. London seemed *en fête*, and rightly so, it was her wedding day. She was to be the bride of the man she had chosen. At last she would be free to lead her own life beside a beloved husband, who would guard her from further tyranny.

During the magnificent ceremony, the princess seemed to radiate ecstasy, gazing with adoration at Leopold, he correct, rigid and embarrassed.

Later, as they drove away through the crowded streets, the enthusiasm of the people was overwhelming. Blessings and good wishes were cried out to them. At this time, with a demented King and an unloved Regent, this young girl stood as the symbol of sovereignty.

The other marriage was different. The Duchesse d'Orléans describes it in her journal:

"On 22nd July, the marriage took place of Princess Mary and the Duke of Gloucester." The French princes left Twickenham and arrived at the Grillon Hotel in Albemarle Street, where they changed into *grande toilette*.

The Duchesse continues:

At eight o'clock in the evening, we drove to Queen's

House, where we found many people already assembled. Then we entered the Queen's private sitting-room, where only the family were gathered, except the bride. The Prince Regent embraced the Duke of Gloucester and his sister, and bestowed on them the title of Royal Highness.

At nine o'clock, the Regent offered his arm to his mother, the Queen, and so, in procession, we entered into the Grand Salon where, at the far end, had been erected a beautiful altar; in front of it was a long stool for the bride and bridegroom. The Princes stood on the right of the altar, the Queen sat in a large armchair on the left; then came the Court and the Ambassadors.

When all were seated, the Duke of Gloucester entered, followed by his suite. After bowing low to the Regent and the Queen, he stood on the left of the altar. At this moment the Dukes of Clarence and Cambridge left to bring Princess Mary.

As she made her appearance, the Regent took her by the hand and led her to the altar. Never had we seen Mary so lovely and interesting; she wore a simple gown of silver tissue, a garland of diamonds in her hair. Her eyes were cast down, and she was almost unable to give the responses. The Regent seemed to hold her up, otherwise she would have fallen: really more like a victim than a bride.

Seeing her so desolate, those present could not refrain from weeping. All knew that she had fought against this union, but as she refused to live out of Great Britain, this was the only possible marriage.

After the ceremony, we entered the Queen's large Salon, where most were able to regain their composure. The new Duchess of Gloucester made a great effort and was charming to all present.

At length, the carriages were called and the bride and bridegroom left for Bagshot, the country home of the Gloucester family: this union remained childless.[1]

These two ceremonies impressed Marie Amélie, and in later

[1] *Journal de Marie Amélie* (ed. la Duchesse de Vendôme). Librairie Plon.

years she often alluded to the contrast; the happy one lasted a year, the unhappy one eighteen years.

*   *   *

In 1817 Princess Charlotte, under the pretext that her house in London was not ready, remained at Claremont, Esher, with her beloved husband, saying that in her state of pregnancy she could not attend any functions; yet she would invite the chosen few to dine.

The Comtesse de Boigne tells us that she attended a dinner party there with her parents, the Marquis and Marquise d'Osmond. They arrived at Claremont, which was a rather long drive from London; they were received by Lady Glenbervie, Mistress of the Robes, and by Baron de Hardenbrock, Aide de Camp to the prince.

> Some of the guests had preceded us, others followed. Prince Leopold appeared, and then immediately, without greeting anyone, he left. After waiting a long time, we heard heavy footsteps which we could only compare with those of a sergeant-major; all around the whisper was heard, "It is the Princess".
>
> Indeed, the Princess appeared, magnificently dressed, covered with jewels, a grand air, aping the manner of the great Elizabeth with this decided walk and the poise of a haughty head.
>
> As she entered, leaning on her husband's arm, the door at the other end of the room was thrown open and she walked straight through without looking at anyone. Once in the dining-room, she summoned two Ambassadors to sit one on each side of her. The Prince was placed opposite with the two Ambassadors' wives next to him.
>
> The Princess had only eyes for her husband and, as the monumental centrepiece on the table prevented her seeing him, she simply gave orders to have it taken away.
>
> She smiled sweetly at him during the long dinner, but never looked at anybody else, and rarely addressed the Ambassadors, who were sweating in their strenuous attempt at conversation. Yet rarely has anyone had a more mobile

face; it was full of expression, her red lips disclosing perfect teeth, her colouring so fresh and without any shadow of make-up, were a contrast to all the other women.

The dinner ended, the Princess stood up, making a slight sign to the ladies, and passed into the drawing-room, followed by them; but immediately, she sat down in a corner of the room with a married friend of hers who was in the same state of pregnancy. From that moment, Princess Charlotte never addressed a word to anyone else, but sat on, giggling at everything with her childhood friend. All the ladies stood at the opposite side of the room, not quite knowing what to do.

When the Prince entered with the men, he looked worried, and tried to repair the rudeness of his wife. He drew up armchairs for the Ambassadresses, and did his utmost to establish some sort of communication between the Princess and her guests, but to no avail.

At last, Princess Lieven, wife of the Russian Ambassador, more courageous than the rest, went up and sat on the same couch as the Princess, and contrived to amuse her hostess.

So we all waited impatiently for our carriages to be summoned. At that moment, the Princess rose from her sofa and, with barely a bow of her head, dismissed us.

A few days later—we supposed that Leopold had lectured her—she sent again for my parents and myself; this time she was absolutely enchanting, natural and attractive. She kept us until after midnight. Monsieur de Boigne had once thought of buying Claremont, so this interested her, and she begged us to come in daylight, so as to visit the gardens which, she said, had been so much improved by her wish.

So we settled on a day, and returned once more to pay a visit, but this time the Princess's mood had changed again. She received us more than coldly, and said that we could visit the grounds by ourselves. She, who had shown such pleasure at the idea a few days before of disclosing the beauties of her garden, now seemed too anxious to see the last of us.

As we were walking, admiring the lovely flowers, and yet deeply hurt at the Princess's attitude, Prince Leopold came up and said the Princess now felt so much better, and would be delighted to give us tea. The tactful husband must have persuaded her once again for, like a true volatile woman, she met us in the most delightful manner. Tea was brought in, and while my parents were discussing politics with Leopold, we talked.

She depicted to me most unusually the picture of "the Queen's husband", but she added, "My Leopold will never be exposed to this humiliating situation, or my name is not Charlotte", and she stamped violently on the floor with her rather large foot.

"If this was made obligatory, I would not hesitate to renounce the throne and find a hut where I could live like an ordinary woman under the domination of my husband.

"I wish to remain in England, on condition that he and I reign together, he recognized as King, independent of my whims, because I know that sometimes I am not responsible for my actions.

"Remember, he will be King, or I shall never be Queen."

So, still that Hanoverian instability went on. As we were leaving, standing under the portico of the lovely house, once more she turned to me, saying: "My dear friend, come again to Claremont; it shelters perfect happiness." [1]

Madame de Boigne never saw her again. A few weeks after, Princess Charlotte died in childbirth, and in one hour two generations of Sovereigns passed away.

Adèle de Boigne was a brilliantly intellectual and clever woman; she was the chief visitor to the Orléans family, keeping them informed of the different way they were to approach Society. Although very attached to the family, she did not ignore the Duc's ambitions, and the hidden activities of Adélaïde.

She fully realized, too, that Marie Amélie remained apart from all intrigues, speaking little except to teach her children the precepts of religion, and to give them a true value of life.

PUFF PASTRY AT THE PALAIS ROYAL

France seemed to have regained her stability after the turmoil of the Hundred Days. Once again the people breathed a sigh of

---

[1] *Mémoires* of the Comtesse de Boigne. Librairie Plon.

relief. All the enthusiasm they had once felt for Bonaparte had vanished when they realized that Napoleonic rule meant war, war, war.

By contrast, the now infirm old King had become almost a symbol of peace in his very immobility. Louis Philippe's name had faded from the public mind, for the moment. He was far away, and most of the population did not even know his whereabouts.

Then, from Grenoble, whispers began to be heard, at first faintly, but soon to grow louder. At the bottom of this mysterious conspiracy was a lawyer, Paul Didier, a man of frustrated ambition, whose previous career had discredited him among the powerful men who distributed pensions and places.

As Bourbons and Bonapartes succeeded each other at the Tuileries, so Didier had reversed his loyalties to suit his interest. By 1816, ruined and embittered, meeting on all sides with contempt, the lawyer's only hope of rebuilding his fortune lay in intrigue. So he hit upon the fatal plan.

The Duc d'Orléans might be the means of regaining some prestige. Didier had many friends in Grenoble, discontented and ready to start anything to make themselves known, in the hope of bettering their position. They did not care for whom they fought, so when Didier approached them, they consented to follow him.

During the first days of May 1816, Paul Didier, acting on the instructions of a small committee which had its roots in Paris, and worked under the name of "Société de l'Indépendance Nationale", gathered a number of adherents in the Isère province of France. The pretext of the insurrection was to be the deliverance of the King of Rome, son of Napoleon, but in reality its ultimate aim was the ascent to power of the Duc d'Orléans.

Before long, their numbers had grown considerably, supporters flocking from all parts of France, and even from abroad. The whole affair was very shady, and none of the followers were sure for whom they worked. One of Didier's accomplices, named Millet, questioned him on the subject:

"Tell us for whom we are working?"

"Be assured that all we are doing is for someone who is of our

97

generation, and who knows our needs," was the reply, "but, remember, if we had not mentioned the name of Napoleon or his son, we should not have recruited a single man."

When Didier was arrested, amongst his papers was found a letter which gave the key to the conspiracy.

"Monseigneur, our efforts have failed, but the strings are not all cut."

Who could "Monseigneur" be, but the quiet family man *who never mixed in politics!*

Paul Didier was a curious type. A few moments before mounting the scaffold, he spoke of all the benefits he had received under the reign of Louis XVIII, and in his profound repentance, he wished to send a warning to the King: the greatest enemy of his Crown was a member of his own family.

One wonders how Louis Philippe reacted to all these revelations. Outwardly, he changed nothing in his mode of life. It is difficult to reconcile the apparent calm of the Duc with the plot of Paul Didier.

Another curious detail to note is that the Duc Decazes, whose behaviour throughout this episode was just a little suspicious, never ceased, during the reign of Louis Philippe, to enjoy the friendship of the monarch and the privileges the Crown could bestow. Also, the surviving accomplices of Paul Didier, and their children, were named by the Orléans government to important posts.

It is hardly reasonable to think that the Duc had no knowledge of the plot.

*   *   *

The exiled Orléans family had been recalled shortly before the Didier plot came to light, so it was in the early days of February 1817 that Louis Philippe and his numerous family re-entered France after eighteen months' absence.

Paris! What awaited him there? He had felt safe in Britain. All his intrigues could be hidden from the world, especially since the spies of the former French Ambassador, Monsieur de la Châtre, had been removed by his more trustful successor, the Marquis d'Osmond. It had been a pleasant life, the house was easily run, the etiquette not too strict. He could receive whom he chose, unknown to the world outside. The Prince Regent had been friendly.

As he drove from Calais in the large travelling coach, the Duchesse dozing, the children tired and whining, he felt troubled; he realized that he alone was alive to the struggle that lay before them. The Palais Royal was immense, and would require a grandiose establishment. He also dreaded the reaction of the Court.

Yet, as the carriage drew near to the city, his courage seemed to grow. He had a large fortune, and would fill the Palais Royal with officials.

"I shall fill my home with glory and beauty. I will show them all that the first Prince of the Royal Blood knows how to live."

The Comtesse de Boigne related in her memoirs[1] that the next morning she went to the Palais Royal.

The luncheon was waiting on the table for the Duc and his family. They had gone to the Tuileries to pay their respects to the King. As they returned, I could see by their looks that the interview had been rather painful.

The Duchesse looked sad, the Duc troubled; Madame Adélaïde fainted. She had scarcely recovered from a severe indisposition; we surrounded her, and in a few moments she regained consciousness. Pressing my hand, she murmured: "Thank you, my dear, it is nothing, I am still weak, and painful scenes upset me."

Suddenly, thank heaven, all faces lost their morose expression, as a large dish of échaudés, a little cloud of pastry such as only the chef of the Palais Royal could achieve, was brought in. At once the atmosphere cleared, shouts of enthusiasm burst forth. The love of the motherland, and rejoicing in the native soil, brought complete forgetfulness of the icy reception of the Tuileries.

It takes a Frenchman to be soothed by a little cloud of pastry. One wonders if this attitude of Louis XVIII was not partly the result of the intrigues of the clique of "ultra-royalists" who were bent on keeping alive the animosity against Louis Philippe.

[1] Published by Librairie Plon.

Their tool was the pretty Comtesse du Cayla, whom they had bribed to gain ascendancy over the King. Even before the death of his wife, Louis XVIII had abandoned her for this young schemer. His age and infirmity prevented any sexual intimacy, and perhaps the young woman was grateful for this limitation of the old King's caresses, and content that "he knew her not".

It is true that the Queen had never been attractive, but she and her husband had been good friends, and their friendship went on, even after he met Madame du Cayla. She was too wise to resent this *amitié amoureuse* of her husband.

When Louis XVIII returned to France a widower, Madame du Cayla followed him to Paris, and the strange liaison went on. It kept the King happy, and Madame du Cayla busy.

Daily, trifling annoyances continued to disturb the peace of the Palais Royal. It is worth remembering that, when the Orléans returned to Paris, the Didier affair was still fresh in all minds. One day, the Orléans family found themselves excluded from the royal tribune for Mass at the Tuileries, then they were denied their places in the royal box at gala performances. The climax came when, at one of the great religious ceremonies at Nôtre Dame, the King gave orders, as Louis Philippe and Madame Adélaïde were about to kneel on cushions reserved for them as members of the royal family, that these cushions should be removed; they had to kneel on the marble floor, away from the royal carpet. The insult was great, and the Duc's and his sister's fury deepened.

These constant irritations made the Orléans more embittered than ever, and aroused the ire of the Opposition party. The Orléans contrived subtly to canvass for popularity, always stopping just short of open defiance.

One day, Louis Philippe, taking Monsieur de Fontaine, his architect, by the arm, led him to the picture galleries of the palace.

"Mon cher," he said, "do you not think that there are too many empty spaces on these walls?"

"Monseigneur, the remedy is easily found; large and grandiose paintings will fill the spaces, and improve the proportions of these rooms. There exist a number of such pictures, but since they depict mainly the victories of the Revolution, I doubt if they will please his Majesty."

The Duc smiled. "Buy, Monsieur, buy."

Louis Philippe used every method to make himself popular. Already at this time he was paying court to the great Revolutionary leader, General de Lafayette, whose name was like a lighted lamp among the people; and, whenever he dared, cautiously, he gave his support to the new ideas.

Princesse Adélaïde, whose mind was ever working, hit on the astonishing idea that it would be very popular with the people, that the young Orléans princes should attend an ordinary school. Never before had a prince dreamed of such a democratic measure; it would stagger the Court and the Royalists, but what a triumph for her brother! People would be brought to the realization of the fact that Louis Philippe really intended to turn his sons into ordinary citizens, and do away with the barriers which separated his family from the man in the street.

How incongruous it all was—the Duc d'Orléans living in the Palais Royal, amidst unbelievable luxury and splendour, on the one hand, and turning his sons into little bourgeois on the other.

Adélaïde felt that it would take a great deal of persuasion to make Marie Amélie accept such an innovation, as she maintained high ideals on the dignity of the royal family; and what of the King? If the young princes were to attend such a school, the King's consent was necessary.

Before mentioning the proposal to Marie Amélie, the numerous tutors must be consulted, so one day, when the Duchesse was engaged on a mission of charity, the consultation took place. The tutors were all in favour of the scheme, and the Collège Henri IV was chosen. The Duchesse, on her return, although hating the idea, had to agree.

On 15th October 1819, a short announcement appeared in the press. "It is understood that the young Duc de Chartres, eldest son of the Duc d'Orléans, will enter this year the sixth form (the lowest secondary form) of the Collège Henri IV." So the King was confronted with a *fait accompli*.

The trick was a dangerous one, but Louis Philippe knew that, once announced in the press, a thing is half accomplished. So he went to see the King. The monarch received him coldly, and waited for the Duc to inform him of the reason for the visit. Whilst the Duc explained his plan, Louis XVIII remained silent. When Louis Philippe had ended, the King said:

"If you have come to ask me for advice, I advise you not to send your son to college. If you have come to ask for permission, I permit you to put him there, only as a mere day-boy. I want no meals in common, no recreations in common, no communications with the boarders. If you have come to notify me, you may do as you please. But you will remember what I am telling you, and one day you will repent that you did not pay heed."

The King paused, the Duc remained silent.

"You have nothing to say?"

Then the Duc broke his silence: "I ask the King's permission to persist respectfully in my decision."

*   *   *

When the Orléans family returned to France, there was one more baby and nurse, as well as tutors and governesses to install. There were: the Duc de Chartres, born in 1810, Princesse Louise, 1812, Princesse Marie, 1813, the Duc de Nemours, 1814, and Princesse Clementine, 1817; the last named, a baby in arms.

At that time, with the excuse of supervising the entire renovation of the Palais Royal, the Duc and Duchesse rarely appeared at the Tuileries. Louis Philippe was spending eleven million francs on restoring his home to what it had once been— the most magnificent residence of its day. When at last the Palais had regained its ancient sumptuousness, they opened their huge reception rooms to all the celebrities of Paris.

There were the Princesse de Poix, the Comtesse de Boigne, the four famous Marshals whose names began with M— Macdonald, Molitor, Mortier, Marmont; the poet Lamartine, François Arago, the astronomer. Benjamin Constant, whose liaison with Madame de Staël had been the gossip of its day, regretted her as he looked around and found no one to take her place. Theirs had been a curious attachment: she had pursued him round Europe, almost annihilating him with her love; when he had been near her, he had only thought of escape. Yet he could never remain away from her for long, and now that she was dead he felt lonely and craved for her. Among the diplomats, the Prince de Talleyrand would appear, whose face and figure were sensational, and the Russian Ambassador, Pozzo di Borgo.

At the same time, some of the old associates of Jacobin days would be there, such as the Marquis de Lafayette, and others less desirable. Louis Philippe, ever thoughtful of the future, would bring his unwelcome guests up to the Duchesse, and she, although they jarred upon her, received them with enthusiasm, only to please her husband.

In the midst of these receptions, a loud bell would be rung, and the prince and his eldest son would rush to the top of the stairs, for this announced the arrival of the Duchesse d'Angoulême and her sister-in-law, the Duchesse de Berri.

These fêtes quite outshone the Tuileries, where receptions were often dull, full of bigots and ultra-royalists, who had returned from exile "having forgotten nothing and learnt nothing".

The days when there were no receptions, the Duc and Duchesse attended different theatres, especially the Théâtre Français which was linked to the Palais Royal by a private passage. One must remember that Louis XVIII had excluded them from the royal box, so they would arrive proudly to be received by the authorities, and conducted with due ceremony to their own sumptuous box. There they would sit, and smile, and bow, with concealed defiance towards the occupants of the royal box.

What a contrast existed between the two women who dominated the life of Louis Philippe. Marie Amélie, stately, stout, not particularly intelligent but, like many minds which do not shine, capable of seeing things clearly and giving sound advice. Her opinions were rarely considered, as Madame Adélaïde possessed all the influence over her brother and was considered by him to be the only person who understood his mentality, who could decide events and forecast the future. He made her the most powerful personality at the Palais Royal.

We are told that she was plain, with heavy features, a spotty complexion, and a graceless figure. She was intelligent, sharp-witted, and her ambition for her brother, if anything, out-stripped his own.

Adélaïde and Louis Philippe were complementary to each other. She had a sense of decision, and was forceful. He was persuasive and cautious. They formed a perfect team for the end which they had set themselves to attain, the Crown of France.

I I

Death, Birth, and Death

On 13th February 1820, Monsieur le Docteur Deneux had called upon the Duchesse de Berri,[1] and confirmed her hope that she was expecting a child. The Duc and Duchesse de Berri had one daughter living, the Princesse Louise-Marie-Thérèse; none of their other children had survived. They kept this new hope to themselves, praying that this child might be a son, an heir to the throne of France.[2]

The Doctor had given a stern warning: he had said, "Madame is not strong, and must put an end to her life of ceaseless amusement. She must spend her evenings at home, quietly, and go to bed early." What a bore for the lively princess!

That evening, the programme at the Opéra was very alluring—"Le Rossignol", "Le Carnaval de Venise", "Les Noces de Gamache". Everybody was going, the Comte d'Artois, the Angoulêmes, the Orléans, and all the gayest of their circle. Most tempting of all for the Duc de Berri, Virginie, his favourite of the moment, would be dancing. Still, the Berris sat at home, trying not to think of the two seats waiting for them in their box, of the gaiety, the colour, the music. They talked of small things, stifled a yawn, tried to read; finally the temptation was too strong. They jumped into their carriage and went off to the Opéra.

By eleven o'clock, the Duchesse's face was white with fatigue. The Duc leant over her with a worried expression.

[1] In 1816, the Duc de Berri had married the Princess Marie Caroline of Naples.

[2] Louis XVIII was childless. His brother and heir, the Comte d'Artois, had two sons, the Duc d'Angoulême, also childless, and the Duc de Berri, the second son. Unless he had a male heir, the ancient Bourbon line would end, and the Orléans would accede to the throne.

105

"My wife, be wise, go home."

"A few minutes more," came the answer. "I must see Elie."

Elie was dancing, the famous dancer who had studied with Séraphin; so was Virginie who, under her long eyelashes, cast stealthy glances towards the royal box. At last, the Duc insisted that Caroline should go home.

So they walked out, arm-in-arm, towards the entrance, Caroline humming an air from the "Noces de Gamache", the Duc exchanging light-hearted comments with the Comte de Mesnard, who was with him.

The carriage was called, Caroline settled in and leaned forward smiling. The street was deserted, save for the footmen arranging the rugs around their mistress and folding the steps, and for a lonely guard standing stiffly at attention.

The Duc raised his hand to wave: then, at that moment, a man—a mere shadow wrapped in a great black cloak—sprang at the Duc with uplifted arm. The blade of a knife gleamed for a second; it struck at the Duc's chest, then the murderer was gone as quickly and silently as he came.

It all happened in a second. The Duchesse jumped out of the carriage as the injured body of her husband was carried back into the lobby of the Opéra.

Crowds of people pressed into the room as the news spread, making the air stuffy and unbreathable. The Comte d'Artois his father was there, the Duc d'Angoulême, and the Duchesse his wife, the latter silent and sombre under her huge plumed headdress, remembering all the other crimes which had darkened her life; the Duc d'Orléans, lamenting yet thoughtful, Marie Amélie, sparkling in her lovely decolleté and jewels, horrified and anxious for her niece Caroline, and the ever-present Adélaïde, who added to the commotion by fainting as usual.

There were doctors, quantities of them—Dubois, Bougon, the famous Dupuytren, Lacroix, Monsieur's doctor, Blancheton, Drogard—all powerless to do anything.

Priests, headed by Monseigneur de Latil, in violet robes, the "petit prêtre" of Madame de Polastron.

Amongst all these personalities, actors still in costume, attendants of the theatre, passers-by from the street, ladies-in-waiting, policemen, and the Duc Decazes, Chief of the Police, at whom everybody looked with suspicion.

All were standing around, their eyes fastened on the Duc in his agony, on his life-blood oozing out and dropping on the carpet. The Duchesse, dishevelled, lay half across her husband, her white dress covered with blood, whilst the dying man kept repeating:

"The King! I must see the King!"

Still the King remained at the Tuileries; it was all a question of etiquette.

At last, at five in the morning, Louis XVIII was told that the end was near. He drove to the Opéra, and slowly, heavily, was carried up the narrow back staircase. On seeing him, the Duc, in a last spurt of energy, clutched the King's arm.

"Sire! Sire! Spare the man's life."

This he desired as an atonement for the sins of his past life, and the thought never left him while life remained.

"My son," answered Louis XVIII, "we will talk of this later."

The King turned to Dupuytren, the famous surgeon, and whispered in Latin: "*Superestne spes aliqua salutis?*" ("Is there any hope?")

Dupuytren shook his head; the old King brushed the tears from his eyes and leant again over his nephew.

A few minutes later, the Duc de Berri was dead. His last wish was not fulfilled; Louvel, the murderer, was executed.

As he lay on his death-bed, the Duc had gasped to Caroline: "My poor wife, I implore you to take care of yourself, for the sake of the child you carry."

Those words were caught, whispered from ear to ear, beyond the walls of the room, out into the street. Soon the news flashed across France, "The Duc de Berri is dead, but the Duchesse carries his child." Maybe the old dynasty of France was not dying out after all. Throughout the land, prayers were offered up, that the child might be a boy.

Caroline herself longed for a son, for, though she might never be Queen, she might still become Queen Mother and Regent of France, like Anne d'Autriche, Catherine de Médicis, and Blanche de Castille. For, above all else, the Duchesse de Berri was ambitious; she longed to be a figure on the European stage.

* * *

The entrance of the baby into the world was theatrical, as might have been expected of the Duchesse de Berri: it was at two o'clock on the morning of 29th September 1820.

It all happened so quickly that there was no time to call an official to witness the birth, and the Duchesse had to lie unattended with the child still held to her, whilst her ladies-in-waiting rushed madly hither and thither looking for witnesses to verify beyond a doubt that the Princesse Caroline de Bourbon Naples, Duchesse de Berri, had given birth to a son.

Madame de Gontaut found her valet's room, pulled him out of bed, and brought him to the accouchement, but he couldn't act as witness because he belonged to the household. Another of the ladies found two of the Gardes Nationaux on duty at the entrance. They would do, so a private of the guard—a grocer by profession—and a serjeant of the Grenadiers were the first valid witnesses to appear on the scene, red-faced and indescribably embarrassed, while Caroline, not in the least shy, tried to put them at their ease. Finally, Marshal Suchet, an official witness, arrived, and the panic was over.

The whole of France went wild with joy over the birth of the Duc de Bordeaux; the Sovereigns of Europe spoke of him as the Child of France who would preserve the peace of Europe. He was a miracle and a marvel. Strangers kissed each other in the street, and poets, serious and comic, sat down to write poems about him.

In all this delirious rejoicing, one family did not celebrate— the Orléans. Their sorrow and disappointment were too painfully obvious. Their chance of succeeding to the throne had been taken from them. The day they went to make the compulsory visit to the new-born baby and its mother, they could not conceal their temper.

Adélaïde sourly remarked to the Duchesse de Berri: "After all, there was no witness on the scene."

"I beg your pardon, Monsieur le Maréchal Suchet was there."

The Duc turned to Madame de Gontaut, who was holding the child, and made such rude offensive comments that the poor lady burst into tears. The next day, realizing that he had gone too far, Louis Philippe sent his sister to apologize to the Duchesse.

"Please don't be cross with my brother," she pleaded plaintively. "After all, one does not lose a crown for one's children, without regret."

Meanwhile, the Duc d'Orléans went to see Marshal Suchet, and insisted on questioning him grossly.

"Monsieur le Maréchal, your loyalty is well known to us; were you a witness at the confinement of the Duchesse de Berri, and is she really the mother of a prince?"

"As truly as you are the father of the Duc de Chartres."

Louis Philippe was not convinced; he inserted a long and ridiculous statement on the subject in the British paper, *The Morning Chronicle*; then, seeing the unfortunate effect this created in France, and in fact all over Europe, he denied the authorship of the article.

*   *   *

Despite the arrival of this child whose birth had dealt so cruel a blow to the hopes of the Duc d'Orléans, his own children continued to enjoy their lives unperturbed.

The Prince de Joinville,[1] in his memoirs, related that his first vivid recollection, at the age of six, was of the Feast of the Epiphany, on 6th January 1824. In France this Festival is called "le jour des rois".

"A large cake is passed round the table, and the one who finds the small coin which is hidden in it is proclaimed King; he then chooses a Queen. Then they are installed on a decorated throne, and the guests file past, saluting them, amidst much joking and laughter. It is a very old tradition in honour of the Three Wise Men from the East."

Now that day the Orléans family were invited to dinner by Louis XVIII. The Prince de Joinville recorded that, even at a distance of sixty-six years later, he remembered every detail of the party.

---

[1] Born 7th August 1818

They drove into the vast courtyard of the Tuileries, the Gardes Suisses presented arms at the Pavillon de Marsan, and again the Garde Royale at the Pavillon de Flore. As they stepped out of their carriage under the portico leading to the stone staircase, they were deafened by the beating of the drums of the Gardes Suisses, announcing their arrival; then, amidst all this terrific fuss, they had to flatten themselves against the wall to allow "the King's meat" to pass. It was being carried from the kitchen to the royal apartments, escorted by the Gardes du Corps: when it had gone by, with all the honour due to it, the Orléans party proceeded.

They were met by Monsieur du Cosse, wearing a red and gold uniform, then led through the Salle des Gardes, and shown into the drawing-room, where the royal family soon arrived.

The assembly comprised, as usual, Monsieur—later Charles X—the Duc and Duchesse d'Angoulême, the Duchesse de Berri, the Duc and Duchesse d'Orléans, Madame Adélaïde, the two eldest Orléans princes, the Ducs de Chartres and Nemours, the three sisters, Louise, Marie and Clementine, and the little Prince de Joinville, the youngest of them all.

Presently the door of the King's private Cabinet opened; Louis XVIII appeared sitting in his wheeled chair, with his abundant white hair, his handsome features, wearing the blue coat with white epaulettes which his portraits have rendered so familiar.

We shall let the young prince relate, in his own words, the events of the evening:

The King embraced us one after the other, only addressing himself to my brother Nemours concerning his studies. Nemours suffered terribly from shyness, and it was bad luck that the King should have picked him out. Nemours spluttered some words but at that moment dinner was announced, so he was spared.

At the end of the meal, the cake was brought in and, to my dismay, I had the coin. I felt so embarrassed, as I had been told what was expected of me if by chance I should find it. I knew all eyes were upon me. I rose from the table, my legs rather shaky, and carried the coin on a silver plate to the

Duchesse d'Angoulême, thus proclaiming that I had made her my Queen.

I loved her very much; she was always kind to us. She broke the ice by taking up her glass and drinking; then the King called out: "The Queen drinks", and all the guests had to drink at the same time.

I remember the rest of the evening as being rather boring for a child of six years, and still more so for my Queen, as we had to stay together on the throne.

The Prince goes on:

About that time, I was given a room to myself at the Palais Royal. It overlooked the rue Valois and the restaurant "du Bœuf à la mode". Right opposite me lived an old lady always dressed in black who regularly at seven o'clock in the morning, stood her night pot on her window sill, it was so regular, that I always knew the time by it. Later I changed rooms, the next was situated in the Court; facing me was an artist of the Comédie Française named Dumilâtre and his two daughters.

This man had the same habit as the old lady in black; he would stand his pot on the window sill at six in the morning and I had only changed the hour. It goes without saying, that when they were sure of no passers by, they would tip the pots into the streets.

At the end of winter, when the first fine days of spring awoke their longing for the country, the Orléans family would take up their residence at Neuilly. It was one of the most enchanting places which ever existed. It was a large château without any pretension to architectural design; it was merely a series of one-storeyed buildings connected to each other, placed in lovely gardens.

All around lay an immense park on the banks of the Seine; indeed it enclosed a backwater of the river with islands, streams, woods, fields and orchards; all this within only fifteen minutes' drive from the city.

For the children, it was paradise; they helped the hay-makers and dug potatoes. There were flowers everywhere, wild and cultivated; the perfume was almost intoxicating.

Alas, all this, and the château with its valuable treasures, was destroyed and burnt by the crazy uncontrollable mob in February 1848.

*   *   *

On Christmas Day 1822, a solemn council was held at the Tuileries, presided over by the King. The question at issue was the situation in Spain, where a revolution seemed imminent. Ferdinand VII was virtually a prisoner in the hands of the fanatical *Commureros* who had gained control of the country.

It looked like the French Revolution all over again, and Louis XVIII was alarmed lest their success might encourage the Republican party in France. So he declared war upon them. The Duc d'Angoulême was chosen as Commander-in-Chief.

On 21st March 1823, a French army of 80,000 men set off for Spain. The result was almost a foregone conclusion. The Spaniards are a devout people; all the peaceful citizens, headed by monks and clergy, who had been terrorized by the *Commureros* and their new anti-religious edicts, received the French as saviours. In two months the Duc d'Angoulême entered Madrid, to find that the royal family had been removed by the Cortes to Cadiz. So the French besieged Cadiz, and by the end of September the war was over.

The people of Paris went almost delirious at the news and, never losing an opportunity, rushed out into the streets to kiss and dance with all the pretty women.

On the afternoon of 12th October, the royal family went to Nôtre Dame to attend a Service of Thanksgiving. Louis XVIII had been very worried by the event in Spain, and the strain had told upon his health. During the ceremony he kept fumbling, he dropped his prayer book several times, and as he looked about him with vague appeal, those watching began to realize that a reign was ending.

From that day, the King's body seemed to grow weaker, but his will became more imperious. The presence of Louis Philippe seemed to infuriate him, yet when Marie Amélie gave birth to her ninth child, he was pleased and went to Neuilly to congratulate her. That day the King was almost his old self; he showed no animosity to the Duc d'Orléans, who told his wife that he had not seen the King so well for a long time; he seemed to have more strength and to be able to hold himself more erect.

The next day, 1st August 1824, after dinner, Louis XVIII collapsed, and those around thought it was a stroke; at once all members of the family and high officials were summoned.

The King regained consciousness in a rage, accusing everybody of having made a useless fuss. Yet each day his strength grew less; he had fever at night, and most of his days were passed in somnolence. His head would drop almost to his knees, and he could not raise it unaided.

On the Feast of St. Louis, the doctors implored him not to hold his audiences. His reply was: "There are only two alternatives; the King is dead or well."

Those who had the honour to pay their court to him that day, left in great distress; they only saw the crown of his head as it rested on his knees. He was terribly thin, his sight almost gone, his voice scarcely audible. Yet he managed to say a word of kindness to each one, as if he wished to take a last leave. Even then, the Duchesse d'Angoulême, who never left him, dared not ask him about his health.

On 12th September 1824, the Duc d'Orléans, who, with his family, had gone to their château at Eu, was summoned to Paris.

He left at eight o'clock in the morning, and drove to the capital without stopping, in fourteen hours ten minutes.

At the Chaussée d'Antin, his carriage broke down, so he engaged a cab, and arrived at the Palais Royal, where he found his uniform and a private carriage. He drove on to the Tuileries, and saw the Comte d'Artois, who told him that the King was slowly dying.

The Bourse and all the theatres and places of amusement were closed; prayers were being recited in all churches. Abbé Rocher, the King's Confessor, a worthy and dignified prelate, who at first hesitated to appear before the King, saying that he never presented himself before his Majesty unsummoned, dared to enter the royal chamber. The King, seeing him, seemed surprised, saying that he did not think that he was so ill.

The Abbé remained some time, and heard his confession, then spoke to him about the last Sacrament. The monarch replied that the moment had not come for that.

Seeing that time was passing, and the Abbé could get no further, someone had a strange idea; they asked Madame du Cayla to intervene. She entered the room and, with great tact and feeling, prevailed upon the King to receive the last rites. The King opened his eyes and, seeing her, said: "I did not think, Madame, that you would be the one to announce my end."

The next few days passed, and still the King lived; the members of his family spent most of their time waiting at the Tuileries. The meals took place in the ordinary dining-room, the King's place served as if he were present.

On 15th September, at three o'clock in the morning, the Orléans, with other members of the royal family, were hastily called. "The King is dying." But once more his pulse revived and they all went home.

On the 16th, when answering a renewed summons, they were told that there was hardly any pulse.

The King's room was crowded when the Orléans entered. The heat was stifling. The Duchesse d'Angoulême nearly fainted and went to a shut window to try to get a breath of air.

A profound silence reigned; it made it all the more poignant to hear the hard breathing of the monarch. Prayers were being recited in the adjoining room. At last, the breathing became weaker, the Grand Aumonier and the Abbé Rocher began reciting the prayers for the dying.

Then, at four o'clock, the King lay still; alkali was put into his nose, but not a movement was discerned. Then all, with great respect, drew near to the bed. The Comte Charles de Damas advanced towards the Comte d'Artois and said in a respectful voice: "Sire, the King is dead."

Then, after the *De Profundis*, the doors were opened, and the Duc de Blacas shouted to the waiting crowd: "Gentlemen, the King!" At once, the flow of courtiers followed the new King Charles X.

12

France is Sneering

Charles X, formerly the Comte d'Artois, differed in every way from his brother, the late King. Louis XVIII had held the reins of government with tenacious will-power, obstinately maintaining the etiquette of Louis XIV, to mark the distance between himself and his subjects. But in all this, wisdom was hidden.

Charles X was kind, anxious to win the affection of his people, but he was indolent and easy-going, only too ready to leave his responsibilities to others.

One of his first actions as King was to send for Louis Philippe to come to St. Cloud. As the Duc drove alone to the royal residence, he wondered what the interview might bring, so rarely in the last few years had anything pleasant occurred.

He was reassured when he entered the presence, as the King came towards him smiling, and said:

"My dear cousin, I want you to know that in no way do I share the prejudice of my brother, the late King, which estranged the two branches of our family. To prove this, I bestow on you and your children the title of 'Royal Highness'. I do the same for your sister, the Princesse Adélaïde."

Louis Philippe seemed overwhelmed, and once again protested his loyalty to the Crown and to the person of the King.

On 25th October, at eleven o'clock, the Duc d'Orléans, wearing a cloak of deepest mourning, left Neuilly for St. Denis, to attend the funeral of the late King.

The Abbey was magnificently draped with crêpe. The high dignitaries of the realm stood around the catafalque,

115

each holding one of the emblems of the monarchy, the Prince de Talleyrand carrying the banner of France, and the Grand Aumonier the golden casket in which the King's heart had been placed after the embalming. Two guards bore the entrails of the late King, which were enclosed in a golden box, on which was engraved, "Here are the entrails of the high, mighty, most Christian and very excellent Prince Louis XVIII, King of France and Navarre, died at the age of 68 years 9 months and 29 days." As the ceremony proceeded, the prayers and chants could scarcely be heard; the very assistants were hushed by the grandeur of death.

When the service ended, the coffin was carried down to the vault, to be laid on the first step of the stair. It was the custom for it to remain there until the coffin of the next King came to replace it.

Then the Duc d'Uzès, Marshal of the Court, broke his staff in twain and dropped the fragments into the vault, the heralds at arms divested themselves of their tabards and threw them after the staff; lastly, one of them called by name all the commanders who bore the King's insignias, so that each should dispose of them in a similar manner; then the Prince de Talleyrand was the last to salute the dead King, by lowering the flag which he held into the vault. Then, in a loud voice, a herald proclaimed, "Messieurs, la Maison du Roi est dissoute. Pourvoyez-vous ailleurs. Le Roi est mort! Le Roi est mort! Le Roi est mort! Vive le Roi!" [1]

At the last words of this proclamation, Talleyrand lifted the flag, and the whole congregation cried, "*Vive le Roi!*"

This sudden transition from death to life was a shock to many people present, as few could remember a previous royal funeral, and a feeling of sadness crept into many hearts.[2]

Charles X never forgot the reply of Monsieur de Dreux-Brézé, Grand Master of Ceremonies, when, after the funeral of Louis XVIII, the King congratulated him on the irreproachable

[1] "Gentlemen, the King's House is dissolved. Purvey yourselves elsewhere. The King is dead! The King is dead! The King is dead! Long live the King!"

[2] *Journal de Marie Amélie* (ed. la Duchesse de Vendôme). Librairie Plon.

SAINT-CLOUD

From the painting by Daubigny

manner in which the ceremony had been conducted. "Sire, your Majesty is most kind; many things were forgotten, but I can assure your Majesty that next time all will be in order."

"I thank you, Brézé," answered the monarch, "but I am not in a hurry."

The poor Grand Master of Ceremonies collapsed.

*   *   *

Eight months passed between the black crêpe of St. Denis, and the gold and scarlet of Rheims. As it was the last Coronation to take place in France, it is interesting to record it.

On 27th May 1825, Charles X left Paris on his way to Rheims. As he passed through numerous towns and villages, he was welcomed everywhere with shouts and "vivas", town bands and triumphal arches.

He stopped at the small village of Fismes in Champagne, not far from Rheims. It was traditional for the Sovereign to spend a night in this small town on his way to his Coronation, and to sleep in the home of a candle-merchant.

The next day, Charles X was to be crowned. From dawn, crowds had massed in the narrow streets and the Cathedral Square. As the sun rose, so the fever grew, till the excitement was intense. Already, at five in the morning, the Court ladies were dressing. Marie Amélie writes in her Journal, that she and the other members of the royal family wore their gala Court gowns of gold lamé brocade, strewn with diamonds, tiaras on their heads and diamonds covering their necks, arms and fingers.

The Duc d'Orléans wore the costume of the Bourbon Princes, a long tunic of cloth of gold, embroidered with gold, fastened by a blue band powdered with fleurs de lis, a neckband and cuffs of *point d'Angleterre* lace, and a large cloak of gold tissue, opening in front to show his tunic. At the back a long train of velvet fell from his shoulders; it was edged with rich embroidery of golden fleurs de lis, and lined with ermine; this cloak had a cape of the same style, and it weighed forty-five pounds. On his head rested a ducal crown.

The Prince de Joinville, in his memoirs, described his father, Louis Philippe, as looking like a Pharaoh.

Those who were present said that never had they witnessed such a magnificent scene as the Cathedral that day. The walls were covered with light-blue cloth sewn with golden fleurs de lis. All around hung portraits of past Kings of France, who had been crowned at Rheims; above them were medallions of former Archbishops of Rheims. On both sides of the aisle, tribunes had been erected for the ladies, diplomatic corps, peers, ministers and envoys. In front of the altar was a faldstool for the King, behind which stood three similar ones for the Duc d'Angoulême, the Duc d'Orléans, and the Prince de Condé.

The interior of the Cathedral seemed almost on fire with the brilliance of the thousands of candles flickering in the atmosphere of the sacred edifice. At seven o'clock, the Duc d'Orléans rose from his seat, and accompanied by the two Cardinals de Clermont-Tonnerre and de la Fare, left to bring the King to his Coronation. On arrival at the monarch's residence, they stood outside the King's room, and knocked twice. From within, the Prince de Talleyrand cried, "Whom do you seek?"

The Cardinals responded: "Charles X, whom God has given us to be our King."

Then the Prince de Talleyrand cried, "Ushers, open the doors!"

The doors having been flung open, the two Cardinals entered the room, recited a prayer and, offering their arms to the King, supported him to the Cathedral.

The King wore a tunic of cloth of silver, on his head a small cap of black velvet surmounted by white feathers.

The Sovereign having been presented to his people, the ceremony proceeded in all its splendour, made the more solemn by the rich copes of the archbishops, and the beauty of the sacred music which had been composed for the occasion by the greatest musicians of France.

At the actual moment of enthronement, when the King mounted the throne, which was placed on a dais high above the people, wearing his regal robes with the crown of Charlemagne on his head, in his right hand the sceptre, in his left the wand of justice, surrounded by his officers of state in their brilliant uniforms, the Cardinals and the princes cried:

"*Vivat Rex in aeternum.*"

Flags were lowered before him, salvos of artillery were heard, doves were released to fly high over the heads of the crowd, medals were scattered from the throne to all below, and cries of *"Vive le Roi!"* echoed again and again from those sacred walls, where Joan of Arc had raised the same cry four hundred years before.

Thus was consecrated Charles X, the last King of France.

The weeks which followed the crowning of the King were brilliant and wildly gay. The people, rich and poor, danced, sang and amused themselves. The old nobility, who had not entertained for years, now opened wide their doors. Commerce flourished, and France seemed satisfied.

Yet one wonders, is France ever satisfied? Some people praised, others mocked; some prayed, others blasphemed. So it is in all countries, but the French, with their critical outlook on life, carry this very far.

Mingled with the singing and dancing, one heard such remarks as, "Did you hear how, at the Coronation, the Prince de Talleyrand vested the King in violet half-boots, sprinkled with fleurs de lis . . . that his tunic was pierced in six places to allow for the anointment . . . and Jourdan was there, that old Republican soldier, carrying the Crown of Charlemagne before the King . . ." And people sneered and guffawed.

The ancient traditions had been revived, and all France appeared to be cheering; in reality this was only a façade; the spirit had gone, and all was torn to shreds, trampled upon and criticized. Yet, if any foreigner had joined in this chorus of disparagement, he would have instantly been challenged to a duel.

Meanwhile, the King entertained the foreign envoys and ambassadors at the Tuileries, and daily received deputations which came from the provinces to pay homage. Country nobility and peasants flocked to the capital to see the King driving in procession, or reviewing his troops. Paris was crowded; it was difficult for the sightseers to circulate, the streets were so narrow, but all the pushing and jostling added to the general excitement.

On 7th June 1825, the first State function took place: it was the investiture of the King with the Order of the Garter, at the hands of the Duke of Northumberland, acting as special envoy of George IV.

General de Rumigny [1] described the scene, and his remarks show very clearly how strange the traditional ceremonial must have appeared to French eyes.

At one o'clock, Charles X entered the Galerie de Diane, dressed entirely in white—white silk knee-breeches, a large white bow below the left knee, white shoes, a white coat fitting closely at the waist and flaring outwards, fastened by white buttons, his head bare.

The Court was ranged to the left and right of the throne. The British Ambassador was introduced by the gentlemen ushers, followed by the members of his Embassy bearing the robes, hat and insignia of the Order on blue velvet cushions.

The costume of Sir George Maylet was most incongruous. He wore a mantle of red silk, and his white habit, close fitting underneath, made him resemble a sick man escaped from his bed, who had taken his curtain to cover himself.

The bonnet of the Order is a hat surmounted by feathers four feet high, it looks as though a whole ostrich had been placed upon it, it is a real baldachin. I have entered into these details to show that, despite the small importance which, in this century, should be attached to these little things, men love, and will always love, baubles.

At the moment of investiture, there was a solemn address from the Duke of Northumberland, to which the King responded in fitting terms.

This procedure was conducted with so much gravity, that some of the younger courtiers could hardly refrain from suppressed giggles when their King received this strange English honour, a jewelled Garter, with so much ceremony.

The next day the Municipality of Paris offered the King and royal family a fête at the Hôtel de Ville, which was said to have been one of the most magnificent which had ever been given in this celebrated building.

In the famous Salle d'Angoulême where the banquet took place, the King sat on a gilt throne under a blue canopy

[1] In his *Souvenirs*.

strewn with fleurs de lis, at the head of a richly-adorned table, and was served by the municipal Councillors, whilst the royal family and thirty ladies chosen by the King sat on stools at the same table, and had the honour of dining with his Majesty. Round the immense hall, on raised benches, were seated less fortunate ladies.

They had been informed when invited that they should wear their most sumptuous gowns and richest jewels; they were warned that they would not be given any kind of food, but as a consolation, on their arrival, they were offered a rose, and a case containing medals with the King's effigy. Their role was to make a colourful background for the banquet, which lasted nine quarters of an hour.

The heat was so unbearable that, before the end, many places were empty. The background had fainted.

When the ordeal was over, the royal family went in procession to the immense ballroom, where the crowd made the heat worse; there they had to listen to a long cantata. Later, only half alive, the King mounted his throne, and the Duchesse de Berri opened the Ball. Later still, they moved again in procession to another hall, where they had to witness the beginning of another Ball, which lasted until dawn broke over the city.

So Charles X took up his reign in the Tuileries.

The King, as he appeared in public, created a great sensation. He was now nearly seventy, but his enchanting manner and attractive smile made him look almost youthful. One had the impression that he was constantly looking around for those who needed help. Strict etiquette bored him; he submitted outwardly to its numerous rules, but he insisted on leading his private life in the manner he chose. The only person who counted for him was his grandson, "le fils de France", as the people called the Duc de Bordeaux.

Every morning, a cup of camomile tea would be his only breakfast; then, at half-past eight, a gentle knock brought joy to those dreamy eyes, as the door opened and a small boy appeared—the Duc de Bordeaux: he would throw his arms around his grandpapa and chatter, never waiting for an answer.

His grandfather was never willing to let him go, and as etiquette forbade anyone entering the King's room unbidden, the little boy often missed his lessons; his numerous tutors were left waiting, anxiously looking at the clock, wondering when they would see their pupil again.

The Duc at this time was about five years old, and was a handsome, lively child; years later, when the Château de Chambord was presented to him by public subscription, he took the title Comte de Chambord, by which he is generally known.

The King deemed it a loss of time to sit down to a proper luncheon so, hurriedly, he would drink some soup, swallow half a chicken, throw down his napkin, and drive off to Rambouillet, hunting or looking after his horses. In the evening he would visit the Duchesse de Berri. Sometimes he remained late, taking part in the gaiety, and joining in the graceful minuets in which he also excelled. And yet he would blame the Duchesse de Berri for her wild life.

The season, beyond the palace walls, was brilliant compared with the dullness of the Court; at last the Duchesse d'Angoulême realized that, as the hostess, she must entertain at the Tuileries, so she persuaded the King to hold a reception once a week. The Duchesse was hardly the person to enliven a fête; she had no personal charm, and her manner was haughty and unbending; was it from shyness, or the tragedy of her youth? The Princess Radziwill, in her memoirs, tells us that "when somebody was presented to her, the Duchesse would stand, twirling her fan and making munching noises with her mouth, before she could bring forth a phrase".

She decided that the strictest etiquette was to be observed. All the guests had to be in the palace by eight o'clock in the evening, after which the doors were closed, and none could enter or leave. The guests had to stand in two rows, until the King had passed through the galleries to the far end, where he sat down to play cards with a few of the old courtiers. The Duchesses de Berri and d'Orléans played cards, each in a different salon, but the "gay" Duchesse d'Angoulême just sat at a round table and embroidered.

The guests went round these groups, hoping to catch the

royal eye, or a smile from one of the princesses, and they bravely endeavoured to look interested and alive, whilst they longed for the moment when the King would rise, and thus give the signal for their release.

After a few of these intoxicating soirées, the Duchesse de Berri told the King that she was bored to tears; he then confessed that he could not stand them any longer so, to everybody's joy, they were discontinued.

As a contrast to this dull mediocrity, the Palais Royal was a shining light. There, fêtes and receptions were planned to dazzle. The most outstanding politicians, a fair sprinkling of the Opposition, all the great thinkers, authors, poets, artists, were invited and flattered, so that their pens and speech would be used for the greater glory of the Duc d'Orléans.

The Baron de Damas remarked: "What a dangerous double game the Duc d'Orléans is playing. Dazzling the Court, flattering the Opposition and bowing down to the rabble. He may fall between three stools."

In the State Drawing-Room, concerts took place, at which Madame Malibran sang, the celebrated flautist, Drouet, and Hauman, the German violinist, played. At the Grand Balls, the Duc de Chartres, only sixteen years old, but already as beautiful as a Greek god, led the dance with the Duchesse de Berri.

Marie Amélie was gracious, Louis Philippe cordial, but the one who never became quite attuned to these entertainments was the Princesse Adélaïde. She knew too well that, although she was a Bourbon, and now a Royal Highness, the princesses of the elder branch always kept her at a distance; they looked upon her as an intruder, and openly regretted that Marie Amélie, whom they all loved, should be burdened with such a sister-in-law; one who was insidiously influencing the Duc, ever whispering in his ear.

13

"The Child of France"

Unthinkingly, the King was working for the cause of his cousin: each day he pursued a policy which had no definite aim, which was not in touch with reality. Gradually, the reforms which had been proclaimed on the accession melted away—not actually revoked, but certainly not carried out.

Villèle, the Chief Minister, realizing that with this indolent King, whose sympathies lay with the "ultra-royalists", he had a freer hand, began to introduce measures which first surprised the public, then made them anxious, and finally angered them.

The Army was shaken to the core by the decision to place 150 of Napoleon's generals on the retired list. Then there was the *"milliard des émigrés"*, an indemnity paid to those émigrés who, on their return from exile, found that their estates, confiscated during the Revolution, had been bought by *nouveaux riches* of the Empire. For ten years they had harassed Louis XVIII for restitution. Then, in 1825, Villèle conceived this solution to appease the bitterness of the old and the new. It seemed innocent enough, but it gave the Opposition a chance to say that it was infamous that those who had fought against France should thus be rewarded. Louis Philippe and his sister received sixteen million francs, but they were careful not to discourage the resentment.

The law on sacrilege was passed to enable the Courts to inflict the death penalty for profanation of churches. This had been increasing in the last few years. A shocking instance occurred one morning, when thirty young children, in seeming piety, came to the altar rails of a church to receive Holy Communion. They then withdrew the Host from their mouths and, on returning home, used them to seal their letters.

124

Villèle was not the instigator of this law; he knew the fury it would arouse among the atheists, liberals, Republicans and anti-clericals, and dreaded the result. His foreboding proved to be right, the indignation and protestation became serious. So Marshal Oudinot suggested that the monarch should show himself publicly and, by his presence, regain the confidence of the people. A review of the Garde Nationale was arranged to be held and, in spite of rumours that there might be disturbing manifestations, Villèle could not dissuade the King from attending the parade.

In the Palais Royal, Louis Philippe knew what would take place, and was slightly anxious lest the coming disturbance should arouse suspicions against him in the mind of the King. He consulted his sister on the wisdom of excusing himself from attendance, but Adélaïde urged him to go; she felt no embarrassment at the thought of being a witness to a scene which would be painful to the monarch. Louis Philippe must be seen on every occasion, the liberal prince.

At one o'clock on 29th August 1827, Charles X rode in procession to the Champ de Mars. The huge parade-ground was crowded; the whole Garde Nationale in Paris were arrayed in their brilliant uniforms, and spectators were massed around. All went well along the processional route, the King being hailed with shouts of "*Vive le Roi!*"

Then the inspection began. Villèle was watching tensely, Louis Philippe almost holding his breath. The first legion saluted his arrival with "*Vive le Roi!*" Then, suddenly, came a cry of "Down with the Ministers!" "Down with the Jesuits!" "Long live the Charta!"

The King passed on to the second legion, and the same thing happened; the same angry cries, interspersed with loyal shouts of "*Vive le Roi!*" And so it was throughout the inspection.

Imperturbably, Charles X pursued the review to the end, acknowledging the loyal cries, ignoring all else.

In the carriage from which they were watching, four royal ladies showed more emotion. All four were sitting very erect and silent. The Duchesse d'Angoulême, red-faced and breathing heavily, was glaring at Princesse Adélaïde who sat opposite her, tight-lipped and inscrutable, taking in every detail of the scene. The Duchesse de Berri was almost weeping with anger, feeling the insult as if it were addressed to her son. The fourth, the Duchesse d'Orléans, unutterably embarrassed, was staring straight in front of her, seeing nothing.

The following day, 30th April, the Garde Nationale was disbanded.

General de Rumigny was in Louis Philippe's study when the *Moniteur*, then one of the leading newspapers, was brought in. The Duc unfolded it, read, and then turned to Rumigny with a startled look, his arms dropping to his sides as he let the *Moniteur* fall to the carpet.

"Great Heavens!! What blindness!" he cried.

He sent Rumigny to gather more information, and to see how the men involved were taking it. As his Aide de Camp left him, he showed no sign of his real emotions. He sat at his writing table, his head between his hands, motionless.[1]

For Louis Philippe, the next few days were full of uncertainty. He felt annoyed that he had not been consulted over such an important decision. And now that it had been taken, Charles X showed no inclination to discuss it with him; as if his opinion were of no consequence. He was also anxious. Why was the King leaving him out of his confidence? What did he suspect? Always this fear of being found out!

At last the summons came: the King was going to Compiègne and wished to take leave of his cousin. When Louis Philippe was ushered into the King's study, Charles X was standing near the open window, speaking to the Baron de Damas. The Duc could not help noticing that, although the monarch looked tired, he held himself erect and slightly defiant. He did not ask the Duc to sit down, but motioned him to wait.

Discreetly, Louis Philippe withdrew to the far end of the room and looked around. How well he knew this room; in each reign it assumed a fresh personality. Under Louis XVI it was always filled with flowers; their scent mingled with the perfume of Marie Antoinette, who often entered it. Then, with Louis XVIII, the flowers had gone, and the wheeled chair of the King had made lines in the pile of the carpet. Now Charles X had revived the flowers, but a new odour had come,

[1] *Souvenirs* of General de Rumigny.

the prevailing aura of incense, brought by the many bishops and priests.

Finally, Baron de Damas was dismissed. The King walked slowly to his writing table, sat down and, turning, said:

"I have taken a great decision since I last saw you, my dear cousin; but it was necessary. I am, as you know, slightly deaf. I only heard the cries of '*Vive le Roi!*', but the ladies assured me that they had heard very different shouts."

"Indeed, Sire," said Louis Philippe, "but the mass of the people were shouting '*Vive le Roi!*' "

"I cannot allow the armed forces to dictate the law, and if I had any wish to alter the Cabinet, which I have not, I should certainly not have done so for that reason. Rather than give way to such demands, I would resign."

"Sire! For a King there is no resignation, only abdication."

The King brushed the remark aside; he had spoken lightly. Yet how deeply he was to feel the bitterness of that word three years later.

Amid all his worries, the King had a great consolation. Often when the many ministers and advisers had taken leave of him, he would relax for a few moments; then slowly walk to the fireplace and pull the long strip of embroidery of the bell, with which he summoned an A.D.C. He would tell him to offer his compliments to their Royal Highnesses, his grandchildren, and ask them to give him the pleasure of their company.

"La petite Mademoiselle," Louise Marie Thérèse, daughter of the Duchesse de Berri, was now ten years old. She promised to be very pretty; she was graceful, accomplished and, although as yet very young, she already took an interest in public affairs.

She knew how to entertain and be gracious to any political personage, without being prompted. Her governess, the Comtesse de Gontaut, had taught her that a royal personage should be able to speak on every subject, and the child had learnt this quite naturally.

The day that her small brother, the Duc de Bordeaux, had been separated from her and placed under the care of his tutors, the little Mademoiselle had a shock. When she was taken to see her grandfather, the King, the sentinels did not present arms;

she was so surprised that she stopped short, looked up with an angry frown, but passed on.

Later the same day, she was going for a drive but—another blow—there was no escort. This hurt her feelings so much that she refused to enter the carriage.

The following day, a sentinel who had not received the new order, seeing her, cried out "To arms!" The little princess looked at him and, making a deep reverence, said: "I thank you, but it is only me." [1] The feeling that all the fuss and ceremony which had hitherto surrounded her, had only been meant for the small brother upon whom she had looked down, hurt her deeply.

In the meantime, the household of the Duc de Bordeaux had been formed. It consisted of six Aides de Camp, two honorary Aides, a staff Colonel, a Colonel-in-Chief of the Gardes Suisses, four titulary Aides, two orderly officers, one Secretary-General, one Commissioner-General, a tutor, two under-tutors, a preceptor, an equerry, a valet, two servants, two ushers, and four footmen.

In the midst of this crowd of officials, the little boy was often lonely, as he was allowed few playmates. The Duchesse took little part in her son's education. She lived on the ground floor of the Pavillon de Marsan, he on the first floor, where all orders came from the King.

The truth is that the gloomy life at the Tuileries bored and frustrated the Duchesse beyond words. There was no outlet for her energy and intelligence. She who loved adventure and gaiety, was penned within these dull walls, where there was nothing to keep her alive. Little by little, her authority over the lives of her children was taken away, until, having no responsibilities, she embarked on a life of pleasure which gradually began to cause a scandal.

It was whispered that her country house at Rosny had become a centre for wild orgies. Nothing seemed to satisfy her craving for excitement. Even when her son, the Duc de Bordeaux, was dangerously ill with measles, she did not stay with him in Paris, but left for Rosny with a party of notorious friends.

All this disturbed the King, and enraged her sister-in-law,

[1] *Mémoires* of the Comtesse de Boigne. Librairie Plon.

the Duchesse d'Angoulême, but, careless of all, she went her own way.

The little Duc usually dined alone, while his tutor, the Baron de Damas, dined also alone in another room, at a table laid for sixteen people: the preceptor and under-tutors, each in separate apartments, sat at the head of a table laid for eight. All these tables were sumptuously provided, except that of the Duc de Bordeaux himself; his menu consisted of some stodgy, but fill- ing, soup; one main dish which was made to last two days; vegetables; and a few sips of a rather inferior, well-watered wine. The fare was so scanty that when, occasionally, the little Duc had a friend to dine, the Baron de Damas would send a supplementary dish from his own table. Such was the life of the heir to the throne of France.

In vivid contrast, the life of the young Orléans princes was luxurious. Ostensibly they were being brought up as demo- cratic citizens, attending classes at the Collège Henri IV, tak- ing their meals in the refectory, sharing their recreation with the other pupils. But in reality they had their own appointed places in class, special dishes were served at table, they each had their own private apartments in the Collège, and were accompanied everywhere by their respective tutors.

The Prince de Joinville in his memoirs tells us that the sons of the bourgeoisie were not taken in by this pretence of equality; they delighted to give them kicks or punches on the sly, during recreation, muttering, "*attrape petite majesté*".

Each of the elder brothers had his own partner amongst his sisters, and the pairs were called "ménages", like married couples. Thus the Duc de Chartres and Princesse Louise were known as "le ménage Chartres"; each "ménage" danced to- gether, walked in to dinner together, sat together at the theatre. How different all this was from the dull life of the heir to the throne.

One evening, the Duc de Bordeaux was having his dinner, as usual alone, when he heard light footsteps approaching along the corridor. The footmen, gazing at him, bored and indifferent, as he ate his one dish, suddenly stiffened to attention as the door opened, and the Duchesse de Berri entered.

With a word, she dismissed the servants and, to the joy of her small son, she embraced him, drew up a chair to the huge table, and sat down facing him.

"Give me a piece of your meat; I am so hungry."

The child could scarcely believe his eyes; he so rarely saw his mother, and now she was actually sitting with him, eating part of his dinner.

As she tasted the somewhat dried-up piece of mutton, which had been cooked the day before, she made a grimace.

"It is rather hard; but never mind the food. I have come to invite you to your own Ball."

She stopped to note his reaction, then continued:

"I am giving it for your sister, and you must do the honours for her."

The child was almost overwhelmed when she told him that she had already chosen the fancy costume that he would wear —that of a thirteenth-century knight. Suddenly the smile faded from his face, and he said:

"What will Grandpapa, and Monsieur de Damas say?"

For a moment the Duchesse was silent; only that day her father-in-law had complained to her of her frivolous mode of life; but she had answered that she could not survive in the boresome and lethargic atmosphere of the Tuileries, in which others seemed to thrive. To her it meant death.

She turned to her son and said: "You will ask your grand-papa's permission tomorrow morning."

To her surprise, the King was most gracious, and told the boy that he would even be present at the Ball himself.

On 25th January, the Pavillon de Marsan was ablaze with lights and flowers, as equipage after equipage drew up at the entrance, and little figures stepped out in powdered wigs and satin, or gay peasant costume with clogs. They were received by the Duc de Bordeaux in his coat of mail, and by the little Mademoiselle as a Neapolitan peasant of her mother's home-land.

At four o'clock, the Orléans children arrived. So much trouble had been taken with their costumes that, as usual, they outshone everybody else; most enchanting of all was Princesse Clementine, the youngest daughter of the Duc and Duchesse d'Orléans, wearing a rich dress of the Court of Louis XV. As she danced a minuet with her brother, the Prince de Joinville, in a costume of the same period, they looked exquisite, as if they had stepped from a Nattier painting. When the dance was over, Charles X was so carried away that he led her to her father saying:

"Monsieur mon cousin, were I forty years younger, I would ask you for the hand of your daughter, to make her Queen of France."

Then he kissed the little girl, and handed her back to Joinville.

The children danced whilst their parents exchanged compliments. Louis Philippe excelled in his role as devoted papa, and displayed every sign of the most obsequious loyalty towards the King. All this was the visible world of the Duc d'Orléans.

Another aspect of his life was not so wholesome. Let us peruse some of the secret police records at about this time. There is a confidential report on the state of mind of the country, which put the King on his guard against Dupin, Laffitte, Casimir Périer, Sebastiani—all eminent liberals who became Ministers under the July monarchy: but it added: "The King need have no fear of H.R.H. the Duc d'Orléans, his good and devoted cousin." This is curious, as all these were the close associates of the Duc.

The report goes on to cite an impressive list of active opponents of the royal government, including several of Napoleon's Marshals, but it always omits to note that all the persons mentioned received the most courteous and flattering attention at the Palais Royal. This strange omission has led many authors to wonder which side the police favoured.

In another paragraph, we are informed: "The Protestants have joined the Orléanist camp. . . . The Republicans and Bonapartists would, in a crisis, have the Marquis de Lafayette, and Jourdan for their leaders." [1]

Lafayette, Jourdan and the great Protestant Duc de Broglie, were all well-known adherents of the Duc d'Orléans. But let his Majesty have no fears, his good cousin is so loyal and devoted!

There is also the "black book" of the police of the period, which reported in detail the movements of eminent personages.

_____
[1] *Louis Philippe*, by J. Lucas-Dubreton.

There is recorded the fact that Louis Philippe had secret relations with the British Foreign Office, with the Spanish Ambassador; employed a professional intriguer named Müller; and that he had, on a number of occasions, gone alone, in the evening, to the house of the Duc de Dalmatie, to meet the leaders of the Opposition.

In reality, Louis Philippe had decided that, for the moment, his best course was inaction. There seemed to be no lack of people anxious to work in his interest, so why not wait?

Madame Adélaïde thought differently. She had all the boldness which her brother lacked, and little of his caution. To her, intrigue was the breath of life; she was happiest when she was presiding over some secret committee, or exercising her influence or power behind the scenes. She cherished the notion that she was the centre of everything, the unofficial leader of her brother's party, the "Grey Eminence" of the Orléans.

The Royalists, who hated Louis Philippe, took very little notice of Princesse Adélaïde. This obscurity left her free to act.

Madame de Boigne noted that Adélaïde received many people, sounded the opinions of important men, and obliged them to take sides, when they would have preferred to remain aloof. She cajoled Talleyrand, bullied Laffitte, flattered Sebastiani; and summoned them to committees where the policies of the Opposition were discussed.

14

Cupidity

Few of the citizens of Paris realized that another reign was ending, not by death, but through the influence of one man; one who had worked since his early youth to destroy the monarchy in France—the General Marquis de Lafayette.

To some, he was a hero; to others, he was a man who ever destroyed, and never created. Once, he had toyed with the idea that he was in love, first with the Comtesse d'Hunolstein, and then with Madame de Simiane; these, according to the Prince de Ligne, were the two most beautiful women in France; in reality, he had only one love in his life—America; and George Washington had been his guiding star. He tried to bring to the French the stable Constitution of the American people, quite forgetting that what suited the simple, earnest Americans, would never fit the cynical, rebellious French.

Before his time, democracy was a fashionable toy, safely held within the bounds of philosophy. To Lafayette it was no abstract ideal, but a vibrant, living creed. He dreamt of it, lived by it, until nothing could hold him back—mistress, country, not even the gay life of Paris.

On his return from the war of American Independence, he made it his mission to carry the seed of liberty to France; that seed took root in fertile soil, and spread until even he was dismayed at the result.

Although Lafayette was an enemy of monarchy, he realized that France needed a King, but a King who would be the servant of a republican nation, a man whom he, Lafayette, could lead and use as he had always dreamt.

In the Chamber, Lafayette never lost an opportunity to make himself conspicuous. The old Revolutionary ideals permeated every paragraph of his speeches and, amidst the applause which followed, cries of *"Liberté!"* were often heard.

With Thiers, Guizot and Laffitte, he often visited the Palais Royal, and then toured the provinces, discreetly spreading his ideas. These journeys revived his personal popularity, and everywhere he was enthusiastically acclaimed. Even the secret police sometimes forgot to report these damaging speeches.

He was the beacon for those idealists whose dreams could never come true, but those dreams, while they lasted, seemed so real. Victor Hugo, Dumas, Gautier, Lamartine, would listen with rapt attention to the words of one who had known the American Revolution. Always it was the name of Louis Philippe which closed the discussions; he alone was deemed worthy of the throne of France, he who had learnt from the Jacobins, fought with the revolutionaries, and was educating his children in the democratic ideals; that simple, unambitious man.

How little they knew him!

As these men were shaping his political future, Louis Philippe was shaping his financial one. He had one great weakness; a passion which dominated all others—his pride in his wealth.

Since his return to France in 1814, he had striven ceaselessly to increase his fortune, disputing claims in the Law Courts, poring over his household accounts, watching over his estates with the care of a lover, even pestering his neighbours at Neuilly to sell him their lands, so that he could extend his already vast domains.

In 1830, this cupidity caused his name to be whispered in connection with the tragedy of the Prince de Condé. This prince, father of the ill-fated Duc d'Enghien who had been shot by order of Napoleon, had never recovered from the shock of losing his only son. Now aged seventy-four, his mind was slightly dimmed by the fog of age and sorrow.

He lived in his two beautiful palaces, the Château de Chantilly and the Palais Bourbon in Paris, surrounded by all the luxury that his riches provided. Dominating the scene was a woman, an adventuress named Sophie Dawes, the daughter of an Isle of Wight fisherman. In 1811 she had become the mistress of the Prince de Condé, then living in London; in 1818 an officer of the royal guard of Louis XVIII, the Baron de Feuchère, married her, believing her tale that she was the illegitimate daughter of the Prince de Condé. On discovering the true story of her life, the Baron left her, and she returned to the prince, now an old man, to dominate his life. She still posed as his mistress though, considering his age and the state of his health, this liaison could only have been a memory.

The Prince de Condé had long ago decided to make the Duc de Bordeaux heir to his vast fortune. This did not suit the Baronne, whose one ambition was to be received at Court, and to be accepted by Society.

So one day, through an intermediary, she approached the Duc d'Orléans with the suggestion that she could perhaps persuade the prince to alter his Will in favour of the Duc d'Aumale,[1] his godson. She laid down her conditions—the Orléans must accept her, invite her to their home, return the visit by dining openly at Chantilly, and ultimately present her at Court: a hard nut to crack with the Duchesse d'Angoulême. The Duc d'Orléans accepted the bargain without hesitation; the fortune was worth grasping, and Chantilly worth possessing.

Feeble though he was, the old prince protested, and would not hear of altering his last testament. Then a veritable siege commenced; daily he was nagged by his *soi-disant* mistress, coerced by repeated visits from the Duc d'Orléans, often accompanied by the young Duc d'Aumale, brought to pay court to his godfather.

The bullying and persuasion daily became more menacing and cruel. Constant messages passed between the Palais Royal and the Palais Bourbon. At last, tired and terrified, the Prince de Condé took a pen in his aching fingers, and signed the revised Will by which the Duc d'Aumale would become one of the richest Princes of France, and future owner of Chantilly.

That night, the messenger sent by the ex-Sophie Dawes to the Palais Royal was well rewarded.

Madame de Feuchère was received at Court; the Duchesse d'Angoulême, who always refrained from even touching anything unclean, at first resented the very thought of shaking hands with this blatant creature. But Louis Philippe persuaded

[1] Seventh child of Louis Philippe, born in 1822.

Marie Amélie to plead for d'Aumale; as Madame d'Angoulême loved this boy, she consented, but made a condition, she would only bow and not give her hand.

Now the pleading continued, would her dear cousin speak to the King? Marie Amélie, by now, was almost in tears. The Duchesse, touched by so much anguish, said that she would try. To the relief of everybody, Charles X declared he would rather enjoy seeing the famous mistress of his cousin Condé; it would bring him once more in touch with his youth. So Madame de Feuchère achieved her heart's desire.

Cuvillier Fleury described Madame de Feuchère as "a tall, handsome woman, perfectly preserved, with a proud, vain, amiable face, speaking bad French. She has a way of showering gifts upon the children. . . . She gave a magnificent déjeuner to all the company, the Duc d'Aumale on her right, the Duc d'Orléans on her left. The Prince de Condé sat in a corner; he seemed worried and sad, as he always is when not in the country. He had red eyes, a pale face, a slight limp, and only spoke a few words of greeting to keep up the appearance of a host."

To most people, even to those of his family, Louis Philippe's relations with Madame de Feuchère were a source of embarrassment: in another paragraph Cuvillier Fleury gives the attitude of the Duchesse:

"Madame de Feuchère has been received at Neuilly. She sat at table on the right of Monsieur le Duc d'Orléans. . . . She was less amiable than she had seemed in her own house. . . . When she arrived she was not the only person to be embarrassed; Madame la Duchesse d'Orléans took two steps towards her, complimented her, then returned to her place, and her ladies did the rest."

While Madame de Feuchère thus insinuated herself into the royal circle, the Prince de Condé remained alone in his lovely residence, and brooded. He realized that his signature on the new Will had robbed him of his personality, in the eyes of those who had alternately bullied or flattered him to achieve their ends; now they did not even notice him.

Suddenly he rebelled; why should he submit to these scoundrels, no better than extortioners. If only he could get away from them, he could change his Will again, and regain his self-reliance and liberty of thought. He must escape.

He sent for his faithful valet, and told him that they were going abroad, but that the journey must be organized with the utmost secrecy. He did not know, however, that the "faithful" man was in the pay of Madame de Feuchère. So the prince remained a captive.

Notwithstanding this sordid intrigue, life at the Palais Royal remained serene and unruffled on the surface.

One evening, Louis Philippe and the Duchesse de Dino sat together in his study. It was a relaxation to him to talk with her, since she had known him from her childhood. He could fully trust her judgment and her affection.

That night, the conversation turned upon the children. Louis Philippe had a great affection for each, but he was not blind to their faults.

"My angelic Louise is wise and good, but will never shine. Marie is a delightful imp, with no thought but for laughter, brushing boredom aside; but she will become known as a great artist. Clementine is ambitious; if she bears a son, she will teach him, perhaps, to be too ambitious to be trusted.[1]

"Now for my sons: Chartres, delightful but too impulsive. Nemours, so deep that one can never know what he wants—I often wonder, does he ever want anything? Joinville, '*Je m'en fiche*' would be a good name for him, but straight as an arrow, and the most popular of all. Aumale's riches will never spoil him, but his 'grand seigneur' manner will prevent people from approaching too near. Montpensier is too small, but I predict he will go far and cause much controversy—mon pauvre petit Ton Ton."

Louis Philippe continued: "I must tell you a little anecdote about Ton Ton. Very much against his mother's wish, I insist that now he is six years old, he should begin to attend some of our dinner parties.

"Three nights ago, he sat between two admirals; as you know, he never stops talking; so this midget chattered and chattered; the poor admirals, bored to death, could not get

[1] This forecast is interesting. Princesse Clementine did have a son who became King Ferdinand of Bulgaria.

away from his incessant prattle, but out of respect they appeared to be full of interest.

"Montpensier's valet, seeing the plight of the two men, came up to him and, in a voice loud enough to be heard by his neighbours, said: 'Monsieur Ton Ton, here is your beefsteak—eat it and stop talking.'

"The poor child turned scarlet, and I could see tears spring to his eyes, but he never opened his mouth again—I feel sure, to the great relief of the admirals!"

The Duchesse de Dino enjoyed these intimate conversations with Louis Philippe. She loved royalty, and he loved familiarity. So both had a delightful time when they were alone together.

Louis Philippe's life was a perpetual attempt to disguise his true feelings. His aim was to make England believe that he was a strong Anglophile, France that he was the greatest patriot, the Royalists, a staunch Royalist, and the Republicans, one of themselves. It was a difficult role to keep up. The result, none trusted him.

Not to lose caste with English society, whenever any prominent personality arrived from that country, he would overwhelm them with lavish entertainments. When Lady Jersey came over for a short visit, she was absolutely stormed by invitations from the Palais Royal. She returned home after two weeks, having been nowhere and having seen no one except the Orléans family and the interior of their sumptuous abode.

Louis Philippe felt that entertaining English society was not enough; he, himself, was losing touch with England. He had not seen George IV since his accession, and some of those who now counted in political circles were comparatively unknown to him. It would be difficult to persuade Charles X that he needed a change of air, but he had an excellent excuse now that Chartres was eighteen years old; an age when travel was needed to complete his education.

Chartres was remarkably good-looking, tall, slight, graceful —"un enchanteur", Paris exclaimed. With all this, he was strong-willed and already showed an independence of spirit, which later grew stronger and caused a certain amount of anxiety for his father.

His parents thought that the time had come when their

favourite son must begin "to live" as the French say. So he went forth to sample the pleasures that Paris is ever ready to give. Society went wild, and every temptation was offered to him; but he had already tasted the existence of the *grand monde* at the Palais Royal; he wanted to enjoy the other aspect of life, so far withheld from him.

Often Marie Amélie lay awake praying that no harm should come to her darling.

Soon, stories spread that he was behaving rather unwisely; it was known that he was frequenting houses of dubious fame. His father becoming anxious, tried to warn him not "to live" too rapidly, but the young prince answered in a respectful manner that he was now his own master.

The visit to Great Britain was an excellent pretext to wean him from his dissipations; so, amidst tears and blessings from Marie Amélie, father and son set out for London.

On arrival there, they were received by George IV, whom they found very changed. He had grown enormous, and was almost helpless at times. The King, the Court, and the whole of Society were enchanted by the extreme courtesy of the Duc de Chartres. His delightful manner towards young and old, the kissing of hands, his gentleness, his intellectual conversation, made him stand out amongst the other young men of his age.

To the British, Louis Philippe was an enigma; he still retained that charm which had captivated so many, and yet repelled others; nevertheless he was accepted as an authority on French politics.

Certainly the Government showed no great enthusiasm for the present unsettled French policy, and although Wellington and most of those who had known the Duc d'Orléans, still distrusted him, they dreaded still more the unbalanced régime of Charles X. They were worried by the French designs on Algeria, France was growing dangerously friendly with Russia, and the Ministers felt that Louis Philippe, with Britain at his back, might prove to be a useful pawn in the hands of the Cabinet.

Greece had at last achieved her independence from Turkey, and the chancelleries of Europe were vibrant with the wrangling of monarchs and ministers, in the search for a King for that troubled country. A King had to be found, and that speedily. Candidates appeared on every side, one of whom was the Duc de Nemours; but there were many rivals.

Louis Philippe, ever alert to seize an opportunity, sent agents to Greece to canvass secretly in favour of his son, but eventually the throne was offered to Leopold of Saxe-Coburg, the widower of Princess Charlotte of Great Britain.

Louis Philippe was bitterly disappointed, as even Charles X had expressed a keen desire to see his young cousin crowned King of the Hellenes; but it was some consolation when a letter came from Prince Leopold, asking for the hand of Princesse Louise d'Orléans' in marriage. The princess was just eighteen, her suitor forty-two. The Duc was delighted at the possibility of his daughter becoming Queen of Greece, but the Duchesse hesitated; she had always hoped to marry Louise to her nephew, the Duke of Calabria.

The unselfish nature of the princess suffered at the idea of causing pain to her father by refusing, for she knew that such a marriage would be a brilliant asset to the Orléans. Yet she was terrified of becoming the Queen of a nation still in a state bordering on civil war, and where the customs, language and religion were alien to anything she knew. Above all, Leopold was twenty-four years older than herself.

She kept asking for more time to consider the question, always hoping that the Duke of Calabria might, in the meantime, decide to marry her. Leopold, on his side, still weighed in his mind whether to accept the stupendous task of bringing order out of chaos in Greece.

The other children were too young to figure much in public affairs; occasionally they appeared with the Duc and Duchesse in the Orléans box at the Opéra or the Théâtre Français. Then an immense "Aah!" would arise from the audience—"*Comme ils sont beaux!!*" And it was true.

Only one tragedy had dimmed this perfection. The small Duc de Penthièvre, the sixth child of the Orléans, had been born prematurely on New Year's Day 1820, and his mind had not fully developed. In 1828 he died, and Marie Amélie, who had adored this pathetic, helpless child, had to hide her tears to escape the comments of Adélaïde: "Don't be silly. It was the best thing that could happen to him."

By the year 1829, Charles X was tired of being buffeted between the opposing parties. He had tried a strong Government with Villèle, he had tried relaxation with Martignac. Neither had satisfied the Opposition; indeed, he had begun to realize that nothing he could do would satisfy the Opposition. He only longed to be able to dismiss them all, so that he could find peace to be able to sleep, eat, and enjoy life.

In desperation, he removed Martignac from office and chose, to replace him, the one man who was least likely to pester him, the Prince Jules de Polignac, his dearest friend, the boon companion of his wild early life. With him, there would be no arguments, no contradictions. The prince was well known as a great charmer, "un grand seigneur", an amusing conversationalist, but in politics, a complete nonentity.

He was the son of that Princesse de Polignac who had been the confidante of Marie Antoinette, on whom her Majesty had showered all the gifts in her power. This friendship had brought odium on the Queen, and the princess had been accused by her enemies of every vice and corruption. Among all the friends of Marie Antoinette, she had been singled out as the evil genius. The very name of the new Minister stood for all the errors of the old régime.

Up and down the country, people who rarely thought of politics were shaken to the core. The Orléans were staying at the Château d'Eu at the time, and Cuvillier Fleury described the scene:

"On entering the drawing-room, I perceived a certain preoccupation. Madame de Montjoie handed me the *Moniteur*. 'POLIGNAC MINISTER . . .' Madame de Montjoie was groaning: Princesse Adélaïde, already ill, had collapsed."

During the next few days, various newspapers were condemned for attacking the Ministry, and the Duc de Chartres was severely scolded by the King for having protested against this condemnation.

Yet it was this Government which won for France that loveliest of all prizes—Algeria.

15

The Ball at the Palais Royal

The spring of 1830 was radiant. The brilliant sun was forcing the chestnut trees of the Luxembourg Gardens to show early pink and white blossoms. Under them children were running to and fro, in light colourful dresses; gardeners bent over the flower-beds, tending their dazzling display; in the parks military bands played.

Yet, over all, there was an oppressive feeling of unrest and agitation; it was as if people, seeing the clouds gather, were hurrying to do all they had to do before the storm broke.

As the day approached on which Charles X was to open his new Parliament and pronounce his speech to the Chambers, the ferment grew in Paris; all were intent on seeing how Polignac would face this new role.

The day came, 2nd March 1830; the Chamber was packed, the royal family, peers and deputies all anxious and expectant, listening to the speech from the throne.

The King's nervous condition was noticed, as he stumbled hesitatingly through his address, to utter the threatening words: "If disloyal manœuvres create obstacles for my Government, I shall find strength to overcome them in my determination to maintain public peace."

At that moment the monarch threw back his head, his hat fell off and rolled down the steps of the throne. The Duc d'Orléans picked it up and held it until the end of the speech.

The words seemed to re-echo, "If the crown falls from the head that wears it, I shall pick it up."

The Chamber retorted by the famous address inviting the King to dismiss his Ministers. In return Polignac, in his blind obstinacy, advised the King to dissolve the Chamber; then people began to murmur, "They are paving the way to the Throne for Orléans."

In the midst of all this tension, the King and Queen of Naples announced their visit, and for a short interlude all else was forgotten in the excitement of entertaining them.

At the opening reception given by Charles X, for the first time for several years the Orléans family appeared in the royal box. The day before, the King had said that he regretted that his box was not large enough to include Louis Philippe and his family. This was repeated to Monsieur de Glandevès, Governor of the Tuileries.

He decided that the exclusion of the ducal family on such an occasion would be a great insult, especially as Marie Amélie was the sister of the visiting monarch; at once he gave orders for the box to be enlarged. All night, work went on; by morning it was ready. When Monsieur de Glandevès informed his Majesty, the King smiled sarcastically, then said with a frown, "Thank you, Monsieur le Gouverneur; now I have no alternative; the Orléans troupe can be admitted."

Of all the entertainments given for the Neapolitan monarchs, none excelled the Ball at the Palais Royal. The King of France rarely attended any function outside his residence, but as the King and Queen of Naples were his guests, he condescended to be present.

During all the preparations, there was an undercurrent of anxiety. George IV was dying, and the thought of everyone at the Palais Royal was—would he last long enough to allow the Ball to take place?

On Monday, 31st May 1830, from early morning, crowds invaded the gardens and courtyard of the Palais. Numerous workmen could be discerned scurrying to and fro inside the building and on the terraces, but alas, it began to pour, the rain pattering loudly on the stone parapet.

The crowd still remained, in hopes of a break in the grey sky. They were rewarded a little later when blue patches appeared and the rain ceased; the sun came out, and in a few moments it was a radiant Parisian spring day—and George IV was still alive!

At half-past five in the afternoon the Orléans, with the King and Queen of Naples, sat down to dinner. The weather had become still more beautiful.

At eight o'clock, the guests began to fill the numerous reception rooms, and a little later the illuminations began. The whole Palais was outlined with fairy lamps, and festoons of brilliantly coloured lights which seemed to float in the air, stirred by the evening breeze. Between these, vases filled with exotic flowers, surmounted by pyramids of fire and huge candelabra were reflected in the innumerable windows.

The garden was a dream of beauty; garlands of lighted lanterns linked the trees, sweet-scented flowers proudly showed their gorgeous hues, butterflies of every colour flying around attracted by the bewildering brilliancy of the lights: amongst all this, a countless mob were already showing signs of agitation at the foot of the terraces.

Within the walls of the Palais was a very different scene; men in uniform, every seam of their coats covered in gold braid, and almost smothered in decorations, women in ample, ungainly gowns, their heads bent under the weight of diamond head-dresses, their necks, arms and fingers loaded with precious stones, showing more dignity than those outside, but just as eager for the King's arrival.

The Comtesse de Boigne, who had arrived early, managed to stand near the Duc and Duchesse as they greeted their guests, and noticed with horror the mixed nature of the assembly. She was so astonished that she asked one of the household how it was possible that so many well-known members of the Opposition were present. He answered, "Monsieur le Duc d'Orléans has made no distinction; he has sent the invitations indiscriminately."

At eleven o'clock, outriders, guards on horseback, and the beating of drums, announced the arrival of the King of France. Charles X made his entrance into the State Rooms of the Palais Royal, preceded by his brilliant suite.

Who could have dreamt that night that any cares troubled the monarch? He smiled and bowed right and left to the assembled guests; even when his eyes alighted on such men as Lafayette, Guizot or Thiers, not a flicker of his eyelids showed that he had even noticed the insult of his cousin.

At this moment, Louis Philippe felt proud; the dresses, the jewels, the magnificence of the rooms, hangings, pictures, bronzes, the gilded ceilings reflected endlessly in the mirrors. The dazzling panorama delighted him, he felt triumphant. At last he was able to show what the First Prince of the Blood could command; even the King, in his dislike for his host, could not refrain from envying him his unique abode. He turned to the Duc, and said, "In truth, Monsieur mon cousin, you have made it your business to be better housed than I!"

As he continued his walk through the rooms, he paused to look out of the windows, and, turning to the Duc, said: "Where the devil did you find such a fine courtyard?"

Then he called Monsieur de Fontaine, the architect: "You have never done such beautiful work for me."

As the King's glance travelled down the long vista of salons, one thought dimmed his mood of admiration, the number of his enemies who were standing in groups, their very presence a slight to his person; he then understood to the full the Baron d'Haussey's meaning when he had said:

"At the Palais Royal, one only meets the enemies of your Majesty!"

As the royal party entered the ballroom, the quadrille in fancy dress began, and Monsieur de Salvandy made the famous comment:

"This is truly a Neapolitan ball; we are dancing on a volcano."

Madame de Boigne, who still managed to keep close to the royal party, related that the crowd had become so dense that she was unable to move, so she passed her time scrutinizing the faces of the principal figures. She noted that the Duc looked perturbed; even Cuvillier Fleury, who never criticized Louis Philippe, made the same remark and added: "I wonder why?" Madame de Boigne had no hesitation. She knew why!

"The King looked in a good temper, the Neapolitans astonished, Madame la Dauphine rather upset, and," added Madame de Boigne, "I quite understand her; the Duchesse looked angry and Princesse Adélaïde embarrassed.

"As the evening wore on, the attitude of the Duc changed

and gave way to a sense of satisfaction; his smugness rather disgusted me; a feeling of fear and sadness overtook me. I left. On my arrival home, my mother asked why I had left so early. My answer was: 'I am too fond of the Orléans to have been pleased with my evening.'

"For the first time I could not help believing that the Duc d'Orléans had certain intentions which terrified me." [1]

She had read between the lines, and certainly that night the true aim of the Duc was manifest. He had filled the Palais Royal beyond its capacity with a crowd, mainly composed of the King's opponents.

He had appeared alone on the terrace, knowing that the cry "*Vive le Duc d'Orléans*" would reach the King's ears. It all seemed part of a conspiracy to undermine the popularity of the monarch, and to evoke the affection of the mob for Louis Philippe.

Still the dancing continued; supper was served, each dish a miracle of art; and when, at last, the famous *échaudés* appeared, the King again complimented his host.

At midnight, the monarch walked out on to the terrace; a slight breeze stirred the air.

"This wind is good for my fleet of Algiers," [2] he said. The night was perfect, the sky a deep sapphire; the stars seemed like peepholes, compared to the lights in the trees. As the King appeared, he bowed to the mob; not a cheer, not a sound of welcome in return. Charles X stood for a few minutes waving his hand; still no sound came from the gaping throng so, half-smiling and half-seriously, he waved once more, saying:

"Good morning, my people!" Then he turned and walked back to the ballroom, his head slightly bowed, but as he saluted the guests on his departure, he had regained his serenity.

When Charles X left the Palais, the unruly mob piled up the chairs and benches in the gardens and set fire to them. The statue of Apollo was badly scorched, flowers were uprooted, clothes strewn about, children were trampled underfoot and women shrieked. The people also were having their fun. At last,

[1] *Mémoires* of the Comtesse de Boigne. Librairie Plon.
[2] That very night, a fleet was sailing to undertake the conquest of Algeria.

troops were called in to clear the grounds. This was the first riot of 1830.

*   *   *

In all this turmoil and excitement, Louis Philippe yearned for Britain. He often dwelt on the life he had led at Twickenham; it seemed so peaceful in comparison with the one he was now leading—plans, intrigues, threats and schemes, all with the sole purpose of placing him at the head of the State. Was it worth it?

On the morning of 26th June 1830, as he sat writing at his desk, the Comte d'Houdetôt entered. Louis Philippe hated being disturbed when he was busy, but something in the manner of his Aide de Camp made him look up.

"What is it?"

"Sir, the King of England is dead."

For a minute, Louis Philippe was stunned. George IV, the man who had befriended him in exile, his only supporter among the monarchs of Europe; it seemed as though his query had been answered. "All must end in death."

16

The Great Gamble, 1830

The place that the Princesse Adélaïde occupied in her brother's life was never so publicly demonstrated as during those fateful days from July 26th to 29th, during which the future of France was decided.

The Duc was at Neuilly with his family, and it was about eleven o'clock on the morning of 26th July, holiday time; the long windows of the drawing-room were wide open, the heat of the day was already to be felt.

Marie Amélie was glancing through some accounts, the children, with their tutors, were making plans for the afternoon; Louis Philippe alone seemed preoccupied; Marie Amélie looked up at him, and said:

"Are you feeling the heat of these last few days, mon ami? Really we should go to Eu; the air there would revive us all."

The Duc did not reply, but, as if thinking aloud, remarked:

"The *Moniteur* is late; what can be delaying it?"

Usually, the family waited until the paper arrived, to hear any news of interest. At this moment, the *Moniteur* was handed to the Duc. It was his custom to look through it quickly, and read aloud anything spectacular before dismissing the children. But today, as he unfolded the paper, he uttered an oath, for there, across the front page, were published the three royal ordinances:[1] one dissolved the recently elected Chamber, another swept away the liberty of the Press, whilst the third—perhaps the most staggering—was the new electoral law which reduced the freedom of voting almost to vanishing point.

"They are crazy!" cried Louis Philippe. "They will be driven

[1] Royal edicts promulgated by the King without the approval of the Chambers.

out again!" He threw down the paper, stood up and shouted: "Adélaïde, Adélaïde!"

Everyone in the room was startled. Consternation was general, each thinking only for himself. The situation was critical; it seemed sheer folly to enact such laws at such a time. The young princesses began to sob and the smaller children joined in, not having the faintest idea what it was all about. Tears rolled down Marie Amélie's cheeks.

Then the door flew open and Princess Adélaïde rushed in, her lace headdress in disorder. She had heard her brother call, and the tone of his voice made her run straight to him, oblivious of her appearance.

He handed her the newspaper. Without making any comment, she turned to Marie Amélie and the princesses. "Quick—the cockades."

Followed by Louise and Marie, she dashed out again, flew to her wardrobe, pulled out all the clothes that were red, white or blue; back into the drawing-room, laden with needles, cotton and scissors, and very soon tricolor cockades were strewing the floor; just as, fifteen years before, the noble ladies of the Faubourg St. Germain had sewn white ones.

Château de St. Cloud, same day, same hour
  Residence of the King

Charles X received the *Moniteur* and, without opening it, summoned an Aide de Camp to take it to the Duchesse de Berri. As the King was entering his carriage, the princess ran into the courtyard, carrying the paper. She knelt before him and, kissing his hand, exclaimed: "You reign at last, Sire. My son will owe you his Crown, and I, his mother, thank you!"

The King embraced her tenderly, pushed the gazette into his pocket and, without a word to his suite, drove to Rambouillet to hunt.

Paris. Later in the same day

No details of the discontent and agitation which stirred the capital reached St. Cloud. Why was the King left in such ignorance? Already, in Paris, the citizens looked different; they were in a solemn, gloomy mood. People stopped to talk to one another, or eyed the passers-by with looks of enquiry. If any man seemed unperturbed it was thought that he had not yet grasped the gravity of the situation.

Neuilly, same day, evening
Residence of the Duc d'Orléans

Louis Philippe and his family remained at Neuilly; news kept on arriving from Paris—"Nothing serious; only a few slight clashes have taken place."

After dinner, the family assembled in the billiard room. The Duc invited his Aides de Camp and the princes' tutors to join them that evening, as he wanted to hear their opinions. He said little, only listened.

Then a message came that forty-four journalists had rebelled against the suppression of the Press, and were preparing serious resistance. Cuvillier Fleury started shouting insults at the Government. This excited the children, who applauded.

Princesse Adélaïde talked loudest and most, but at the same time she enjoined caution on all. Marie Amélie alone said nothing, but continued writing without raising her head.

Neuilly, 27th July

There was a strange atmosphere at Neuilly. As messengers arrived with the news, it affected each of the inhabitants differently; in reality, it meant so much to them all.

The revolt was growing hourly, and the King's troops had been ordered to preserve the peace; but how long would they continue to do so?

At length, a messenger arrived, who asked to speak to Marie Amélie. In greatest secrecy he told her that the colonel commanding the regiment at Courbevoie had received orders that, if the rioting continued, the Duc d'Orléans was to be arrested.

The Duchesse hesitated to inform her husband, but later, when it appeared that the rebellion was gaining strength, she asked him to hide for a while in the "Petit Château", a pavilion in the park, until events became clearer.

At four o'clock, the Comtesse de Boigne was announced. The Duc was nowhere to be seen; the Duchesse was walking in the gardens, but the visitor found the Princesse Adélaïde at home, very anxious and especially afraid lest her brother's name should be compromised. Madame de Boigne, who realized that the princess knew everything that was happening, was so interested in the course of events that she hoped the princess might confide in her. But Adélaïde, sitting in her large armchair wearing, as usual, her frilly lace bonnet, her hands stroking her cat, only muttered: "My poor brother; I hope he will not be implicated," and asked her to comfort Marie Amélie who was very agitated.

Paris, same day

The morning passed fairly quietly. But when the workers did not return after their midday meal, and the shopkeepers put up their shutters, people began to feel nervous, missing the familiar noises of the streets.

Some of the daily papers had been published, in defiance of the ordinance, so the Prefect of Police decided to have their printing presses smashed. When this became known, it caused an uproar; men of every class marched up and down the boulevards, shouting and shaking their fists. Barricades were erected composed of chairs, paving stones, tables, mattresses and upturned carts.

Then the order went forth that the Garde Royale should be put under arms. A battalion with two guns took up position in the Place du Carrousel, and at the Palais Royal. Two more were stationed in the Place Louis XV—now Place de la Concorde. Infantry lined the Place Vendôme, the boulevards St. Martin, St. Denis and the Place de l'Eléphant.

The rioters appeared to have no chance, but they ignored the troops and rushed to the rue Richelieu and rue St. Honoré where, at seven o'clock, the mob was so great that no one could move. The gendarmerie and some of the Gardes tried to clear the road quietly without violence, but they were assailed with a hail of stones and tiles. The Gardes still refrained from reprisals.

Suddenly a shot came from the Hôtel Royal, rue St. Honoré. That shot, the first of the Revolution, had been fired by Mr. Fox, a relative of the British Minister. The soldiers fired back and he was killed in his room, as well as two of his servants.

151

A little further down the same street, a barricade was forced. This made the crowd angry. Near St. Roch, one of the best-known churches in Paris, the troops, hoping to disperse the unruly mob, fired twice into the air; the crowd hurled at them everything they could find, pulling up the cobbles and even entering houses to collect iron pots and pans—any missile obtainable—until darkness brought fighting to an end.

Paris, 28th July

At dawn crowds began to gather on the Place de l'Hôtel de Ville. By eight o'clock they had taken possession of the whole building: the Arsenal, and the great powder magazine "des Deux Moulins", which had been left practically unguarded, had been looted by the mob during the night, as well as several gunsmiths' shops.

The Garde Nationale, disbanded in 1827, reappeared on the streets; their uniforms, which had been retrieved from old boxes or the depths of cupboards, although still smelling of camphor, were hastily donned. Wherever they presented themselves, they were welcomed by the mob and supplied with arms.

At nine o'clock, five battalions of the King's troops emerged from barracks and Marshal Marmont, Duc de Raguse, who had been given command of Paris, proclaimed a state of siege.

The royal troops, usually so well equipped for reviews or parades, found themselves almost without officers; some had no horses, others could not find their uniforms. The men had been without food since the previous day, as all the army stores had been looted by the people.

In contrast to the chaotic state of the military, the insurgents seemed to have a certain hidden organization, as though there had been definite preparation. Groups passed from door to door, collecting arms. Men walked the streets carrying covered baskets, like those used by the errand-boys of the pâtisseries, filled with cartridges which they distributed surreptitiously.

Women waited on their doorsteps for the carts to bring

Note. Principal works consulted on the 1830 Revolution: Th. Anne, *Journal de Saint-Cloud à Cherbourg*; Prince de Joinville, *Vieux Souvenirs*; Comtesse de Boigne, *Mémoires*; Cuvillier Fleury, *Journal*; General de Rumigny, *Souvenirs*; Michaud, *Louis Philippe*; Boullée, *Louis Philippe*; Trognon, *La Vie de Marie Amélie.*

powder looted from the magazines, then sat down to make bullets; others went to destroy the emblems of royalty over shops.

Soon the streets were strewn with broken glass and splintered wood.

By midday, having collected all possible munitions, the people began to fight in earnest. Soon it was evident that an intelligent, concerted leadership was behind the uprising. The royal troops were drawn away from the wide boulevards into the narrow streets. Once there, they were opposed by a crowd of insurgents, a few shots were exchanged, then the mob fled, some along the street, others into the houses to fire down upon the advancing soldiers. When the troops passed, barricades were thrown up in their rear so that the military, unable to retreat, were lured deeper into the tangle of streets and alleys. Soon Marmont had to call out the artillery.

As the afternoon melted into dusk, the boom of cannon, the toll of the tocsin from Nôtre Dame, the beat of the drums sounding the "Générale", calling all citizens to arms, the black flag flying from the Church of La Madeleine, drove terror into every heart.

St. Cloud, same day

At the Château St. Cloud, few had slept; those whose duties did not permit them to leave their posts around the King, were anxious concerning their families in Paris, amidst the fighting.

For the King, nothing had changed; his valet brought him, as usual, the cup of camomile tea at half past eight, and the Duc de Bordeaux and the little Mademoiselle wished him good-morning. The monarch seemed quite unperturbed.

At nine o'clock, the King received Monsieur de Vitrolles, one of those who had never ceased going to and fro bringing news of the rioting. He told the King that fighting was continuing more fiercely than the previous day. The King consulted his advisers, who assured him that all this was exaggerated. His Majesty then sat down to lunch.

At three o'clock, it was reported that the people had seized the Hôtel de Ville, over which the Tricolor flag was now flying. But the high officials responsible for the ordinances still smiled and said this was just a puff of hot air; the army was strong, the Duc de Raguse was in control of the situation.

At four o'clock, the news was slightly disconcerting: General Gérard and General Lamarque had accepted to lead the mob. To raise the disconsolate spirits at St. Cloud, Monsieur de Peyronnet appeared in the drawing-room in his brilliant ministerial uniform.

Somebody said: "How can you show yourself at this moment in those clothes? You might be attacked by the mob."

"And why not?" answered his Excellency. "Good gracious, it will all be over by midnight."

That evening, while the King was playing whist with some of his suite, a gentleman asked to be received in audience; the monarch, with a bored expression, turned to the Aide de Camp who brought the message.

"Tell him to wait; I must finish my game."

Without more ado, he returned to his cards. When he had finished, he pushed back his chair, and said: "Now I am ready."

Then Baron Weyler de Navas, *Sous-Comptroller* of the Military Household, entered his presence, dishevelled and dusty. In a few words, he related the naked truth—the massacres, the butchery going on in the capital, corpses lying unattended, the military fighting on empty stomachs, ammunition becoming scarce, and the people determined to win the fight.

The King stood and listened; his Ministers had duped him to the very end, assuring him that there was nothing to be feared. He could not believe this sinister picture.

"Mon cher Monsieur, you exaggerate the danger."

"I exaggerate so little, Sire, that unless your Majesty negotiates, within three hours, the crown that your Majesty wears will have fallen from your head."

This warning, unfortunately, had no effect, and the King sat down to another game of whist.

17

Procession in the Night

Neuilly, same day

The windows were still wide open, the garden was bathed in hot sunshine. While the cannons could be heard over Paris sending forth their disastrous mission, Marie Amélie sat alone in the large drawing-room endeavouring to finish her letters, but she could not find the words to write; apprehension of the future and all it held blurred other thoughts. She dropped her pen and walked out into the garden.

A blinding struggle raged in her mind. She realized more than ever at this moment that she, the niece of Marie Antoinette, could never become part of the Orléans. Since childhood she had learnt to venerate the name of Bourbon and all it stood for. As she wandered into the park, turning these things in her mind, she hardly knew how to pray—for exile, or for a crown which would bring with it the contempt of Europe.

At length a messenger sought her; he had come from Monsieur Laffitte to inform the Duc that events were moving in his favour, and to warn him "to be careful of the nets of St. Cloud. We are beginning a drama, the end of which will be a crown for the Duc d'Orléans."

As dusk fell, cannon boomed without cessation. After dinner the Duc and Marie Amélie went out on to the terrace, and there they walked backwards and forwards discussing the future. At midnight Mr. Tuthill, an Englishman, arrived, panting and perspiring: "The people have not lost hope, but munitions are running low; it is feared they may have to retreat."

Everyone went to bed in gloom and anxiety.

During that night the Garde Royale fell back upon the Tuileries. They had fought bravely for two days without food or

155

rest; they had been promised bread on their return, but none was to be had; now, surrounded by the insurgents, nothing could be procured. Some of the regiments of the line had managed to get food by exchanging munitions with the citizens for bread, but the Gardes were loyal to their monarch; they had lost three hundred of their comrades, but had been supported by the hope that, when they returned, the King would be there to welcome them. Instead, they heard that Charles X and the Duc d'Angoulême were at St. Cloud. They did not conceal their disgust that, when men were dying for the Bourbon cause, the Bourbons themselves slept in safety, well away from all danger.

It seems inconceivable that none of the gold-laced councillors of the monarch had the intelligence to urge Charles X to return to Paris. At St. Cloud a guard of about two thousand men surrounded the King; if his Majesty had ridden into the capital at the head of these troops, several regiments that were gradually giving ground for lack of support and encouragement, might have rallied, and the King might have calmed the people and saved the throne—if not for himself, at least for his grandson to reign as Henri V. But no wise man came forward to advise the monarch.

Paris, 29th July

When dawn broke, the troops in the capital returned to the positions they had occupied the previous morning. At first the streets were comparatively empty; gradually they filled, as the people awoke refreshed, ready to renew the fighting. About eight o'clock, a crowd of rioters had gathered around the officer commanding the regiment guarding the Palais Bourbon, and roughly insisted on his promising to remain neutral; but soon becoming bolder they threatened his life so, to save himself, he treacherously allowed them to climb on the roof of the palace, and thence to shoot on the royal troops in the Place Louis XV. The 5th and 53rd Regiments of the Line guarding the Place Vendôme were ordered to reinforce those who were being fired upon in the Place Louis XV; instead, they fixed their bayonets, held their weapons above their heads, and joined the mob.

The Duc de Raguse immediately ordered a battalion of the Gardes Suisses, defending the Louvre, to go into action. In the confusion, instead of sending the battalion which was defending the gardens, he sent the men who were keeping the mob at bay by firing from the windows of the Louvre, with the result that the people entered the palace without opposition, rushed to the windows, and fired down upon the Gardes Suisses in the garden. These fled in disorder to the Carrousel, thinking they had been attacked by their own comrades.

Wild confusion ensued, and more regiments went over to the insurgents, until the Duc de Raguse gave the order to evacuate the city and fall back on St. Cloud.

St. Cloud, same day

Meanwhile, at St. Cloud, all was quiet. When the King awoke, the news from the Prince de Polignac was reassuring; he reported that no incidents had occurred in the capital during the night, and that the insurgents lacked powder and were ready to negotiate.

As the monarch sat drinking his tisane he smiled. How right he had been not to give in to all those frightened fools, who yesterday had kept arriving from Paris with alarming tales! No! His brother Louis XVI had tried negotiating, but he, Charles X, preferred to ride on horseback rather than in a tumbril.

At that moment there was a rumble of wheels in the courtyard below; the King leisurely placed his cup on a small table and walked to the window.

A shabby-looking carriage was drawing up at the entrance. The King watched, and, to his astonishment, one by one his Ministers stepped out of the vehicle. For a moment his heart almost stopped; but of course, it was only his Government bringing him news of the defeat of the people.

The King stood waiting to hear confirmation of Polignac's good news, but his expression changed when the Ministers entered, pale and dejected. They had heard a menacing crowd screaming for vengeance on their heads, and stealthily they had fled from the city through the back streets.

Whilst they were speaking, the Marquis de Sémonville, a

deputy, arrived and begged an audience. He threw himself at the King's feet and besought him to revoke the ordinances and dismiss his Ministers.

"If your Majesty will not take this advice, all is lost; to-morrow, Sire, your Majesty will no longer be King of France."

Throughout that long day, similar warnings shook the optimism of St. Cloud, but Charles X and his Ministers seemed paralysed. At last, the King faced the truth. He signed the dismissal of his Ministers and named the Duc de Mortemart Président du Conseil.

Then he summoned Messieurs de Vitrolles, de Sémonville, and d'Argout, and authorized them to inform Paris of his change of Government. Having done this, he regained his composure, and assured the Duchesse de Berri that in twenty-four hours all would be settled.

The evening passed as usual. The King played his game of whist in the Salon de la Vérité. Paris seemed calm. But that night, Alfred de Vigny, the poet, wrote in his journal: "Ils ne viennent pas à Paris, on meurt pour eux, race de Stuarts." [1]

Neuilly, same day

Louis Philippe had not slept. In truth, his role was difficult; to his family he affected to be deeply troubled by all these events, and in great anxiety concerning the King's crown; in reality, had he not decided upon his future actions?

Hope, ambition, pride and anxiety fought for possession of his soul. The coming days would be a gamble, and he meant to win; yet he feared, as he knew that St. Cloud was well aware that his name was being hawked round the streets of Paris, and he had been warned that the Ministers were pressing for his arrest.

When the sun rose on that morning, the painter, Ary Scheffer, arrived with crushing news:

"The people are defeated."

Something near panic came over Neuilly, and some began to think of flight.

But at nine o'clock, Princesse Marie burst into a room where the family were assembled, crying, "Victory! The Garde Royale have surrendered." This phrase seemed to contain the

[1] "They do not come to Paris, people are dying for them, race of Stuarts."

essence of the Orléans policy. The abscess had burst, and the ducal family had shown their true colour.

From all parts of the château, the inhabitants, without distinction of rank, poured into the drawing-room. Monsieur Badouin, who had brought the news, was surrounded by the Duc, his family, and even the chefs, who appeared in their tall white caps, still holding the utensils with which they were preparing the déjeuner.

Yes, it was glorious; the royal troops had been defeated, and, in disorder, were trying to reach the King. Paris had capitulated, the Tricolor flag was flying over the Hôtel de Ville; those of the soldiers who continued fighting after the order for retreat was given, had been massacred.

Yes, it was glorious news!

Already the road from Paris was encumbered with people making their way to Neuilly, on foot, in carriages, in postchaises. The heat was unbearable, but still they came—hot, dusty, perspiring, smelly, all intent on seeking something for themselves from the rising star, Orléans.

Terrified by this invasion, Louis Philippe's one idea was flight. After all, he did not know how all this would end, and the idea that he might become a hostage in the hands of either Charles X or the Republicans, frightened him.

On the pretext of taking his children to safety, he set off with them to Villiers, but before nightfall he decided to return to Neuilly and, for greater safety, to pass the night in a small building called "the little château" in the park.

Paris, 30th July

When the citizens of Paris awoke, all traces of royal authority had vanished. The people were victorious. For a few hours, Paris was theirs; Paris, with all its treasures, lay at the mercy of violence, pillage and destruction.

At an early hour the Tuileries was invaded by a screaming, delirious mob. Ancient portraits were cut to ribbons, furniture was broken up, tapestries torn down, women in tattered clothes covered their arms and necks with priceless jewels, and others, despite the heat, paraded in valuable furs and Court dresses, cackling and swaying their hips.

In the Throne Room, the mob pushed each other to reach the throne; one by one, they sat on it and buffooned before the roaring spectators. When they grew tired of this, they hoisted the dead body of a rioter on to the throne, covered him with bits of crêpe, and forgot him. So the madness went on, and those who had unleashed it began to feel afraid, wondering how to control it.

Victory was glorious, but to keep the glory from growing tarnished, someone had to direct the rays. Lafayette, who had arrived two days before from his home in the provinces, directly the smell of revolutionary powder reached his nostrils, visited some of the barricades. He was recognized and given a faint cheer; that faint cheer was heard, and it resounded far and wide, until the fighters of the revolution called for him to lead them.

Once more Lafayette was a general; they brought him a white horse to ride through the streets; the people screamed for him, and the echo ricocheted from walls and housetops. At the Hôtel de Ville a vast crowd milled around shouting, "Lafayette and Liberty!"

All through that night, the new leader sat battling with his conscience. He had tasted revolution, but he could not help feeling that monarchy was the only solution for France; yet the Bourbons were finished.

Only two solutions lay before him. A republic headed by himself? No, he felt too old. Or a Republican monarch—Louis Philippe?

By seven o'clock in the morning, he had decided—Louis Philippe.

St. Cloud, same day

At one o'clock in the morning Monsieur de Vitrolles, returning to St. Cloud, found the château in darkness. From King to kitchen-boy, all were asleep. With infinite trouble, he managed to penetrate to the apartments of the Duc de Mortemart, to announce the failure of his mission.

The insurgents had refused to receive him or his companions. The revolutionary commission, assembled in the house of Monsieur Laffitte, the banker, insisted on seeing the new Président du Conseil, the Duc de Mortemart himself, before deciding upon the attitude they would adopt; but a change of ministry was not enough: immediate repeal of the ordinances, re-establishment of the Garde Nationale, and the convocation of a new Chamber were essential.

The Duc de Mortemart listened to Vitrolles, and said that only the King could decide what should be done. His Majesty was asleep, and etiquette forbade entry into the King's room without being summoned. So, before doing anything further, several high functionaries had to be consulted and, as they were all asleep in different parts of the building, it would take time.

At last, after much discussion and loss of precious hours, it was decided to over-ride the rules and awaken the King. Dawn was breaking when at last Mortemart entered the bedroom. His Majesty was asleep, his head covered by a cotton nightcap. He was not over-pleased at being awakened, but his temper increased when Monsieur de Vitrolles, who had followed the Duc, began to explain the failure of his mission. As he went on, Charles X became still more angry. "Who do they think I am?" But Vitrolles did not falter, and declared that even now it might be too late. The only hope was to give in to the insurgents.

It was a strange scene; the room dimly lit by a few candles, and the two men standing in a respectful attitude before the bewildered and angry monarch.

Gradually the King gave way and agreed to sign the new decrees, but there was no pen in the room; Mortemart rushed to find one. Then the King, sitting on the side of his bed, his head sunk on his chest, signed without even looking at the paper.

At seven o'clock in the morning, the Duc de Mortemart left St. Cloud, carrying the new decrees—a last hope!

In the meantime, Thiers, Laffitte and their friends were proclaiming in the capital the name of Louis Philippe, Duc d'Orléans, as a candidate for the throne of France. They plastered the walls with huge posters, acclaiming the virtues of a prince so devoted to the cause of the Revolution.

So the day passed: by evening, the whole Court at St. Cloud was chaos: no news had come from Mortemart. In the Salon de la Vérité the whist table had been thrust into a corner; at the gates, wounded soldiers were asking for bread.

Then an officer galloped up with the report that fifteen hundred armed insurgents were marching towards St. Cloud. The King, worn out, had retired; his bed curtains were drawn and he was sound asleep. His valet woke him.

"What is it?"

"Sire, the Duc d'Angoulême begs your Majesty to leave at once for Versailles."

"I will get ready."

At that moment, there was a disturbance outside the room; the voice of the Duchesse de Berri crying, "I must see the King!"

Then, without waiting for permission, she flew in, dressed in a green frock coat, a short velvet cape, a wide pair of trousers, two pistols in her belt, on her blonde hair a soldier's kepi. The King peered at her through his sunken eyes.

"Why this extraordinary get-up?"

"To defend my children," cried the undaunted little Duchesse.

"I beseech your Majesty to allow me to drive to Paris with my son; the people love him as 'L'enfant de France'; a child disarms anger, the crowd will be pacified, and the Throne will be saved."

Charles X raised his long thin hand in protest.

"I refuse. My grandson must be kept safe for the future. I cannot allow him to risk death from a stray bullet."

"Then let me go alone."

"Never!"

And so the very last chance of saving the Crown slipped away.

In the palace, all were now astir; yet there was complete silence. Every passage was encumbered by servants carrying trunks, boxes, parcels, to huge wagons waiting in the courtyard.

At three o'clock in the morning of 31st July 1830, the King climbed heavily into a carriage with the Duchesse de Berri; Marshal Marmont was on horseback near the door. In considerable disorder, soldiers, Gardes du Corps, Chasseurs à Cheval and other regiments followed.

Gradually, order was restored and it was no longer a wild flight, but, in the silence of a lovely summer night, the long convoy resembled a funeral procession.

18

The Evil-Smelling Crowd

Neuilly, same day

Out in the park, sleep had been impossible. The animals were listless, the grass was the colour of hay. The countryside seemed gasping for water.

The Duc d'Orléans rose from his bed, bewildered from want of sleep, fear in his heart and the thought repeating itself in his brain: "I must get away." "I must get away." At le Raincy he owned a small château, where no one would think of seeking him. He must reach its safety before it was too late.

He looked at his watch; it was four o'clock. A knock at the door, and a valet entered bringing an armful of peasant's clothes, a soiled blouse, a pair of old trousers, heavy boots and a cap which could be drawn down to hide his face.

So dressed, with a tricolor cockade well displayed, he slipped into the garden to begin his tramp to the Château du Raincy, three leagues away. There he would be safe until the Revolutionary Commission made its decision. With his Aide de Camp, Monsieur de Berthois, as his only companion, he trudged in the sultry air, sweating, stumbling, uncertain and wondering.

So Marie Amélie and Adélaïde were left alone—the first trusting to her husband's honesty, the second to his ambition. At ten o'clock they met in the great salon, Marie Amélie sitting at her embroidery, Adélaïde moving restlessly from window to window, waiting for news from Paris.

At last, even their stilted conversation ceased: the silence was heavy, broken only by the sound of the thread slipping through the canvas of the embroidery.

Then a distant rumble, as a post-chaise came up the avenue. In a few minutes, Monsieur Thiers, a rising politician, and Ary Scheffer, the fashionable painter, asked to be received. They had come to warn the Duc that in a few hours the leadership of the country would be offered to him; but before their mission could be fully explained, a stream of people burst in, pompous, important, urgent—all demanding to see the Duc. The crowd invaded the salons; even the staircase was full of people saying "the Duc must come or France is lost"; while, in the capital, the deputies argued incessantly, and decided nothing.

The crowds of visitors grew larger as the hours passed by. Marie Amélie, dignified and outwardly calm, repeated to those who assured her that the Duc ran no danger:

"Dangers are nothing; honour is everything. My husband is experiencing the scruples of an honest man; it is his honour which makes him hesitate."

The Princesse Adélaïde adopted a very different tone; her voice went forth as a challenge:

"First of all, the Chamber of Deputies must make their decision. Once this is done, my brother will not hesitate. If necessary, I will myself go to Paris to accept the power in his name."

At five o'clock, the news reached Neuilly that the Duc d'Orléans had been proclaimed Lieutenant-General of the Kingdom. Marie Amélie received the message in silence; then, in a few moments, she turned to Monsieur Thiers and, with sobs in her voice, said:

"My happiness is ended; the future will prove a torture for me."

But Adélaïde, triumphant, and with a look of utter disdain at her sister-in-law, said:

"This is the event for which I have striven all my life—the glory of my brother."

Thiers regarded her with admiration. "Madame," he said, "you bestow a crown upon your House."

At ten o'clock that night, the Duc was back at Neuilly. He did not show himself openly, as he felt that he must weigh up the course of events; in reality, he knew that he would accept office.

He summoned his wife and sister to meet him in the lonely dimly-lit pavilion in the park. It was a historic scene.

K.F.—M   165

Louis Philippe, tired after all the excitement of the last two days, the two women standing before him, one clinging to his arm, imploring him to reflect and be guided by his conscience, reminding him of his oft-repeated oaths of loyalty to his King; Adélaïde, listening with ill-concealed impatience, then pushing her sister-in-law aside as she uttered only *"Marche en avant!"* (go forward!)

At that moment, Monsieur de Berthois entered, saying:

"Monseigneur, word has come from Monsieur Thiers that your presence at the Palais Royal is imperative."

At once, Louis Philippe set off, on foot, with Monsieur de Berthois. It was midnight before he reached the Palais Royal. Almost prostrate with fatigue, without taking the trouble to undress, he threw himself upon a couch and tried to rest.

This proved impossible: too many thoughts passed through his mind, conscience fought with ambition. He recalled that he had sworn fealty to Charles X. The monarch had been kind, even generous and forgiving. Should he betray his King, as his father had betrayed Louis XVI?

At four in the morning he rose; he could bear the tension no longer. He sent General de Rumigny to bring the Duc de Mortemart to the Palais Royal, telling him that his safety was guaranteed.

When Mortemart arrived, the Duc d'Orléans had returned to his couch where he lay, his face red, his eyes full of tears.

"Monsieur," he cried, "find the King, and assure him that never will I accept the Crown—No! Never!!" And he put his hands to his head, and repeated: "Nothing in this world could persuade me to do such a thing."

"But, Monseigneur," said the astonished Mortemart, "you bid me carry this message to the King: what proof will he have that your statement is really true?"

Louis Philippe walked hurriedly to his desk and, taking a piece of paper, wrote an assurance that it was his firm resolution never to accept the Crown if it should be offered to him.

Mortemart received the precious document, folded it into the pleat of his cravat, and took his leave. Yet, a few hours later, Louis Philippe's ambition had over-ridden his conscience. In great haste he sent a messenger to recover the letter. The Duc de Mortemart in disgust handed it back.

At seven o'clock, a group of deputies arrived to beg him, in the name of France, to accept the position of Lieutenant-General of the Kingdom. Without a moment's hesitation he accepted, knowing full well that this was the path which led to the Throne.

Now at last, he could almost call himself King of the French.

31st July 1830

Cuvillier Fleury described this day of days for Louis Philippe: "Paris seemed 'en fête', the barricades had been hastily removed, women in their Sunday clothes paraded the streets, accompanied by every sort of male; they felt that they were the masters of France; there seemed no authority to restrain them."

At the same time, slightly overshadowing the elation, Paris was burying her dead. In front of the Louvre, they had dug a deep trench, and the bodies of those who had died were tipped into it from carts. Quicklime was poured over them, then earth hid the hideous spectacle from the fascinated gaze of the onlookers.

The Curé of St. Germain l'Auxerrois read the burial service, and orators poured forth a torrent of impassioned speech.

Cuvillier Fleury entered the Palais Royal with the people, all crowding in pell-mell, milling through the Great Hall; the smell of humanity was suffocating; everywhere people filled the salons—no one could keep them out. The staircase was full of strange individuals, all intent on guarding the Duc d'Orléans. The army had disappeared, and self-appointed protectors claimed the right to protect the Duc. Meanwhile, more and more ragged hordes made their way into the rooms.

Louis Philippe sat on the edge of his couch, unwashed, dishevelled, his coat still on the chair upon which he had thrown it the previous night. The noise of the mob invading the Palais seemed like the hum of angry wasps.

He roused himself; he felt that he must make the first move. So he sent Rumigny to inform Lafayette that he would receive the General and the deputies at two o'clock that afternoon.

Then Louis Philippe donned the magnificent uniform of a Lieutenant-General, and sat waiting.

But two o'clock passed, and no delegation arrived. At three o'clock still no one had appeared. Once more he sent word that he was waiting; again, no one came. Then he understood. "It is for me to go to the General."

So he informed the deputies that they were to come to the Palais Royal to escort him to the Hôtel de Ville.

Later an extraordinary procession set out, which grew in numbers as it passed through the hot crowded streets. In front went four Gardes Suisses, and a drunken drummer who beat his drum spasmodically; then Louis Philippe, wearing a wide tricolor sash over his uniform, mounted on a white horse, and followed by a medley of deputies—some in sedan chairs, some on horseback, others on foot, all bellowing: "*Vive le Duc d'Orléans!*"

But the temper of that sea of humanity in the streets was not reassuring. Many screamed insults and shook their fists; some even pointed muskets at the Duc.

By now the sweat was trickling down his collar; he tried to wipe it away, but it was useless, so he smiled and waved, his one idea to reach the Hôtel de Ville—and Lafayette!

At last he was there; he dismounted. For a moment he swayed; the heat, the stench of the people, his own emotion, betrayed him. Then, with a supreme effort, he regained his composure, and entered the celebrated building.

Lafayette stood waiting. For the old General, this was the moment of his life: he was creating a monarch, and that monarch had come to him to 'fetch his crown', that monarch would obey him. In effect, he was creating a Republican King. Still the crowd showed no enthusiasm; something must be done. So, dragging the Duc to the balcony, in full view of the thousands below on the Place, Lafayette thrust a Tricolor flag into Louis Philippe's hand and, putting his arm round the Duc's shoulder, kissed his sweating cheek.

The effect was immediate. The people went crazy with delight, and shouted "*Vive le Duc d'Orléans! Vive le Général de Lafayette!*" The tumult and excitement were overwhelming—Louis Philippe was made.

He descended to the street, and fought his way back to his white horse, to make a triumphant return to the Palais Royal. His charger was literally carried along by the throng. At the head of the procession went a man, almost naked, twirling a halberd plundered from the Tuileries, clearing a way for a new era.

When the new Lieutenant-General of the Kingdom reached the Palais Royal, the very dregs of society rushed in to fill the corridors; the Grand Staircase became impassable with people trying to reach the Duc, to touch him, to press his hand; he was nearly suffocated in the mêlée.

With a struggle, he reached his Cabinet; then a ragged body-guard formed outside to hold back the crowd. As he entered the room and shut out the nightmare, all strength seemed to leave him; he looked old and grey as his head sank, and a ghastly look of disillusion passed across his face. Only Cuvillier Fleury, who was with him, understood what Louis Philippe was going through. All his life he had craved for the grandeur and dignity of kingship, and now that he was nearly there, he knew that he was nothing but a puppet of the people, a rag doll. Then he was brought to his senses by the shouts of the crowd in the courtyard below, calling for him to appear.

Clutching a Tricolor flag which stood in a corner, he walked to the balcony and, with a fixed smile, he bowed, waved, and threw kisses to the screaming people.

Towards evening, Marie Amélie and the children arrived from Neuilly. The Prince de Joinville, in his *Vieux Souvenirs*, described the scene:

On 31st July, in the evening, my mother told us that we were to leave for Paris to join our father at the Palais Royal. We all, including Aunt Adélaïde, got into an ordinary omnibus so as not to attract attention. At the barrier of the Etoile, we began to find barricades, but a space had been cleared to allow one carriage to pass at a time. This was guarded by armed citizens, playing at soldiers, others pretending to be police, all self-appointed.

After much questioning, we were told to proceed, but our carriage had to stop at the Place Louis XV on account of the obstructions; my mother made us get out of the vehicle and walk in groups to our residence.

Paris that night presented a curious sight. It was entirely illuminated with lanterns, and Tricolor flags were at every window. . . . Stones had been dug up and piled into barricades, mingled with overturned carts, barrels, and any obstacle that could be found. Behind these stood guards, some walking to and fro, others firing off their muskets for no reason at all, the whole population adorned with tricolor cockades, in caps, hats, and even in their hair.

On the Place du Palais Royal a crowd surrounded a mail coach which, overturned, had been used as a barricade; it had been put back on its wheels, filled with people, and was being pulled, rocking crazily, round the Place.

It was late when we reached our home, and the Palais was entirely lit up. People were installed on the steps of the Grand Staircase, ready to spend the night.

We saw our father in his Cabinet, where all who wished came in and out. Some came to offer their services, such as Anatole de Montesquiou, who brought Chateaubriand into my mother's boudoir. People pushed and squeezed themselves in different corridors, peering into the rooms, and helping themselves to anything they fancied.

That evening we were all sitting together when we heard an awful pandemonium. We rushed out, to find, mounting the staircase, a huge struggling procession with lighted torches and flags. At the head walked students of the Ecole Polytéchnique, their tricornes on their heads, brandishing swords in their hands. They brought in triumph a woman dressed in men's clothes, red sash, tight-legged trousers, a heroine of the barricades whom this howling mob insisted on presenting to my father. Although I was only twelve years old, this scene gave me a feeling of utter disgust.

Later there was another uproar. General de Lafayette was being escorted from the Hôtel de Ville to the Palais Royal. The crowd had lost any remnant of control, and were clutching one another in a wild frenzy of kissing.

The General had managed to reach the salon where I had taken refuge; he stood in front of me. Several thousand people pressed forward, and a feeling of nausea came over me when he started to embrace these creatures as they passed before him—unknown, unwashed, smelling of drink. He went on kissing each one with enthusiasm.

I recognized several individuals who passed again and again before the famous old man, only to be kissed once more, and each time he pressed their cheeks with the same emotional, tearful attitude.

Lafayette's habit of kissing on every occasion won him, amongst the populace, the nickname of "Le père baiseur"— the kissing father.

19

A Parody of Majesty

Meanwhile, Charles X was making his way to Rambouillet. The royal family travelled by night so as to avoid the heat. An immense procession accompanied them—ladies, Aides de Camp, Gardes du Corps, a few regiments of the line, valets, footmen, butlers, under-butlers, chefs and scullions, hairdressers, doctors, tutors, intendants—the whole royal household, with wagon after wagon of luggage, horses, guns, ammunition. The only commodity which had been forgotten was food!

They arrived at the Château de Rambouillet at ten o'clock at night on 31st July. Nobody expected the tired, sleepy crowd; no food, no forage was available, and all went to bed hungry.

On Sunday morning, 1st August, silver plate had to be sold in exchange for meat, vegetables and bread, and permission was given to shoot game in the royal preserve.

The King heard Mass in the little chapel near his bedroom. Then he took his breakfast at a small table by the open window. He heard the soldiers shooting his game, and the thought came to him that there would be no more hunting for him at Rambouillet for many months.

At last, family, Court and Household had satisfied their hunger, and a sense of well-being replaced the anxiety of past days. The Duc de Bordeaux and his sister were swinging happily on the same swings that had once been the joy of the Duchesse d'Angoulême. It was like a Fragonard picture—the lovely garden, the swing, the little boy pushing his sister; her hat had fallen off and one of her shoes dangled.

A carriage came in view and stopped; an elderly gentleman alighted and made a deep bow.

"Who are you?" said the little prince.

"I am General de Girardin. I bring a message from Paris to his Majesty."

"I will show you the way," and, preceding him, the boy led the way to his grandfather's study.

The King looked astonished, but rose graciously from his chair.

"You desire to speak to me, Monsieur?"

"Sire, I have brought the latest news from Paris." And the general handed the King a paper on which was written the full story of the events which had taken place the day before at the Hôtel de Ville. For a moment, Charles X seemed stunned; then, recovering his composure, he said: "Thank you, Monsieur le Général; I will acknowledge the message."

The general, bowing very low, left the room, and the small Duc returned to his sister and his swinging.

The King sat down slowly, the paper in his hand. The whole treachery of Louis Philippe stood before him—those words, those vows, those protestations of loyalty!—it must be stopped. He summoned the family and held a conference. It was decided to preserve a semblance of power by appointing the Duc d'Orléans as Lieutenant-General of the Kingdom, ignoring the fact that he had already been appointed by the Chamber. A document was sent to Louis Philippe to that effect.

The next morning a letter came from the Duc d'Orléans. It was written in an affectionate style, but refused the royal nomination, saying that he had already received his power from the Chamber.

Once more, a family council was called. The King, his son, and his two daughters-in-law assembled at eleven o'clock in the salon which had once belonged to Marie Antoinette. The doors were locked, and the last monarch of the ancient France made his final decision as King. The tears of the Duchesse de Berri, the protests of the Duc d'Angoulême, were futile. Less than an hour later, Charles X opened the door, and summoned the Baron de Damas.

"You will draw up a document requiring my cousin the Duc d'Orléans to proclaim the accession of my grandson to the throne, under the title of Henri V, and informing the Duc that I appoint him Regent during the new King's minority."

When the famous document had been written, and Charles X and the Duc d'Angoulême had put their signatures to it, the Baron de Damas solemnly repaired to his pupil's room.

As he entered, the small King, ignorant of his new dignity, was on all fours on the floor, and his sister, sitting on his back, was kicking him vigorously. The Baron bowed deeply before the dishevelled little boy, and ceremoniously announced to him that he was now King of France. When he had finished, the new King laughed outright, and simply said:

"Impossible! Come on, *ma sœur*, your turn to be horse."

A moment later, he suddenly pulled her up: "After all, if I am King, you will have to obey me!"

She answered: "This is what I think of you!" and leaping on him pulled his hair.

Throughout that afternoon, his new dignity was like a delightful game to Henri V. The cries of *"Vive Henri V!"* echoing round him when his grandfather presented him to the troops; giving the password that evening in the place of Charles X; all gave him a sense of his new value. That night, when his valet had undressed him, he stood on his bed in his nightshirt, and, looking down at the man, said: "You must be proud of being the valet of a King."

On 3rd August, the very day upon which Louis Philippe was to perform the first function of his new office—the opening of the Chamber—the commissaires who had been sent to Charles X returned to the capital. They had gone to inform the King that he had been deposed, and to request him to hand over any crown jewels in his possession, and to allow himself to be escorted to the coast. Charles X had flown into a rage, refused to see them, and formally cancelled his abdication.

Odillon Barrot called on the Duc to discuss the situation.

"The only solution, Monseigneur, is to frighten the King away. With your permission we will organize a demonstration."

Louis Philippe pondered for a few moments, then said:

"Do as you think best."

In a short while Paris was covered with huge posters announcing that Charles X, with his army, was about to march to Paris, to have the Duc de Bordeaux proclaimed King. To add to the fever, the "Générale" was beaten on the drums throughout the city.

From attics and cellars, as soon as they heard the call to arms, rushed all the idlers and trouble-makers of Paris, snatching the first utensil which came to hand. Armed with old swords, guns, cudgels and kitchen knives, they converged on the Hôtel de Ville: there they piled into the strangest assortment of vehicles, ranging from cabriolets to dust-carts, and set out for Rambouillet, twenty thousand strong, a filthy, disorderly rabble, a masquerade of an army; a few hundred trained soldiers could have scattered them like sparrows.

But when they arrived at Rambouillet at two o'clock in the morning, there were no soldiers. The palace was empty. Rather than allow more bloodshed, Charles X had begun his journey to the coast.

Frustrated, the mob broke open the coach houses, and harnessed eight white horses to each of the seven gold carriages of state; some put huge carcasses of raw meat upon the white satin seats, and thus, as many as could cram themselves in, feasted on their way back to the Palais Royal, howling and shouting, and waving empty bottles from the windows. They had found and brought back with them the crown jewels. It is curious to note that not a single piece of jewellery was missing, yet the rabble had them at their mercy for hours.

On reaching the Orléans residence, the crowd called for their new Lieutenant-General to appear, but apparently a feeling of disgust came over him; he felt that he could not witness the degradation of the Bourbon Monarchy, although he had sanctioned the act. Perhaps the evidence in his courtyard was too realistic.

For a week, the debates had continued; deputies went to and fro between the Chamber and the Palais Royal, hammering out the new Charta. The leaders of the revolution had to give their opinion on the form which the new monarchy should take.

The Duc de Broglie and Monsieur Guizot pressed their Lieutenant-General to maintain the ancient style of "by the grace of God, King of France", to use the term "subjects" in all decrees, and to assume the title of Philippe VII.

But Louis Philippe dismissed all this with a wave of the hand.

"No, I have chosen to be known as 'Louis Philippe Ier, by the will of the people, King of the French'—and there will be no more subjects, but only *concitoyens*."

On 7th August 1830, the new royal family assembled in the magnificent hall of the Palais Royal, the Salon des Batailles, to await the arrival of the head of the House of Orléans.

The doors were flung open by lackeys and Marie Amélie entered the hall, followed by Louis Philippe: it was the last time that this would happen; the next time it would be the Duc who would lead the way, as King of the French.

After a short pause, a group of deputies, led by Laffitte, were announced. They brought with them the new Constitution, and the Resolution by which Louis Philippe was called to the throne. It was an emotional scene; with great dignity, Monsieur Laffitte read the declaration of the Chamber, the whole assembly standing stiffly erect. When he had finished, the Duc, in a flood of noble and patriotic words, accepted the Crown, frequently interrupted by the applause of those present in the salon and the frantic cheering of the crowds outside in the courtyard, until all eyes seemed shining with tears.

Then the Duc, with well-rehearsed majesty and benevolence, approached those assembled in the great hall, extending his hand to all. Marie Amélie, conquering her repugnance, followed her husband, expressing her devotion to her country, and the pride she felt in her husband having thus been honoured by the whole nation.

Then a curious incident occurred. Lafayette came up to Louis Philippe, the man whom he had placed on the throne of France, and whispered, "This is the finest republic of all." These words, heard and repeated, were the means of rallying many to the new régime.

In response to cries from the crowd outside the Palais, the Duc and Duchesse appeared on the balcony, but shouts for Lafayette resounded from every side. As the General came forward, Louis Philippe, in sight of the enthusiastic mob, threw his arms emotionally around the neck of the beaming Lafayette and gave him a resounding kiss. A Tricolor flag was produced, which the new Sovereign, with tears flowing down his cheeks, seized and pressed to his heart.

The new habit of embracing on the slightest pretext appealed to the people, who, shouting with delight, commenced hugging one another without restraint. From this time a perfect mania started, crowds filled the courtyard and surrounding streets, whistling, screaming, and singing the "Marseillaise"; day and night the din continued; it seemed as if the people relayed each other.

After a whole week, these savage coarse voices created an atmosphere of hell. What had begun in rejoicing was ending in rioting. Louis Philippe, exhausted and hoarse, would have to come out onto the balcony and join in the "Marseillaise", beating time with his extended hand and leading the crazy choir.

That night of the 7th to 8th, the Duc d'Orléans sent secretly for the Russian Ambassador, Pozzo di Borgo, who wrote an account of the interview.

> I found the Duc d'Orléans filled with fear and hope. He repeated that he had never wished for the Crown, that he had often warned Charles X of the coming danger, but no heed had been paid to his words; that his desire would have been to continue a peaceful life amidst his family, that he was sacrificing himself for the salvation of his country.
>
> Now he requires the indulgence of Europe to maintain France in peace and, above all, the goodwill of the Emperor of Russia, to whom he abandons himself without reserve.

The Ambassador's reply was cautious. It seems that he personally sympathized with Louis Philippe, but he had few illusions on the reaction of his Imperial master. He could only advise Louis Philippe to keep the revolutionary spectre out of sight as best he could, for it was this, far more than the change of monarch, which alarmed the foreign powers.

As usual, the Duc d'Orléans had taken the precaution to make excuses beforehand for the treacherous act of usurpation which he was about to commit.

Louis Philippe had been proclaimed King, but it required some kind of enthronement before he could be declared, officially, the King of the French. This was a simple ceremony, so different from the ancient rites of Rheims.

On 9th August 1830, the Duc drove alone to the Chamber. On arrival, he was met by Monsieur Laffitte and a crowd of self-important men who led him to the Salle des Séances, where a throne, draped with Tricolor flags, had been erected.

The Duchesse, with the princesses, were seated in the tribunes facing the dais. Whilst the audience rose in greeting, the Duc and his two elder sons entered, and took their seats in front of the throne. Then Monsieur Casimir Périer read aloud the declaration of the Chamber of Peers embodying the Constitution, and Monsieur Pasquier that of the Chamber of Deputies.

The Duc d'Orléans signed both documents; then, assuming an air of majesty, he ascended the throne and seated himself, whilst heralds proclaimed him as "Louis Philippe Ier, Roi des Français". A few cries of "*Vive le Roi*", then it was over.

The new King left the Chamber, shaking hands ostentatiously with the Gardes Nationaux as he passed. He mounted his horse and, accompanied by his sons, returned to the Palais Royal.

One wonders what thoughts filled the mind of the new Queen Marie Amélie, as she drove from this travesty of a coronation. Did she recall the solemn ceremony which took place at Rheims, just five years before, when, with all the ancient rites and ceremonies of the Church and the royal prerogative, Charles X was truly anointed King of France?

Louis Philippe was now King, but he still had anxious moments; he knew that he would never be at ease until the rightful monarch had left France. But neither threats nor intimidation could hurry Charles X, who was making his departure with all the majesty of a royal progress.

During his journey to the coast, a strange incident had happened, on the night of 6th August, the very eve of Louis Philippe's acceptance of the Crown.

The royal party were in the small town of Merlurault. The King had already retired for the night, when an Englishman arrived very secretly, and asked to speak to his Majesty. He revealed that he was Colonel Craddock, and that he had been sent by Lord Stuart, the British Ambassador, with a message for the King.

Charles X agreed to receive him, and the messenger entered

178

one of the rooms, where two or three candles, hastily lit, gave a feeble flickering light.

The monarch watched, puzzled, while the Colonel slit the lining of his coat and produced a small piece of paper. Completely mystified, Charles X held it near the light of one of the candles and read a few words in the handwriting of Louis Philippe.

"Believe, Sire, all that Colonel Craddock will tell you on my behalf."

"What is it, Monsieur, that you have to tell me on my cousin's behalf?" asked the King.

"Sire, his Royal Highness suggests that you entrust Monsieur le Duc de Bordeaux to my care, and that I should take him to Paris where, as Lieutenant-General of the Realm, the Duc d'Orléans will do his best to have him proclaimed King."

Charles X was deeply touched. He hesitated.

"I cannot take such a step without first consulting his mother," and he summoned the Duchesse de Berri.

The Duchesse arrived, and Craddock repeated the proposition. She looked at the King for a moment, then both shook their heads.

Colonel Craddock understood, bowed, and left the room. Before the Colonel could have returned to the capital with Charles X's answer, Louis Philippe had accepted the throne.

What could have induced Louis Philippe to make such an offer, at the very moment when all details of his own accession were settled? Could it have been remorse? Or the knowledge that the people of Paris would never acknowledge the Duc de Bordeaux, and that by making this gesture Louis Philippe could establish that he had taken the only possible course in accepting the Throne himself? Or perhaps he wanted a hostage, to ensure that he should have nothing more to fear from the deposed Bourbons?

However this may be, Lord Stuart received a severe reprimand from the Duke of Wellington for having interfered in the affairs of the French.

Charles X continued his leisurely progress through the country, towards the sea.

At last, it was 15th August, the Assumption of the Blessed Virgin, Charles X's last day in France. On that day, it had been the custom for the Kings of France to attend in great ceremony the High Mass at Nôtre Dame. Charles X must have remembered this as he walked sadly into the drawing-room of the Château de Valognes, where he was to take leave of his guards, those men who had given up all to follow him to the last.

The guards were drawn up around the room, their officers in front of them. No sound, except their deep breathing, could be heard. Charles X walked to the far end of the room, and waited with a heavy heart for the staff officers to hand over their standards to him; they would be only useless symbols after the King's departure. He wore a shabby coat, no decoration, nothing to denote his rank.

As the first officer came towards his Majesty, and, kneeling on one knee, made the gesture of delivering his flag, there was a burst of sobs, and suddenly, all the guards were weeping, protesting, entreating. The King, whose eyes were full of tears, bent towards them, saying: "My sons, is it for me to console you at this moment, when I am the one needing the strength to say farewell?"

As the men passed by, he merely touched the white silk of the flags. Then, he thanked them for their loyalty, and bade them keep their standards for the day when his grandson Henri V would need them. This last appeal was too much for these loyal men. They lost all control, rushed down the grand staircase, talking wildly, shouting, beside themselves with grief. Later that evening one of them shot himself. All that they had honoured, loved, and worked for, was leaving them, and now they realized that the Kingdom of France was no more.

Before ten o'clock the next morning, four carriages arrived to take the royal family the last few miles to Cherbourg.

It had been a long time, since that last night at St. Cloud, but the King had travelled leisurely, retaining his dignity to the end. He had expressed his desire that during his departure, the Tricolor flag should not be flown on land or sea at Cherbourg. This wish was observed.

At one o'clock in the afternoon, he stepped out of his carriage in front of the harbour. The weather was beautiful, the sun seemed to send forth its rays in farewell to the King who was leaving his Kingdom.

A crowd had gathered, and many officers rushed forward to kiss the hands of the royal ladies, who broke down and, forgetting all etiquette, embraced the men, the last of their faithful bodyguard.

As the King moved forward, bugles sounded, and four companies of the Garde du Corps, which had escorted him all the way from St. Cloud, ranged themselves in battle order, facing the sea. Charles X saluted, then slowly mounted the gangway.

The Duc de Bordeaux, in a light-blue coat, his white collar turned down, his white trousers buttoned to his jacket, followed his grandfather.

Then came the little Mademoiselle, charming in her striped dress of blue and pink muslin; the Duchesse d'Angoulême, hiding her despair behind a face completely devoid of expression, followed by the Duc d'Angoulême in black, and, last of all, the Duc de Raguse.

On deck, the King stood alone, wearing an ill-fitting blue coat and an old round hat. None approached him as he stood with his back to the shore, looking out to sea.

At half past two, Charles X gave the order for the departure. As the ship moved away, the monarch turned towards the land he was leaving—perhaps for ever—and made a sign: was it the sign of the Cross? The Gardes du Corps stood silent, watching, guarding, till the ship was lost to their sight.

That night the new Sovereign received a report of this last scene, and he sighed with relief. One more thorn had been removed from his crown.

20

The Ill-Fitting Crown

Now that Charles X had left France, the usurper began his reign. Gradually Paris regained its composure; streets were re-paved, shops reopened, and traffic moved freely once more.

The most turbulent citizens were organized into "regiments of the Charta", and sent to join the army engaged in the conquest of Algeria;[1] but it was difficult to get rid of the fanatics who still haunted the Palais Royal.

One night General de Rumigny was awakened at midnight by two murderous-looking individuals with cadaverous features, and long matted beards, their shirts covered with blood.

"General, we must see the King. His life depends on it." Rumigny tried to parley, but they insisted, and seemed so wild that he went to awaken the King.

It was a strange scene; the King and his Aide de Camp, their coats only half-buttoned, their eyes full of sleep, hair unbrushed —and the two fanatics, looking like hungry wolves.

"We come from the Société des Amis du Peuple, to tell you now that the old régime is dissolved, not a trace of its former customs must remain. All must be swept away; the people demand it."

Louis Philippe looked enquiringly at the general, who nodded.

"Messieurs, I feel sure his Majesty agrees with you, and thanks you for such good advice. It is too late to hold a conference. Will you accept his hospitality, sleep under his roof? Tomorrow your proposition can be discussed more fully."

The two men withdrew, grumbling, and one was heard to say:

[1] It was in June of that year, during the Ministry of Polignac, that an expedition had set sail to undertake the conquest of Algeria.

"The King is cleverer than we are." [1]

No peace by night, and during the day the ordeal continued. Day after day, the King and Queen, following the example of Lafayette, stood giving audience to all who chose to come. Endless processions passed before them, chiefly of beggars and vagabonds, riddled with vermin and disease, exuding an awful odour of destitution, filth and drink. Most of these, as they filed before the King and Queen, thrust out their cheeks or soiled lips to those of the Sovereigns. We are told that Marie Amélie offered this ordeal to God, as a sacrifice for her husband's broken faith with Charles X. From the repulsive to the grotesque, the King had become the favourite toy, or perhaps the stock-in-trade of the urchins of Paris. They had discovered that every time they called for him, he would appear tamely on the balcony and wave to them. So they would charge the passers-by thirty sous to show them the King, and perhaps another thirty sous to make him sing the "Marseillaise". The Place du Palais Royal had become a fairground, and the King of the French its principal showpiece.

The Palais Royal was unrecognizable. All refinement had gone. Etiquette had vanished. Anyone could walk in and wreck the rich carpets with dirty boots. All uniforms and Court liveries had disappeared from the entourage of the new King; so had most of those who wore them. There was one master of ceremonies left, but no ceremonial, and instead of the aristocracy who surrounded Charles X, a rabble!

But Princesse Adélaïde thought that all this was not enough.

"You must not rest, Philippe; remember, you must keep the people interested and amused."

So it was decided that, two or three times a week, dinner for sixty to eighty people should take place at the Palais. Anyone could attend; there was no distinction of class or rank. This brought many more adherents than any other act, but to some this became a matter for laughter.

Cuvillier Fleury overheard one deputy of very modest origin say, "One can no longer dine with the King; the company is too low." And the Prince de Joinville, in his memoirs, related that these dinners were an odious ordeal for the family. It must have

[1] *Souvenirs* of General de Rumigny.

been fantastic to see the King and Queen, richly dressed, presiding at these meals surrounded by such an indescribable medley of ill-suited company. What suffering to have to undergo for a shaky, uncertain crown.

The corridors and staircase of the Palais Royal were still filled by the self-constituted guard, the ragged scum of Paris, armed with weapons and armour stolen from the military museum. No one dared to remove them; things were still too insecure.

When the King drove to the Chamber, they beat drums and saluted with the stolen arms according to their fancy. It was really an *opéra bouffe*. This band of vagabonds had elected as their leader a young officer, Damiguet de Vernon, who later became a general. To be rid of this undesirable protection, their leader was named "lieutenant of the municipal guard on horseback" in reward for his services, and uniforms were distributed to his followers. At this first sign of discipline, most of the riff-raff bolted with their new clothes, and the Palais regained its dignity.

During the effervescence at the beginning of the new reign, on 27th August 1830, horrible news reached the Palais Royal. The aged Prince de Condé had been found hanging from a window latch in his room at the Château de St. Leu. Those who knew the manner in which he was treated by his mistress, Madame de Feuchère, at once suspected that she was implicated; even Louis Philippe was not above suspicion. It was obvious from the position in which the body was found, with its knees touching the floor, that the prince could not have taken his own life.

It was also known that he had been planning to join Charles X in England. Had Madame de Feuchère feared lest he should again change his Will when he was free?

Suicide or murder, the truth will never be known; but the real story is probably that told by Madame Etchevery, a daughter of Monsieur de Préjean, Equerry to the Prince, who was twelve years old at the time and was staying at St. Leu.

She recounted that the Baronne often hit the old man brutally, leaving him bruised and sore. Once his valet Manoury, seeing a mark on his face, had asked him if he had knocked into something. "I did not knock into anything," answered the prince, "it's that hag again."

On the morning of the 27th, Mademoiselle de Préjean was awakened by cries, and by people rushing to and fro. She went to see what was happening and, in the midst of the wild confusion, became aware of the truth.

During a violent quarrel with his mistress, the prince, who had been beaten cruelly, had fallen and died in a few minutes, probably of shock. Terrified, Madame de Feuchère sent for a servant who was devoted to her, and together they staged this semblance of suicide, which deceived nobody.

The whole affair was hushed up. No murderer was sought. No trial took place. But Madame de Feuchère continued to frequent the Palais Royal, where Adélaïde and Louis Philippe gave her every honour and attention, and the small Duc d'Aumale inherited the vast estates of the House of Condé.

Now that the first days of the reign had passed, the new dynasty was more or less accepted by the different provinces of France; certainly, without much enthusiasm, but also without serious opposition.

Many considered it to be an expedient which ended an unhappy struggle. Thiers called it an "administrative monarchy"; this phrase became a byword.

The first act of Louis Philippe was to instruct Monsieur Laffitte to form a ministry. The new Conseil named on 11th August 1830 consisted, amongst others, of Monsieur Guizot, Marshal Gérard, the Duc de Broglie, Messieurs Molé, Casimir Périer, Dupin and Thiers, while General de Lafayette, whom the King did not disdain to call his "friend and protector", was given command of the Garde Nationale, a formidable post which put under his immediate control about three million citizens.

It had been intended to include Marshal Sebastiani, father of the ill-fated Duchesse de Praslin, but he was the sworn enemy of Pozzo di Borgo, the Russian Ambassador; a simple reason, they were both Corsicans. As soon as he heard of this intention, Pozzo, who had been enthusiastic in the cause of Louis Philippe, became noticeably cool, and it was felt that he must be placated at all costs because of his influence at the Court of the Czar.

The Comtesse de Boigne was sent to him. She was staggered by the change in his attitude; he seemed hesitant, uninterested, until she casually remarked: "By the way, I meant to tell you, Sebastiani will not be included in the Ministry."

She writes: "He stared at me for a moment, then taking both my hands in his, cried, 'Then I am the friend of Orléans till death'." [1]

Strong words, considering the hatred of the Czar for Louis Philippe.

The ministry of Laffitte soon ran into difficulties, at home as well as abroad. The foreign powers, slowly recovering from the shock of the July revolution, were preparing a menacing protest against the expulsion of Charles X.

Louis Philippe knew the full meaning of this antagonism: it was only fifteen years since another usurper, greater than he, had been sent to a far island in the Atlantic; and the legitimate dynasty had been restored in the person of Louis XVIII, putting an end, so people hoped, to revolution. Now there had been another revolution, and another usurper reigned—what did the future hold for him? Once again the whole problem lay before the great rulers.

Louis Philippe had always admired Great Britain, and he suspected that her Government would not be too displeased by the change of dynasty. But in the rest of Europe, he stood alone, a mountebank. From the Czar, outraged, came orders to all Russians to leave the infected country; Frenchmen were to be refused admission into Russia, and the Tricolor flag forbidden to enter her ports.

In Austria, Prince Metternich was advising the Emperor to be prepared for war, but the King of Prussia, terrified of a revolution in his own country, hastened to recognize the new régime. Sensing danger, Louis Philippe humbled himself to write to the Czar Nicholas I, pleading that he had only accepted the throne to save his country from civil strife, and begging for the protection of the most powerful monarch in the world. But the Czar never deigned to reply.

[1] *Mémoires* of the Comtesse de Boigne. Librairie Plon.

To please the British, he brought the aged Prince de Talleyrand from his self-imposed retirement, and named him as
Ambassador to the Court of St. James's.

Just as he thought that he had reassured Europe, revolution
broke out in Belgium. It seemed to justify every misgiving. The
epidemic was spreading!

A far greater trial had to be faced within the country, that of
rescuing the Ministers of Charles X from death. Three had
escaped abroad, but four had been caught and brought to
Vincennes for judgment—amongst them Prince Jules de
Polignac. The mob were determined to have their blood, and
the King was equally determined to save them.

On 18th October 1830, a frenzied mob attacked the Palais
Royal, shrieking "Death to the Ministers! Death to Polignac!"
The Garde Nationale drove them off. Undaunted, they set off
to Vincennes to vent their lust for revenge on the prisoners.
But, as they reached the fortress, they were met by one brave
man—General Daumesnil—who said calmly:

"You shall not have them! Rather than give them up, I will
set fire to the powder magazine; then we shall all die together!"

That night Madame Adélaïde was awakened by shouts of:
"Death to the Ministers of Charles X—or the head of Louis
Philippe!"

Finally the Ministers were condemned to imprisonment for
life in the fortress of Ham on the Somme.

(Some ten years after, another political prisoner was incar-
cerated in the same gloomy castle—Louis Napoleon, later Emperor of the French. He was horrified when he met these men;
they resembled ghosts when they were eventually released from
this living death.)

During those first months of the reign, General Marquis de
Lafayette was the focus of all flattery at the new Court. The
King treated him almost as an equal, but the General realized
that Laffitte was really the man at the head of the Government, and with him stood the bankers and speculators profiting
by the new régime. The July days had not benefited the people;
once more Lafayette's illusions were shattered.

The King and his Ministers were really anxious to be rid of

Lafayette; he posed too much as a king-maker. One day, when he and the King had disagreed, the General threatened, "I shall leave you, Sire, and return to my château at La Grange; and what will you do then?"

Louis Philippe reflected for a moment, then said: "Eh bien, mon cher, I shall leave you there."

A short time after this, Lafayette learnt that the Chamber had voted for the abolition of the High Command of the Garde Nationale. This was a means of depriving him of his official position. Indignant and hurt, undeceived by the King's affectionate regrets, he retired to his château at La Grange, where he died on 20th May 1834. The King ordered all the pomp of a national funeral, but a vague uneasiness was lifted from his mind as the last clod of earth fell on the coffin of the man who had made him King.

21

A Symbolic Umbrella

On New Year's Day, 1831, Marie Amélie wrote in her journal:

Nothing reveals the void of worldly things more than the present times. On this day last year, the Tuileries shone in all its splendour and prosperity: today it is empty and forlorn. Then, crowds filled it, bringing their affection, their respect and homage to Charles X. Today, the same servile courtiers fill the Palais Royal. God alone knows where they will turn their steps next year. . . .

How much happier I was when I was the one to offer homage, than today, when I am the one to receive it.

But I am ready to accept all for my God, and only ask in return that He should send peace and religion back to the people of France.

This prayer came too soon; the venom was still in the serpent.

On 14th February a few Royalists gathered in the Church of St. Germain l'Auxerrois for a Service in memory of the Duc de Berri, assassinated eleven years earlier. It was Shrove Tuesday, Carnival Day.

Outside, a crowd was watching, threateningly, knowing that it was a Royalist ceremony. The Service began: then, suddenly, as a young officer came forward to pin a picture of the Duc de Bordeaux on the catafalque, a cry arose from the mob outside, and immediately the Church was invaded. An appalling scene ensued. The crowd rushed to break down the altar; they threw the sacred vessels at the stained-glass windows, and tore down the lovely iron Cross which crashed heavily into the organ loft.

While the loyal followers of Charles X fled in horror from this ghastly scene, the insane mob invaded the vestry and, donning the vestments, made a parody of the Mass before an applauding audience.

In a few hours, nothing was left of St. Germain l'Auxerrois but bare walls and shattered ruins. That was the carnival of 1831.

The next day the rabble broke into the palace of the Archbishop near Nôtre Dame. It was a scene of rage and fury; like men possessed, they broke windows and threw into the Seine the furniture, the sacred objects, the rare books and ancient manuscripts from the library, the banisters, the floor boards and even the tiles from the roof. It was incredible that neither the police nor the deputies did anything to stop the frenzy for destruction.

On the previous day, the police had been at St. Germain l'Auxerrois. The Prefect of Police had talked to the leaders, politely requesting them to desist. He knew that the Archbishop's palace was the next target, but he made no preparations to defend it.

The Garde Nationale appeared occasionally at the pillage of the palace, then went away again without making a move to intervene. Thiers wandered amongst the crowd; it was even rumoured that Louis Philippe was there; but no one intervened. The police received only one order—"Keep the people away from the Palais Royal."

Now that the Palais Royal had been freed of the crowd of hangers-on and its self-appointed guards, the King and his family were able to resume their somewhat humdrum private life.

At ten o'clock all took déjeuner together, except Louis Philippe, who was already too occupied to be punctual. At eleven, they moved to a salon, where the princesses took up their sewing. The Queen would direct their work—night shirts, layettes, etc., for the poor. As a break in the monotony, billiards might be suggested, or a walk.

With all the excitement of the past months, the great question had been forgotten—what must the children call their father and mother now? After consulting the Queen, Louis Philippe gathered his family into his Cabinet, and told them that they must choose. Princesse Marie, who spoke for them all on these occasions, declared, "I will call my father 'Papa', and my mother 'Chère Majestée'." Everybody laughed, but this mode of address was adopted. "Chère Majestée". Those words were later to torture Marie Amélie.

At first it was difficult for the new King to decide what attitude he should adopt towards his *concitoyens*. At heart he revelled in the regal purple, but to remain secure on his somewhat plebeian throne, he had to descend to the level of his electors.

At this time he was fifty-six years old; he had a corpulent figure, his head reminded one of a large pear, he wore side-whiskers, his eyes and nose were truly those of a Bourbon.

To attain his purpose, he began to affect a certain "*laisser-aller*", an unkempt style of dress, a slightly vulgar "hail-fellow-well-met" attitude. Instead of gold-trimmed uniforms, he chose to wear civilian clothes; a blue habit with gilt buttons, vast white waistcoat, and a pair of nankin trousers strapped under his shoes; on his head a grey top hat. And he always carried his celebrated large umbrella.

He walked about Paris like an ordinary "Bon Papa", some-times accompanied by Marie Amélie who would have to take his arm, although she hated this undignified role; at times his children trailed behind them. Anybody who chose came up to shake hands with them, some even insisting on giving them a familiar embrace. He sincerely imagined that all this would make him popular, but he quite forgot that sometimes famili-arity breeds contempt.

Adélaïde wore the colours of the Revolution on every occa-sion. A blue dress, a white sleeveless lace jacket, a cherry-coloured bonnet. At first, knowing the important part which she played in the July days, the people alluded to her as "the august sister of our citizen King", "the liberal, charitable, en-dowed with all the virtues".[1] She seemed to puff out in her glory.

But all this had its counterpart amongst the Opposition. Nothing was too vile to appear in their papers. It went so far that she was accused of an incestuous liaison with her brother. Of all the insults which she suffered, this was the worst, as she felt that her love for Louis Philippe was the purest and most self-sacrificing of all her virtues.

[1] *Adélaïde d'Orléans*, by Raoul Arnaud.

191

Princesse Louise, "the angel of the family", as her mother called her, had become very attractive. Her complexion, as the French say, resembled "a rose petal and a drop of milk"; a mass of golden curls framed the lovely oval face. She resembled her mother in character, ever ready to suffer for others, but her mentality was far beyond her age.

Secretly, she dreaded her marriage to Leopold of Saxe-Coburg, although she realized that it must come; perhaps this affected her health, and caused her illness and early death.

Marie was not such a paragon of beauty or virtue, but she was an artist, witty, and full of mischief. She used to say that, "to know all, to become part of all, without being attached to anyone—that is supreme happiness". No one knew her real character. She played up to this saying; in reality she felt deeply, and suffered keenly.

Both were interested in politics; the elder strongly criticized her father's Government for not being sufficiently liberal; Princesse Marie went further, and one day openly professed her republican faith before Madame de Dolomieu, her mother's lady-in-waiting, who nearly fainted.

Princesse Clementine had become very beautiful, a most lovely face, chestnut-coloured hair and large blue eyes. She was then just fourteen, and it was only a few years before that she had captivated Charles X when she danced at the Ball of the little Duc de Bordeaux, at the Tuileries. The King's remark to her father: "Were I forty years younger, I should ask for the hand of your daughter, to make her Queen of France", had become imprinted on her mind, and already she dreamed of power and intrigue. Eventually her ambitions were fulfilled in her son, who became King Ferdinand of Bulgaria.

All three princesses had slight and graceful figures. They loved dress and were known for their exquisite taste. When they appeared at any public function, accompanied by their brother, people exclaimed: "Quelle belle famille!"

The princes were as remarkable as their sisters; but the handsomest of them all was the eldest, who was still called Chartres by the family, although he had become Duc d'Orléans on his father's accession to the throne. He was a being apart, beautiful as a Greek god, but by no means as lifeless. He was restless, violently republican in outlook, constantly clashing with his father's views.

"Beauty", as he was nicknamed by his brothers, objected to Adélaïde's politics, and clamoured to go to the assistance of the Poles in their revolt against Russian rule.

The Duc de Nemours was good-looking, with dreamy eyes and blond wavy hair, but so shy that no one ever knew what he wanted, or if he wanted anything, and to play his part in public was agony to him.

The Duc d'Aumale at this time was still studying at the Collège Henri IV. His brothers called him "the gold mine" because of his Condé inheritance, but he was too young to know or care about riches.

The great charmer was the Prince de Joinville. In looks, he reminded Louis Philippe of his father, as he first remembered him. He was gifted, and became the most popular of the brothers. More sailor and painter than royal prince, he was careless in dress, drank and swore like an old sea-dog; later he wrote a charming book entitled *Vieux Souvenirs*.

"Ton Ton", the Duc de Montpensier, then only a small boy, was full of life and vivacity.

This brilliant cortège always surrounded Louis Philippe when he appeared in public; they smiled, he smiled, and the public smiled.

The afternoons were often spent at St. Cloud or Neuilly, but generally everyone returned in time for dinner at six o'clock, when twenty-five, or even more, guests would be present. Louis Philippe liked to invite the heads of the Opposition and Government alternately, thinking to placate all parties by his geniality. At about half past seven, the royal family entered the Grand Salon for the evening reception at which one met deputies, artists, musicians, writers and leaders of the bourgeoisie and their wives, but never at this time any of the great names of France came to the Palais Royal.

*   *   *

For some time the family of Bonaparte had receded far into the shade. So many absorbing events were taking up Louis

Philippe's thoughts that he was almost startled by an episode which took place in May 1831.

One evening, the Comte d'Houdetôt, one of the King's Aides de Camp, received a mysterious communication. "If the Comte d'H. wishes to meet an old friend, who will be pleased to shake his hand, he is invited to go tonight to the rue de la Paix, Hôtel de Hollande, where he must ask for the lady who occupies Room No. 3."

Greatly intrigued, he went to the given address, and was taken to the room. The door opened and a tall woman stood before him. At first, in the dim light of the corridor, he could not discern her features. Then she put out her hand and laughed, and that gay laughter recalled to him at once a woman he had once known so well—Hortense, Queen of Holland, step-daughter to the Emperor Napoleon.

So much had happened since they last met, but she was as handsome and charming as ever. She explained that, with the aid of Russian passports obtained for her by Prince Gortchakoff, she and her son Louis Napoleon (future Emperor of the French) had fled from Italy, where Louis Napoleon had been implicated in a Carbonaro intrigue. She desired to reach England, and wondered if the Comte, in memory of their past friendship, could secure for her French passports for that purpose, of course in assumed names.

The Comte replied that nothing could be easier, but that he must obtain permission from the King. He returned to the Palais Royal and told Louis Philippe of his adventure.

"How delightful; I must see her! Is she as pretty as ever? Ask Queen Hortense to come, show her into your apartment, and inform me as soon as she arrives."

Twenty minutes later, the King and the Comtesse de St. Leu (as she now called herself) were reminiscing gaily, whilst Houdetôt kept watch in the corridor, wondering how long this tête-à-tête would last.

There was no chair for him to sit on, and his legs were not his strong point, so at last he sat on the floor and dozed. Suddenly the door opened, and the King whispered:

"Houdetôt! Where are you?"

Then the eyes of the monarch alighted on the figure stretched across the floor fast asleep; he roared with laughter and called Hortense to see her old friend. They woke him and sent him to fetch the Queen and Madame Adélaïde.

During the conversation which ensued, Louis Philippe asked for news of her son, the young Prince Louis Napoleon. Queen Hortense looked distressed, and said how deeply her son felt at not being able to present his homage to the King but, poor boy, he was ill in bed with fever.

As Hortense was leaving, the King assured her that she should have the passports, but added kindly:

"Do not hurry; let your son regain his strength; only do not show yourself too much in public."

The King, delighted with his evening, mentioned the visit at the Council of Ministers the next day, and concluded:

"I did not see Prince Louis; poor boy, he was so disappointed, but he is ill with fever and had to keep to his bed."

Concealing a smile, the Président du Conseil replied: "Sire, the young man is not ill, and did not keep to his bed. He left the hotel at nine o'clock last night and returned at five this morning. During that time he attended the meetings of three secret societies and had a long conference with a dangerous character, a Pole named Zaba."

The King remained pensive. The friend whom he had received with open arms had proved treacherous.

"If this is the case, it is better that the passports be sent at once."

"Sire, the Comtesse de St. Leu has already received them, and she and her son will be out of the country in a few hours." [1]

Louis Napoleon's night activity was only a small part of Louis Philippe's difficulties. One day, soon after this episode, in a conversation with Casimir Périer, perhaps the most talented and honest politician in France at this moment, he put his whole problem into a single sentence:

"The Legitimists are hostile, the clergy are legitimist, the Bonapartists are for war, I stand for peace, the Republican claims are impossible, and their wish is to make me fall out with

[1] This anecdote is from *Souvenirs d'un Demi-Siècle*, by Maxime du Camp. Librairie Hachette.

the middle class. In these conditions, I cannot see how I shall govern the country." [1] When Louis Philippe said these words to Casimir Périer, his mind was already made up. Laffitte, the blundering First Minister, must go.

There was rioting daily; every anniversary was an excuse for a demonstration, and every demonstration ended in disorder. Many desired to send help to the Poles, then striving to free themselves from the yoke of Russia; but Louis Philippe opposed this resolutely, fearing to antagonize the Czar.

When the end came and the Poles were defeated, the King felt justified, but the people were not easily appeased, and fresh riots broke out.

Laffitte had to go, and Louis Philippe offered the post of Président du Conseil to Casimir Périer, already a very sick man. But the mere change of ministry could not check the daily disturbances. On 17th September 1831, the King had at his table Lord Granville and other distinguished Englishmen. Suddenly the room seemed to shake with the tramp of feet below, and piercing cries almost drowned the conversation. A band of ruffians had invaded the corridors beneath the dining-room. Louis Philippe continued placidly eating his dinner. Etiquette forbade the guests from rising before their host, so they sat, trying to swallow their lobster, shivering, aghast, and choking, but pretending to ignore the noise beneath them; until at last, the guards drove out the rabble. After that incident, it was decided that the King must move to the Tuileries.

It was pointed out that, apart from the difficulty of guarding the royal family in the Palais Royal, Louis Philippe would not be really King in the eyes of France until he resided in the ancient royal château of the Tuileries.

On 29th September 1831, the Orléans family sat down for the last time at that table where for fifteen years Louis Philippe had presided. Tears were very near, few spoke. Marie Amélie had asked that no guest should be invited; she felt it would be impossible to make conversation. They had loved their home; it had been their creation; every room, every picture, every ornament had been a matter for thought. The Tuileries, to them, was only associated with grief and defeat. Nothing there

[1] *Louis Philippe*, by J. Lucas-Dubreton.

was part of them; they would leave a place of beauty, light and sunshine, for a dark, prison-like château on the Seine.

Even when the *échaudés* were brought—a last offering from the famous kitchens of the Palais Royal—they scarcely brought a light into the children's eyes.

After dinner, Marie Amélie retired to her chapel, and there remained alone. Memories of past days flitted through her mind. Well, now it was over. As she was leaving her home, Marie Amélie turned to General de Rumigny saying: "Little did I dream, when I entered the Palais Royal, that I should leave it as a Queen."

*   *   *

The next day, 30th September 1831, the Tuileries was once more a royal residence, the Tricolor flag flew gaily over the roofs, and the Tricolor King was at home.

The Queen took up her residence in the apartments which had been used by Marie Antoinette. The King, a devoted husband, shared these with her; he was proud of this, and when he showed his guests round the Tuileries, he never failed to point to the large double bed: "You see, I sleep with my wife."

The Queen chose as her private drawing-room the room which Charles X had used as a state bedroom. Once asked why she had especially chosen this room, she pointed to the emblem over the chimney, the Sun of Louis XIV, with the legend *"nec pluribus impar"*. Marie Amélie still clung to the old tradition. The walls of this lovely room were hung with satin in gilt panels, the ceiling was richly painted. Yet, as some remembered that room in the period of Louis XVI, they sighed, and said that it lacked the elegance of that time.

Louis Philippe transformed the whole atmosphere of the Tuileries. Even the ushers, who still, under Charles X, had worn the blue and silver uniforms of the *ancien régime*, were now in black frock-coats; he confided to a friend that, for a citizen-King, the Bourbon uniforms were too flashy.

Yet he entertained royally. During the winter he gave four grand Balls, two smaller ones for the Queen, several concerts, and numerous gala dinners. All these fêtes were extremely brilliant. Three thousand guests crowded the salons, the women in *grande toilette*, but not Court gowns. The men, except those in uniform, wore a blue frock-coat, collars and cuffs embroidered with gold braid, white cashmere trousers trimmed with a gold braid stripe, and buckled shoes.

At the end of the long suite of salons was the hall where concerts took place; on these occasions it was used as a dining-room where a thousand guests could be seated at small tables for supper and listen to the strains of a military band which provided a background for the hum of conversation.

Mingled with the "liberal" nobility were shopkeepers and clerks, the "petits bourgeois", their wives in ostentatious finery, rather self-consciously huddling in corners.

The Duchesse de Dino remarked: "Many things are a contrast: some magnificently gowned women, others in caps; no distinction; one no longer walks in procession before the Court; it is now the Court that walks in procession before the guests. There is a small gentleman in uniform, who precedes the King and Queen to ask each person for his name; but this is a farce, as the names are completely unknown, and the Sovereigns will never remember to whom they belong."

22

The Cholera

It was a superhuman task which Casimir Périer had undertaken; there was constant strife in the Chamber between the different factions; jealousies and hatreds were rife; disorders and riots broke the traffic in the streets.

The Président du Conseil worked day and night, to the detriment of his health, but the undaunted energy of his spirit sustained him for a while.

He set himself the task of reassuring Europe, without humiliating France. At home he vainly attempted to pacify the passions. He became known as the "energetic maniac"; he seemed obsessed with a passion for work, for he felt that he had not much time before him. His health was failing daily.

In contrast, Louis Philippe sat alone at his desk; he was often alone now, ministers rarely visited him. He felt resentful. Everybody was talking of Monsieur Périer. Whenever he spoke to one of his ministers, whatever the subject, the answer would always be: "Yes, Sire, Monsieur Périer suggests that . . ."

He must regain his power, or Périer would reign in his stead; yet who could replace the "energetic maniac"?

Then suddenly, the echo of fear ran through the city: "the cholera is here!" The people, as they heard the dreaded word, stood still; it seemed as if they were turned to stone. Slowly, the horror of what was coming towards them drove all to panic. They knew that it was impossible to escape the scourge.

For a year, the authorities had known that the epidemic was approaching. At this period, 1832, Paris was one of the most unsavoury towns of France.

The narrow streets, which never saw the light of the sun, were bordered with overcrowded, damp, crumbling houses, often five storeys high, with no ventilation. The holes which served as lavatories had no water, the filth which accumulated flooded the floor, and trickled its way down the dank stone stairways. The people often did not take the trouble even to use these holes, simply emptied their refuse from their windows into the streets.

The streets, never swept, were a breeding ground of vermin and disease. Even the hungry dogs skirted the market places, ankle deep in decaying meat and vegetables. The stench could often be noticed at the Tuileries. When Louis Philippe complained, the answer was "there is no remedy". The King could do nothing, the population could do even less! This degraded state of living was the only one they knew, and they did not even notice it. So, on that early morning in March, when that dreaded cry broke forth, they did not know where to turn.

It began on 26th March 1832, when four victims were reported near the Hôtel de Ville; three days later, three hundred cases, and on 1st April it was in every quarter of Paris. Then started a tragic period. The people died in agony, often whole families would lie unburied, forgotten, in some room. In one case, a small child was left alone amid a pyramid of decaying remains, too weak to cry; he in his turn crawled to the heap and lay still.

The hospitals were full, three men to a narrow bed. Often, one would be pushed out by his bedfellows, and lie in his agony on the floor. Then, as the men died, they in turn would be thrown out, and perhaps lie rotting for days. No nurses, no means of obtaining food or drink, few doctors, no medicines, no one left to prepare them; these hospitals were an inferno.

Carts would pass, and gather as many corpses as they could hold. No coffins; the better class would sew up their dead in sacks, and scribble a number on them, in the vain hope of one day finding the remains, and burying them with decency.

At last, the authorities decided to clean up the streets of the city, working at night, employing large farm carts. This created a riot among the rag and bone men, who saw their means of living being taken from them. On the one hand, the people sympathized with the rag and bone men, and on the other, they cried out that the brutal, heartless government were poisoning the population by allowing the filth to remain lying in the roads. As the disease proceeded, the panic grew, until the people lost all sanity, and rushed about the streets, killing and wounding haphazard, crying out against they knew not whom.

Casimir Périer felt that all the tremendous efforts he had made during the past year amounted to nothing. He could hear the people in the streets crying out against him and his colleagues. He was so tired, so ill, yet he must battle on until his strength gave out.

The King and his family had refused to leave the Tuileries during these disastrous months, so one day, Périer, accompanied by the young Duc d'Orléans, went to visit the cholera-stricken patients at the Hôtel-Dieu. Forgetful of their safety, they drew near to the beds and spoke to the victims, trying to bring comfort and reassurance where terror and despair reigned.

A few days later it was officially announced: "The Président du Conseil is ill with the cholera." At once, panic spread. Périer had brought a certain financial stability in this difficult period; who could replace him? From that dreadful scourge, there was no remedy, and in the eyes of the public, he was already dead. He himself knew as well as they did that he could not be saved, and that in a few hours or days his body would be thrown on that great heap outside the city where so many of his friends already lay. Well, he had done his best for the country, but there was so much more to be done. He murmured to a friend: "I am very ill, but France is more ill than I."

One day, two friends were watching over him, as he lay apparently unconscious. Was this the end? The hours dragged by, night was falling. Outside, a passer-by cried: "Mort à Périer!" At this moment, Périer sat up in his bed, his eyes flaming, his thin hands clutching the sheet. He screamed: "Oh! if the Président du Conseil was not mad!" He fell back. He was dead.

* * *

The weeks passed. Gradually, the flames of civil strife died down; the cholera was waning, and July 1832 seemed to bring hope and peace to the tired citizens; the people were grateful to the King and his family for having shared the dangers of the scourge. The sun shone, warming all hearts, but Louis Philippe seemed doomed never to know the blessing of peace for long. Disturbing news reached him—the Duchesse de Berri was in the Vendée and had proclaimed her son, Henri V, King of France.

Holyroodhouse, that grim royal palace lying almost in the shadow of Edinburgh Castle, had been lent to Charles X by the British Government. The King, tired and resigned, reigned in that cloistered atmosphere where etiquette was observed as rigidly as it had been in the Tuileries. The same routine continued; the King played whist every evening, the Duchesse d'Angoulême sat at a round table embroidering, the Court stood about, still hoping for a word or look from one of the royal personages.

The Duchesse de Berri, young and full-blooded, felt suffocated in this milieu.

To the outside world she appeared a frivolous woman, who only lived for sex and vanity: in reality, behind her frail form and seemingly empty life, there existed a strong personality. She was truly a King's daughter; and perhaps one of the last who believed in the Divine Right of Kings.

In those last days at St. Cloud, she had tried to rouse Charles X to action: there she had failed; now she was the only one who did not take it for granted that nothing could be done.

A few years before, when visiting the Vendée, the whole province had welcomed her enthusiastically, almost deliriously. She had been acclaimed as the mother of the future King. Surely the Vendéens would be loyal to their vow. If she could rouse them before the usurper was firmly seated on the throne, whilst there were riots in the capital, she might be able to save France for her son.

She left Scotland in disguise, crossed to Rotterdam, and journeyed to Geneva. From there, she wrote to all the monarchs of Europe, asking for their help for her war in the Vendée. From some she received large sums of money; others sent flattering letters which encouraged her dreams.

On 7th May she reached her destination—Plassac in the Vendée.

Marie Caroline, Duchesse de Berri, was so sure of the future that she felt that she had only to declare her mission for the whole population to arm for her cause.

"I wish to wipe out the stain of Rambouillet," she said as she took up her pen to write the proclamation demanding the overthrow of her uncle, Louis Philippe, and proclaiming her son, the Duc de Bordeaux, as the rightful King of France.

"Vendéens, Bretons, all you inhabitants of the faithful provinces of the West, Henri V calls you. . . ."

Then disillusion began. Nothing happened.

On 16th May, she went to Nantes, capital of Brittany, and issued the same proclamation. Still nothing occurred.

Then began a wild adventure through the countryside, dressed as a boy, sleeping under hedges, begging a crust from farmhouses, ever pursued through swamps, fields and forests by the troops sent by Louis Philippe, who had now awakened to the danger which threatened his throne.

Every hour she grew more dispirited by the apathy around her. What had happened to the heroic Chouans of 1793, to those who, but a few years before, had offered their bodies and their hearts to the service of her son?

At length, tracked down on all sides, the princess reached her last refuge, the Hôtel du Guiny in Nantes, which stands opposite the famous Château de la Duchesse Anne. There the princess spent her last weeks of freedom, conspiring with the few remaining devotees of her lost cause.

For five months now, Marie Caroline had defied the Government of Louis Philippe. It was 30th October 1832. The rain fell in torrents; somewhere in the attic a shutter was creaking and banging in the wind.

In the drawing-room, the flickering candle-light revealed a row of anxious faces staring at the table, where Chevalier Mesnard, who acted as treasurer, had just thrown down a miserable little pile of francs, the last of their funds.

At that moment, Hyacinthe-Simon Deutz was announced; there could be no doubt as to his identity; he had answered the passwords correctly, and he brought twenty-two letters of recommendation from Spain and Portugal; even one from the Pope himself.

He entered, soaked with rain, his handsome Jewish face strained with exhaustion.

He rushed forward to Marie Caroline, kissed the extended hand, kissed the hem of her dress, mad with emotion. When he had calmed down, he declared his message.

Spain and Portugal were entirely gained to her Royal Highness, and money would be forthcoming in a few days. Immediately, the tired faces of the group lit up. But he had a request to make; hesitantly, he asked for a loan to continue his work for the cause.

This was disconcerting, and they dispersed to consider the matter.

Three days later the door bell rang violently; peering out of the window, Chevalier Mesnard saw that the street was full of soldiers.

"Quick, Madame, the hiding place!" With three of her followers, the Duchesse rushed up the stairs. Their hearts pounding, they ran into a small attic room, over to the fireplace, and opened a panel at the back.

There was a little recess, a rough triangle, about four feet in one direction and three feet in the other. They crammed themselves into it, shut the panel, and began their wait in the blackness, with nothing to do but execrate, in low voices, the name of Deutz; surely it was he who was the traitor!

"Some years ago I stayed in this house and stood in that little attic room. It is quite empty except for that fireplace and the recess at the back of it. I opened the plaque and crept into the little dark hole. It seemed barely large enough to crouch in, and it is unbelievable that for almost twenty-four hours *four* people existed in that hole. Was it courage or fear that allowed them to live through this horrible ordeal—no air, no sanitation, no light, no room to move their cramped limbs." [1]

They remained hidden all that night, whilst the troops of Louis Philippe searched every corner of the house and waited for their prey.

At dawn, the gendarmes, who had chosen for their quarters the very attic room which contained the panel, felt cold and lit a fire. As the smoke seeped through the cracks, the fugitives

[1] Author.

were in agony. Mesnard whispered: "We shall have to get out or we shall be suffocated."

"No! No! No!" answered the Duchesse. "We are still alive; we will battle on."

The panel began to glow red; heat added to their sufferings. Soon the heat diminished, the crackling ceased. Thank God, the fire was out!

After a time it was relit; this time, paper was being burnt; clouds of smoke filled the little black hole. How much longer could they bear it? Then the Duchesse sneezed.

The men at the other side stopped talking and leaped to the chimney. There was nothing more that could be done. Mesnard unhooked the iron panel, which crashed into the fire and, one by one, the four prisoners crawled out, dirty and crumpled. They were taken downstairs and handed over to the Commanding Officer.

Then, with her head very high, the Duchesse allowed herself to be led to the Château de la Duchesse Anne; as she passed a bystander murmured: "She is just like Napoleon!"

Now that she had been arrested, Louis Philippe was perplexed to know how to deal with her. Marie Amélie begged that she should be sent back to Charles X, but Adélaïde had caught her prey and, as usual, she triumphed. The prisoner was sent to the fortress of Blaye.

As the days passed, it became clear that, as a prisoner, the Duchesse de Berri was far more embarrassing to Louis Philippe than free. This was the Romantic age. The thought of a princess, whatever her dynasty, pining away in a large hideous barracks, set in some of the most mournful scenery in France, surrounded by rough gaolers, stirred people's sentiments. Presents began to pour into Blaye, wines for her table, books for her library, slippers embroidered with pierced hearts and fleurs de lis, parrots, monkeys, lapdogs to amuse her. Conspiracies sprang up to deliver her.

Louis Philippe read the reports anxiously. Perhaps, after all, Marie Amélie had been right.

One morning, Louis Philippe found on his desk a report from Inspector Joly, a policeman who had accompanied the princess to Blaye. The Duchesse de Berri, in his opinion, was pregnant:

"If your Excellency could see the walk of the princess: the hips drawn in, the body bearing on the heels, all the signs of an immense lassitude. . . ."

Louis Philippe immediately saw how this scandal could be used. If it were true, the exalted legend which surrounded her would crumple in the eyes of the people, and all her panache and bravado would be nothing.

Orders were sent to Blaye that the truth must be ascertained, and from that moment, Marie Caroline was subjected to a revolting treatment. She was questioned endlessly, put through medical examinations in the presence of the Governor and officers of the prison, watched every moment of the day, spied on by her lady-in-waiting, all to break her pride, and make her confess in writing that she was bearing a child.

On the evening of 22nd February 1833, worn out after an exceptionally painful scene with the prison Governor, she sat at her writing table, and wrote her confession:

Général,

Pressed by circumstances and by the measures ordered by the Government, although I have the gravest reasons for keeping my marriage secret, I owe it to myself and to my children to declare that I was married secretly during my stay in Italy.

MARIE CAROLINE

From the Fortress of Blaye, this 22nd February 1833.

This letter was published the following day in the Government newspaper the *Moniteur*. The public refused to believe it. Such a confession had certainly been obtained from her by force, or by the promise that she would be freed!

So Louis Philippe and Adélaïde began to search for new proofs. She must declare whom she had married, when and where. Numerous witnesses must be assembled at Blaye, to be present at her delivery. Knowing that the Duchesse was liable to give birth in a matter of minutes, the Governor set officers on permanent duty in the corridor outside her bedroom, in the anteroom, and in the room below, and a hole was bored through the floor, so that every movement could be overheard. She was never allowed to shut a door, or to be alone.

On the night of 9th to 10th May 1833, a daughter was born to the Duchesse de Berri, "wife in legitimate marriage to Count Hector Lucchesi-Palli of the Princes of Campo Franco, Gentleman of the Chamber of the King of the Two Sicilies, domiciled in Palermo". Honour was saved, whether Count Lucchesi-Palli was truly the husband of the Duchesse and the father of the child at that time, will never be known. He declared it gallantly.

But it was the end of Marie Caroline's dream. She would never now play a part on the great stage of Europe. All her ambitions were ended when she became Countess Lucchesi-Palli. Her adventure had lasted one year.

* * *

On 22nd July 1832, an emaciated young man with a glorious name, Napoleon Bonaparte, King of Rome, Duke of Reichstadt, on whom the Bonapartist party pinned all their hopes, died ingloriously in his bed at Schönbrünn in Austria, and in Paris thousands of old soldiers wept.

Louis Philippe shrugged his shoulders when he was told. As King of Rome, it might have been important. As Duke of Reichstadt, it was only a pawn less on the chessboard.

* * *

At this moment Louis Philippe was triumphant, one of his daughters was going to marry a King! Princesse Louise had at last consented to marry Leopold, King of the Belgians. So the Tuileries was in a turmoil. In the fear that the future bride might alter her mind, everything was being speeded up. The trousseau would be sent on later. Just the few necessary gowns, linen, etc., for the present use must suffice. Louise was kept busy so that she would not find time to reflect or regret her promise.

The King felt that Paris was too sore, after the plague of sickness and rioting, to face any royal rejoicings, so he decided that the Château de Compiègne would be better suited for the ceremony—less etiquette and over more quickly.

In reality, was it rejoicing? Prince Leopold of Saxe-Coburg had renewed the request for the hand of Princesse Louise, which he had first made in 1826; and now that he was King of the Belgians the alliance was of such obvious advantage, that Marie Amélie and Louis Philippe worked on the feelings of the young girl until she gave in.

Louise dreaded leaving home, and above all, she had a strong repugnance for her proposed fiancé. She sensed that he still mourned Princess Charlotte, and that she personally meant nothing. It was only a political transaction on both sides, and she was the victim.

The marriage was solemnized on 9th August 1832. Monsieur Trognon described the ceremony.

> I do not think that the funeral of the same lovely princess when Queen of the Belgians, could have caused more tears than her wedding. Everyone was inconsolable. The princess was weeping, all the family wept loudly, the King, her brother Orléans, sobbed piteously; even the small Duc de Montpensier howled with all his might.

> On the 13th, at the moment of departure, the grief was still more intense. After the religious ceremony, when Louise knelt at her mother's feet and begged for her blessing, some of the family fainted with emotion.

Poor King Leopold felt embarrassed and tried to shed a few tears, but nothing could bring them on; so he waited in patience until he could take his bride away.

After his favourite daughter left, Louis Philippe shut himself up with Monsieur Trognon and went on weeping; then suddenly he stood up and said: "I ought never to have allowed this sacrifice; it will kill her."

*   *   *

At the end of that year Louis Philippe said to one of his ministers: "The cholera has passed, the Duc de Reichstadt is dead, and the Duchesse de Berri is in prison. Now perhaps we shall have peace!"

Only two days later, as the King rode across the Pont Royal, a shot rang out. Instinctively, he bent over the saddle, then straightened his back and saluted the crowd. He glanced down to see a smoking pistol lying on the ground. Cheers broke out from the people, a tribute to his courage.

This outrage rendered Louis Philippe a great service. For a time, he became an idol; honest citizens were sick of street violence, always perpetrated in the name of the Republic.

Public opinion intimidated the firebrands for a while. Peace returned to the city, and the Parisians began to enjoy the luxury of repose; shops displayed their newest creations, money circulated, and at last people smiled.

On 28th July 1833, the statue of Napoleon, which had lain broken on the Place Vendôme, was reinstated; the King and royal family attended; not a discordant note was heard. Thiers said to the King: "Sire, who could have predicted a year ago that such quietude would exist today?"

Yet, all through these first years of the reign of Louis Philippe, scarcely a month went by without some kind of rising, some serious, some less so. People became so accustomed to them that, hearing a few shots, old women would toddle to their windows, then, with a shrug of their shoulders, return to their stockpots.

For the King, the attacks on his person ever remained a torment. Each day, in his Cabinet, he read the police reports placed on his desk, and there was little to reassure him; threats were continually appearing. His reaction to all this was courageous, but for Marie Amélie life had become a tragedy. Every moment of the day, she was terrified for her husband.

The most tragic outrage took place on 28th July 1835. The King was to review some of his troops. The police had given warning that a plot, more violent than the others, was being organized, but they were unable to ascertain in what manner it would be committed. General de Rumigny, the King's favourite Aide de Camp, described the scene.

We had been told to be on our guard, and it was agreed between the Princes and the Aides de Camp, that his Majesty should be surrounded as much as possible to prevent any bullets reaching him. Our great fear was that a shot might be fired from above, so it was our constant task to watch any half-shuttered windows. The police had been told the probable area where the attempt would be made, and they feared the Boulevard du Temple as one of the worst quarters of the city. From the Porte St. Martin to the Gaîté, the police visited every house, as a vague rumour had spread that a mine had been placed under the road, to blow up the procession as it passed.

This day was perfect; the sun shone enchantingly, the streets had been watered to keep down the dust; flags waved, crowds gathered along the route to see the display.

The King, on horseback, surrounded by his sons and A.D.C.s, made a magnificent picture and, as the cavalcade passed, the people cheered and clapped. One could notice, here and there, a few disagreeable and sinister faces, but they were swamped by the enthusiasm of thousands.

The King had arrived in front of the Eighth Legion, on the Boulevard du Temple, when suddenly a terrific explosion was heard. A hail of projectiles fell among the royal suite. The King's horse was hit in the neck; he reared. Louis Philippe turned to his son, Joinville, saying, "This is for me." Marshal Mortier, hit on the temple, fell dead.

"Get away, Sire," shouted the Préfet. The princes surrounded their father, the crowd panicked and screamed amidst the dead and dying, smoke, dust, and pools of blood.

The King alone was calm; a bullet had grazed his forehead, leaving a black bruise, but he rose in his stirrups, waved his plumed hat and cried, "Here I am!" For a moment the people were overcome, then an immense ovation followed.

Only one young man, standing with a red cap on his head, hissed; General de Rumigny, furious, hit him with the flat of his sword, felling him to the ground.

While the house, from which smoke was still issuing, was being surrounded, Louis Philippe cast a look at the scene of horror, and commanded, "We must pass on; the review is not over."

On the Place Vendôme, the Queen and princesses waited anxiously for the King. On reaching them, he dismounted to reassure them, whilst the ladies of the Court, losing all sense of etiquette, rushed about seeking news of their relatives and friends.

The heat was unbearable. Louis Philippe remounted and took the salute for over two hours. When it was over and he had returned to the Tuileries, he shut himself in his Cabinet and wept.

Three men were arrested: a grocer, Pépin, a rope-maker, Morey, and a professional adventurer, Fieschi. The details of the plot were diabolic; Pépin financed the enterprise, Morey organized it, and Fieschi carried it out.

They had taken a small apartment on the Boulevard du Temple, and brought to it their infernal machine in separate parts. To increase the chances of success, they had placed a row of guns at the window, aiming them beforehand with the help of the fourth conspirator, who rode up and down the Boulevard playing the part of the King; a macabre dress rehearsal.

The most gruesome part of the affair was that Pépin and Morey, anxious not to be compromised, had loaded some of the guns in such a way that they would explode, and Fieschi would never speak again.

Fieschi, although horribly mutilated, survived to tell the whole story, before all three were executed.[1]

[1] This version of the Fieschi coup is based on the *Souvenirs* of General de Rumigny.

23

At Last a Princess is Found

While new laws were being passed to provide for the greater
security of the King, Louis Philippe and his family went to the
Château d'Eu, his favourite seaside residence in Normandy. He
needed a rest after his recent emotions.

But Louis Philippe was never allowed to rest; Madame
Adélaïde saw to that. Two days after their arrival, the King,
the Queen, and Adélaïde, stood in the courtyard waving to the
children as they drove away with their tutors to spend the day
at Tréport.

Louis Philippe sighed contentedly. "A whole day of peace
before us."

"Oh non, mon cher frère, we have a very grave subject to discuss. I have waited for this moment. Chartres' future!"

She led the way back towards the house and, ever docile, her
brother followed.

The Duc d'Orléans, or Chartres—as they still called him
amongst the family—was now twenty-five, and it was time for
the heir to the throne to marry and have children.

He, personally, was not of that opinion; recently he had
joined with his regiment in the Mascara Expedition in Algeria;
he had been wounded, and nearly died of dysentery. But all
this, for him, was part of life.

He was a mass of contradictions. His manner was natural,
he was a good companion, and tried to make excuses for his
rank.

One day, going to pay a visit to Ary Scheffer the painter,
the concierge, not recognizing him, shouted:

"Come here! As you are going to Monsieur Scheffer, just take
up this pair of trousers which I have mended for him. Only be

quick about it; he is in a hurry for them; he is expecting the
Duc d'Orléans."

"Give them to me," said the Duc, "I will hurry."

On reaching the door, rather out of breath, he said to the
painter, "I have come up two steps at a time, to bring you the
trousers in which to receive me." [1]

On the other hand, when the King and Queen of Naples
came to France, just before the 1830 Revolution, he created a
disagreeable scene by refusing to give precedence to the Duke
of Salerno, eldest son of the King of Naples.

So, together, Marie Amélie, the King, and Madame
Adélaïde, discussed his marriage.

First of all, it must mean a useful alliance for France. So,
one by one, they ran through the list of possible brides. Louis
Philippe knew that his son, bearing the name of Orléans, might
not be *persona grata*, but Adélaïde brushed away all such nonsense; after all, was he not a King's son?

Without informing the prince, Adélaïde wrote to Monsieur
de Barante, French Ambassador to Russia, and asked him discreetly to discover if an alliance with one of the Grand Duchesses
would be acceptable. The answer must have been definite, as
no more was mentioned on the subject.

The Comte de Ste. Aulaire, the French Ambassador in
Vienna, was more encouraging concerning the young Archduchess Thérèse, one of the daughters of the Archduke Charles.
She was graceful, amiable, pretty, and, it was whispered, the
prospect of the future throne of France thrilled her.

Marie Amélie longed to see one of her sons allied to the
House of Austria, but Louis Philippe, more far-seeing, was
doubtful. Marie Antoinette and Marie Louise had brought a
curse with them. What would a third bride bring?

As usual, Adélaïde swamped any scruples. So, on 5th May
1836, the Duc d'Orléans, accompanied by his brother Nemours,
left for Vienna.

Nothing but praise for the princes' manners, their charm,
and good looks, reached the delighted parents. Each day the
Archduchess seemed more attracted to her proposed fiancé; the

[1] *Louis Philippe Bourgeois*, by Jules Bertaut. Editions Bernard Grasset.

Duc, in his uniforms, outshone even the handsome Austrian officers.

Then, one evening, the Duc d'Orléans spoke to the Archduke and asked him for the hand of his daughter. The Archduke, who had been expecting this request, consented. But when Prince Metternich was informed, he warned the Archduke that he would have to count with the Archduchess Sophie, who dominated the whole family, and was against an alliance with the rather shaky reputation of the Orléans family.

So, with many kind apologies, the Duc was told that the matter would be considered.

The princes, rather humiliated, had just left Vienna, when the news arrived of Alibaud's attempt on the King's life. A month later another plot was discovered: if it had been successful, the whole of the royal family would have perished.

Hearing of all these tragedies, the Archduchess Sophie put the question to her young relative whether, apart from entering the family of a usurper, she was willing to ride in coaches that were constantly riddled by the bullets of regicides.

So the Archduke Charles and the saddened Duc d'Orléans agreed to release each other from their word.

*　　　*　　　*

The Cabinets of Louis Philippe still succeeded one another with disconcerting rapidity. In September 1836, Monsieur Molé had followed Monsieur Thiers as Président du Conseil, and, as usual, the chief preoccupation of the Government was to thwart in time the innumerable plots against the Sovereign.

Switzerland had always been a refuge for political exiles, and one morning, late in 1836, as the Cabinet were taking their leave after a meeting, Monsieur Molé asked the King whether he could speak to him in private. Together they walked into a small room leading on to the terrace:

"Now, tell me what is on your mind."

With the precise turn of phrase with which Monsieur Molé always spoke, the Minister explained that Switzerland, by receiving political French refugees and allowing them to live in perfect freedom, was becoming a breeding-ground for intrigue against the King. It was desirable that France should be rid of such a menace on her frontier, but it was difficult to intervene, unless it could be proved that plots were being nurtured in Switzerland, against Louis Philippe.

The King answered: "The solution is quite simple. We have merely to arrange one."

He stopped for a moment, went over to the fireplace, and pushed a log idly with the toe of his boot.

"I think Monsieur Conseil would be our man."

Molé was silent. These underhand solutions always made him uneasy, but if the monarch suggested them, they were no longer his responsibility.

So Monsieur Conseil was sent to Switzerland. He was a dubious character, one of those creatures who can always be found in the pay of an unstable government. His mission was to organize a plot against Louis Philippe, and to arrange for it to be discovered with great noise and scandal.

A few weeks later, a dangerous conspiracy was unearthed by the police in Switzerland. The French Government was very indignant and demanded that political refugees should be expelled.

To add weight to the demand, 25,000 men mustered on the frontier. The Federal Republic, too small to withstand such intimidation, much against their principles, had to give way.

*　　　*　　　*

On 6th November 1836, the *Moniteur* published the news that Charles X had died of cholera at Goritzia, near Trieste.

It was only six years since he had made that long progress, surrounded by his Court and his Army; a King to the last. France had rejoiced at his departure; would anybody be found to mourn now?

No one stood any longer in opposition to Louis Philippe. The Duc d'Angoulême did not count; by now he was almost insane. Only the Duc de Bordeaux remained, a boy of fourteen, surrounded by a Court asleep.

For Louis Philippe it was a great shock. He sent for Cuvilleri

Fleury, and asked him to gather all details of the last moments of the late King. Then the question arose, should Court mourning be proclaimed? Charles X was a cousin. Marie Amélie insisted, Adélaïde said it was useless. The King said it was a delicate question. Finally, it was decided that, as the death of Charles X had not been officially announced to the King of the French, it would be ignored.

Privately, Louis Philippe said to Fleury:

"You know, mon cher, that outwardly I am not supposed to express my feelings. I am terribly unhappy; all the uncertainty and anguish which I suffered six years ago overwhelms me now. Did I do right?"

A few days later, the details were received. What thoughts must have passed through the King's mind as he read:

"His Majesty the King Charles X suffered much. He received the last Sacrament with the greatest faith and devotion. As the preparations were being made for the ceremony, Cardinal de Latil, who was to administer Extreme Unction, was beside him. Suddenly the King took the Prelate's hand and, looking up, said: 'Receive my thanks; I owe you a great deal. To you I owe the resignation of my life, and the calm with which I am facing death.' "

At this moment, the King may have remembered the humble young priest at Madame de Polastron's deathbed, and later, that same priest, as Cardinal, receiving the last Confession of the Duc de Berri.

"The King gave the responses to the prayers for the dying. As they ended, for a few seconds he was silent in deep meditation. Then, aloud, he prayed for France and, making the sign of the Cross, he blessed his country.

"The Bishop of Hermopolis, who was present, asked the dying man if at this supreme moment he forgave those who had done him so much harm.

" 'I forgave them many years ago. I forgive them again at this instant, with all my heart; may the Lord have mercy on them, as on myself.' "

The report ended:

"Oh, if those whom he forgave had been able to hear this exiled Monarch, victim of a terrible scourge, who was ending half a century of calamities, uttering his last words—not to curse, but to bless."

Let us leave Louis Philippe with his conscience . . .

*   *   *

"That incorrigible clown", as people then termed Louis Napoleon Bonaparte, had again made a stir. It was hardly worth the effort. He had tried to organize an uprising in the garrison at Strasbourg. People smiled. "When will he learn that he has not the slightest chance of success, either now or ever." This Louis Philippe said to Marie Amélie on 15th April 1837.

Madame Adélaïde took no notice of this episode. She was busy corresponding in great privacy with the Ambassadors accredited to the various countries, and consulting them on a possible wife for her nephew.

At last, Monsieur de Bresson, French Minister to the Court of Frederick William, King of Prussia, who had formed a strong attachment for the young Duc, announced that after a long consultation, that monarch had suggested a charming bride.

A few weeks later, the country was in a state of excitement at the news that the heir to the throne had become engaged to Princess Hélène of Mecklemburg Schwerin, young, clever, very well educated, amiable, and in fact all that could be desired . . . but a Protestant.

Poor Marie Amélie's heart almost stopped. Her very soul seemed to rise in revolt against that cold northern creed; she who had surrounded her children with the glowing faith of her Neapolitan ancestors. But, as usual, she suppressed her sighs and tears and awaited her new daughter-in-law.

It was a critical assembly which awaited the Princesse Hélène as she stepped lightly from her carriage in the grand court of the Château de Fontainebleau on 29th May 1837. It is a curious fact that none of those present were able to describe her. Was she beautiful, pretty, or not even good looking? This question was never answered.

On the last day of May, as the great clock struck half past eight in the evening, the royal procession entered the Salle Henri II for the civil marriage.

The princess looked charming in spite of her thin figure and rather colourless face. Palmyr, the renowned dressmaker, had been ordered to create a gown different from any which had been seen before. The result was a redingote of white muslin, lined with pink, a delicious bonnet of white rice-straw covered with a large marabout feather.

The young Duc looked beautiful in his brilliant uniform; perhaps he looked too beautiful, for all eyes turned towards him, and again the question arose—his wife ought to be beautiful; this princess is only dignified.

Then the bride and bridegroom, followed by the royal family, proceeded to the Chapel for the religious ceremony, which was celebrated with great magnificence but, owing to the difference of faith between the prince and his wife, much of the ritual had to be omitted.

Lastly came the Protestant ceremony, which took place in one of the great drawing-rooms. This was almost beyond Marie Amélie's endurance; her conscience crying out at the profanity of attending a "heretical rite", she lost her self-control and wept bitterly.

After their marriage, the Duc and Duchesse took up their residence in the former apartments of the Duchesse de Berri. In a few weeks, they transformed the Pavillon de Marsan into a perfect museum: one of their treasures was the writing-table at which Louis XVI had sat, day after day, battling with the anguish of despair. It was now the work-table of Egalité's grandson.

The young Duc d'Orléans was gradually changing. Was it the influence of Hélène of Mecklemburg Schwerin? He who had at one time rebelled at his father's luxurious manner of living, now found that the Court liveries were not brilliant enough, and his footmen were put into velvet coats braided with red. The Marquis de Castellane, being invited to the first sumptuous party, remarked: "The throne has risen devilishly since 1830."

The Duchesse glided easily through this setting, which suited her better than the demagogic atmosphere of the Tuileries. It seemed that gradually her influence was acting upon the Duc.

His aggressive, almost republican attitude, was fading to such an extent that, one night, after dinner at the Tuileries, he dared to upbraid his father.

"Mon père, your house is kept in a disorderly fashion."

The King was taken aback and exclaimed: "So! Nowadays, children want to teach their parents; well, talk, talk, Chartres; I will answer you."

"I wish to say this, father; you allow your A.D.C.s to go in and out of your rooms without being summoned."

"Perhaps you are right, my son."

"In my house, my A.D.C.s stay in the ante-room until I summon them: my will is law."

"I know you, Chartres! But I am a simple man."

"What I most object to is that many who have no right come to the Queen's receptions, and many who have the right do not come, for fear of mixing with that awful crowd."

"Well, have you finished?"

"Yes, Sire, I have given you my opinion."

"You think that because you have danced with a few women, you know how to hold a drawing-room: well, I tell you it is impossible for your mother's salon to be held as one would wish. Do you think that in these times the Queen of the French can send word, 'This person may come, but this other may not'?" [1]

But, despite the long argument, the young Duc in his new mood was still unconvinced.

Despite his other preoccupations, Louis Philippe as King pursued more than ever his passion for restoring the historical buildings of France. His greatest triumph was Versailles.

France owes a debt to Louis Philippe, who fought to have the palace dedicated as a museum, when the authorities proposed to turn it into an almshouse!

As he walked through the vast galleries, the palace came to life before his eyes. He recalled every detail as it had been before 1789; the Concert Room where Marie Antoinette had played the harp, while he sat gravely under the watchful eye of Madame de Genlis. The Throne Room, where his father had stood among the enemies of the King. The private apartments of the Queen, where he had sometimes penetrated with his

[1] *Louis Philippe Bourgeois*, by Jules Bertaut.

mother; above all, the Chapel where he had walked between the King and Queen to the font, he the central figure of an unforgettable scene.

But if perchance the thought came to him of restoring the palace as it had been in those days, he brushed it aside. He was the King of the people, and his museum would be a museum for the people, with guides and cords and signs saying "Do not touch".

His ideas on the restoration of Versailles were sometimes unhappy. The Queen's state bedroom, for instance, contained a beautiful chimney-piece of rare red marble, decorated with some exquisite rococo bronze work. This was removed and destroyed. So were some of the priceless tapestries and hangings from the famous silk looms of Lyons which did not fit the walls exactly. And the anecdote is well known of the day when, choosing portraits to complete the gallery of Kings and Queens of France, he found that he had two Catherine de Médicis, and no Isabeau de Bavière: he simply turned one Catherine into an Isabeau.

The King has been described as a mean man, and indeed, in small things he was careful to the point of pettiness: but in the vast building projects which were the passion of his life, large sums did not count. Out of his private fortune, Versailles swallowed twenty-three million francs, and he visited the palace some thirty times in a year to watch the progress of the work.

He loved to show his foreign guests around the halls and gardens, so that he could observe their dazzled eyes when they saw the magnificence which the King of the French could command.

At the time of the marriage of the Duc d'Orléans, the work was still far from complete, but the monarch could not resist the urge to hold the final ceremonies in those matchless rooms. So he ordered the architects to complete at all costs the state apartments, and there it was that the heir to the throne appeared for the first time in public with his newly-wedded Duchesse. The fête was sumptuous, the Duc and Duchesse enchanted the crowd of guests by their amiability, talking to all and greeting each person as if they had known them for years.

KING LOUIS PHILIPPE AND HIS SONS AT VERSAILLES

From the painting by Vernet

The palace shone with a thousand candles, the Galerie des Glaces seemed an endless vista of light. The gowns, the jewels, the uniforms, were regal, and when Louis Philippe, radiant, asked Victor Hugo's opinion, the great poet replied:

"Sire, Louis XIV wrote a beautiful book; tonight your Majesty has given it a magnificent binding."

*   *   *

On 17th May 1838, one of the great lights of Europe was extinguished: Charles Maurice de Périgord, Prince de Talley-rand, Prince de Bénévent, Bishop of Autun, died in his sumptuous mansion in the rue St. Florentin.

For thirty years he had held the formidable threads which ruled the civilized world. He was scheming like Machiavelli, witty like Voltaire, and lame as the devil. Possessing the greatest brain in Europe, he had gone through the whole gamut of scandal as priest, bishop, husband, lover, yet at the end he was grand enough to acknowledge his sins and sign an act of submission to the Pope.

A few hours after his death, the doctors came to embalm his corpse. For this, in the manner of the Egyptians, they had removed the entrails and the stomach, and the brains from the skull.

Having done this thing, and having transformed the Prince de Talleyrand into a mummy, and nailed this mummy into a bier lined with white satin, they went away, leaving on the table the brain—that brain which had thought so many things, inspired so many men, led two revolutions, duped twenty Kings, controlled the world.

When the doctors had gone, a valet entered; he saw what they had left. They had forgotten this. "What shall I do with it?"

He remembered that there was a drain in the street. He went to it, and threw the brain into that drain.[1]

[1] *Choses Vues*, by Victor Hugo.

221

24

The Emperor Comes Home

Ever since Louise had left her father's home to reign in Belgium, Marie was left alone amidst the crowds and ceremony of the Tuileries. The light-hearted princess, who loved life and received its offerings so hungrily, gradually changed. She shut herself up in her studio for hours of feverish work on the sculptures which have become renowned. Occasionally, Marie Amélie went to sit with her, but the Queen, who was not very discerning in matters of art, did not go there to admire her daughter's talent, but rather to watch her own creation—Marie herself.

The princess had become secretive and silent, as if some mystic evolution was taking place in her mind, which preoccupied her so much that she had no time for earthly things. She seemed possessed by a terrible thirst for perfection in her work, her faith, and her ideal of human love which, so far, she had not experienced.

She had begun to cough, and when Louis Philippe heard it, his heart sank; all the fear of the future gripped him. He remembered his brothers, Beaujolais, and especially Montpensier—Marie was so like him; would the same curse kill her?

The malady was as yet in its early stages; death seemed far away. Marie was twenty-four years old, and a husband must be found.

Eventually, the Duke Alexander of Würtemberg was chosen, and they were married in October 1837. Queen Victoria said of him: "He is somewhat colossal, I own, but well proportioned and good-looking, I think."

A heavy, slow-thinking German prince, hardly a match for the wraith-like Marie. Yet she devoted herself to him with all her heart, wanting to be the perfect wife, to live by him, for him, to become German like him, to break all ties with France and her family.

Marie left home coldly and without emotion, talking only of the long journey to the east, where she and her husband could be alone together, forgotten by all.

Within a few months she was back in Paris, emaciated, her face ravaged, almost unrecognizable. Horrified, her parents sent her south, but Louis Philippe knew that it was too late. Like Beaujolais, Marie was making her final pilgrimage to the sun, which would not save her.

In the last days of 1838, news arrived from Italy that Princess Marie was dying. Somebody had to be sent to her in all haste. Adélaïde offered to go, but, on her last visit to Paris, Marie had shown so plainly her dislike of her aunt, that finally it fell to Nemours to be present at her death on 7th January 1839. Her body was brought back to France and buried in the church built by the Queen at Dreux. She left a baby son just six months old. Marie Amélie found a consolation in caring for this child.

Life, for the sons of Louis Philippe, was not all marriages, balls and reviews. One by one, as they left the Collège Henri IV, they entered the Army, all except the Prince de Joinville—the eccentric member of the family—who joined the Navy, grew a thick black beard, and made a name for himself in the Mexican War of 1838.

On a visit to Brazil, he naturally asked to be received by the Emperor Pedro I. During the reception, a door opened, and in walked a dark-eyed girl, a voluptuous beauty, such as is only to be found in sun-soaked countries.

She was the Emperor's sister, the Princess Françoise. Joinville stared at her. A few days later he asked for her hand, and wrote to his parents that he intended to marry the Brazilian princess.

At once Louis Philippe summoned his Cabinet, and it was decided that an Ambassador should be sent, with full pomp and ceremony, to Don Pedro, to ask formally for his sister's hand.

While the envoy was gathering his credentials and supervising the packing of the magnificent gifts which he was to take to the fiancée from her future father-in-law, Joinville, not caring a hang for protocol, arrived in Brest, and saluted the Harbour Master with the words:

"I bring home the sailor's wife. She is attractive, don't you think?"

On the day of her arrival in Paris, the entire Court met her with all the etiquette displayed on such occasions. The reception went smoothly, everybody whispering about her appearance: she was startling, an exotic beauty, which seemed a little out of place in the humdrum Tuileries set.

Whispering turned to amazement later, when she took her place on the right of the monarch at the luncheon and, during a pause in the subdued murmur of conversation, the princess suddenly broke into song. But bewilderment reached its peak at the State banquet that evening, when chicken broth was placed before her; without more ado she turned to the official behind her chair and said:

"Take this away and bring me parrot broth."

Yet, in spite of all this, in a few weeks Louis Philippe raved about her; her bizarreries delighted him.

Nevertheless, the thought struck him, "Mon Dieu! Let us hope Aumale does not bring home a little Arab girl from Algeria!"

*   *   *

It was Charles X who, at the beginning of 1830, decided to conquer Algeria, a country of brigands and pirates who were a constant menace to shipping in the Mediterranean.

A fleet sailed in June 1830, on the very evening of Louis Philippe's Neapolitan Ball, and the town of Algiers was taken just three weeks before the July Revolution.

The conquest of the country continued during Louis Philippe's reign. The King himself hardly cared about Algeria, but his sons, bored with military displays at home, insisted on taking part in the fighting.

The war was different from anything the French had experienced before. It was a war of ambush, pursuit through treacherous gorges and ravines; food was scarce, the language unknown, and the Arabs fought a war to the death against the infidel French.

Gradually, the country was occupied, and General Bugeaud,

who commanded the troops, wrote praising the courage of the
Duc d'Aumale.

* * *

Was it the fortune which surrounded the Duc d'Aumale
which seemed to cast a halo around him? Or was it really his
outstanding personality? In the Army, as well as in every grade
of society, he stood out as the most gallant and attractive young
man in the capital. His love affairs became legendary. All the
demi-mondaines, many of whom he had not even heard of,
posed as his mistress.

Roqueplan the writer stated that one was always greeted by
these ladies with whispers such as, "Quick, get out, the Prince
is here." Or, "If you stay, I am lost; this is *his* hour."

One evening, at a reception given by Madame Adélaïde,
Aumale perceived for the first time a young actress, Alice Ozy,
then taking a small part in a play called "Le Chevalier du
Guet", and from that moment her fortune was made. Soon, the
liaison became well-known. He took her everywhere. When he
did not wish to be seen with her, she used to dress as a man and
pass for Montpensier.

But this passion ended like many others. Alice was tempted
by a banker, Pierre Gaux, who, as a first offering, gave her a
carriage and pair worth twenty thousand francs. Who could
compete with such a Nabob?

The Duc wrote in farewell, "I love you more, since you love
me no more." Later, when he married, she returned all his
letters. In exchange, he sent her a thousand francs. She was profoundly hurt, and refused them saying, "I am not hungry; I
should have preferred a tiny souvenir of the time when I
worked for love."

But when Alice deserted him, it seemed the tragedy of his
life. He could hardly bear Paris. He must go away.

He had been in Algeria, and the barren land, with its blinding contrasts of sun and shadow, gleaming white buildings,
black cypress trees, the rough men in their flowing robes, and
the adventure of the unknown, had stirred him profoundly.

So he returned and plunged into that murderous war against
Abd-el-Kader, the fanatic Emir of Oran. Algeria became the

passion of his life; even his marriage could not overcome the lure of that fascinating country.

When eventually Marshal Bugeaud, the Commander-in-Chief, constantly thwarted in his work by the Government, and embittered, resigned his post, the Duc d'Aumale succeeded him as Governor of Algeria. A few months later, Abd-el-Kader made his submission, and in 1847 Algeria belonged to France.

* * *

Thiers had become Ministre du Conseil for the time being: from now on the Ministry resembled a game, three men disputing the power—Guizot, Molé and Thiers. When one was out, the other was in.

As threats and violence, directed against the King, increased daily, and people were beginning to accept them as a matter of course, Thiers felt that something out of the ordinary must be launched to revive the interest in the King's person. He found this, curiously enough, in reviving the memory of Napoleon, a flame always ready to be fanned.

He had favoured the restoration of Napoleon on the Colonne Vendôme in 1833, had completed the Arc de Triomphe in 1836, and it was known that he was gathering material for his famous *History of the Empire*. Now it was he who advised Louis Philippe to bring back the remains of Napoleon to France.

So, in May 1840, the King informed his Ministers that, with the British Government's consent, he was sending his son, the Prince de Joinville, to St. Helena to have the great honour of accompanying the remains of the Emperor back to France.

On 15th December 1840, Paris was awakened at six o'clock in the morning by the drums beating to arms. It was cold, the gutters were frozen, a slight mist encircled the city.

Victor Hugo describes the scene so beautifully: "On sent que Paris tout entier s'est versé d'un seul côté de la ville, comme un liquide dans un vase qui penche." [1]

On approaching the Invalides, conflicting emotions overwhelmed each person—reverence, sadness, and, at the same time, intense popular rejoicing. "He is coming back!"

[1] "It seems as if Paris in its entirety has flowed to one side of the city, like liquid in a leaning vase."

Victor Hugo wrote:

"Three men, poor, almost in rags—three of the many who are cold and hungry all the winter through—walk before me full of joy; one keeps dancing and jumping, doing all kinds of antics, and crying out '*Vive l'Empereur*'. The snow began to fall; it seemed as though God himself wanted to lay a shroud to receive the hero."

Immense tribunes were erected, from the quayside to the entrance to the Invalides. The cold seemed to increase. As the people sat there, they stamped their feet in unison, trying to bring some warmth to their frozen bodies.

On each side of the broad avenue stood heroic marble statues; they looked so white under the rays of the pale sun. Facing the great central dome, a gigantic statue in bronze of the Emperor Napoleon seemed to dominate the scene; between the statues were gilt staves upon which were torches all ready to be lighted.

Behind the statues, the tribunes and the crowd, in front of them, the Garde Nationale; over all, above the tribunes, high masts; from each mast, sixty oriflames waved in the breeze.

All around, guns pointed their muzzles to the sky and, dominating the scene, the dome of the Invalides, almost hidden in black draperies, strewn with silver stars and crêpe from which metallic rays seemed to pierce the cold white mist; the whole scene melancholy yet infinitely imposing.

At noon, all eyes turned to the corner of the Quai d'Orsay, from which the procession would emerge. Suddenly, the Gardes Nationaux sprang to attention, and workmen climbed long ladders to light the torches.

Half an hour later, a salvo of artillery broke the silence; the procession approached.

The hum of the crowd was silenced; then the steady tramp of feet. First a double file of Grenadiers on horseback. That was the beginning.

At that moment, the sun broke through the clouds and shone in all its splendour. The sun of Austerlitz.

Then came the Garde Municipale with their brass helmets, followed by Lancers, their tricolor pennants waving high above their heads; then fanfares and drums, Marshals, Generals, artillery, infantry, Académie Militaire, and the Garde Nationale on horseback—row upon row, the army passed by.

The interest deepened; in a carriage came the chaplain of the ship *La Belle Poule* who had kept vigil by the dead Emperor on the long voyage from St. Helena.

Then the State coach, covered with black velvet, its four horses almost hidden by black velvet and silver harness, conveying the Commission from St. Helena.

Then a pause: from every quarter of the horizon, guns boomed forth in salute; there was a throbbing of muffled drums. The Emperor's funeral coach appeared—a colossal gold catafalque surmounted the remains of Napoleon I. Even the wheels seemed made of gold. It was a pyramid of gold under a purple pall, strewn with Imperial Bees, the Eagles, the Imperial Crown, Sword and Sceptre. As it passed, the air was filled with suppressed exclamations. It seemed to carry on its way the acclamation of the entire nation.

A trophy of captured ensigns and banners stood on the front of the chariot, which sixteen magnificent horses drew with difficulty as they trod the street proudly, covered with huge white feathers down to their flanks, and beneath these, draped from head to hoof in cloth of gold, only their eyes uncovered.

On foot, pacing slowly beside the catafalque, were the Generals of the Empire, all wearing the Grand Cordon of the Légion d'Honneur.

At length, Napoleon reached his last resting-place. The ceremony within the Invalides was simple: the Prince de Joinville, who had accompanied the coffin from St. Helena, stood before the King:

"Sire! I present to you the body of the Emperor Napoleon."

"I receive him in the name of France."

Then, turning to General Bertrand, the King said:

"General! Lay on the coffin the glorious sword of the Emperor."

And to General Gourgand:

"General! Lay on the coffin the Emperor's hat."

The requiem of Mozart was perhaps a little too thin; fine music, but the sounds could not reach the heights of Napoleon's glory.

So they laid him to rest, the man whom all had feared, and now they feared no more.

The ceremony over, Louis Philippe returned to the Tuileries, and exchanged the heavy gold-braided uniform for a frock-coat and trousers. How much more at home he felt in these clothes!

Yet he was pleased. It had been a bold gesture, to risk re-viving the cult of Napoleon; and it had passed off quite successfully. The people were moved, and Europe could see that the King of the French was truly secure on his throne. Palmerston had laughed and said, "This is truly a French idea." By now, the British Minister must know that, French or not, it had been a brilliant spectacle.

A few weeks later, when the novelty had passed and the crowds had forsaken the dead Emperor for some new excitement, a small ugly man was seen to enter the Invalides, alone, hat in hand. A few guards on duty near the catafalque did not recognize him. He walked slowly round the tomb, the collar of his coat turned up; the cold was bitter in the marble crypt, the candlelight made grotesque caricatures of his shadow on the walls as he walked slowly round and round, deep in thought.

This little man was Monsieur Thiers, come to steep himself in the atmosphere of his hero. He had all the time in the world now to meditate on Napoleon; once again, the game of the Ministries had been played, and he was forced out and Monsieur Guizot was in.

Guizot was as beautiful as Thiers was ugly; but the difference went deeper than that. The voice of Thiers—rich, melodious and mellow—sounded above all others in the drawing-rooms; but in the tribune he seemed to hesitate; he mumbled and lost all authority.

Guizot's voice was monotonous and lifeless, until he addressed the deputies, when it became transformed, eloquent and re-sounding. Rachel, the great actress, said of him, "I long to act a tragedy with this man."

Guizot had been Ambassador at the Court of St. James's. When he returned from England to take over his new post, Thiers met him: "It is your turn: there are only two men in this country; you and I. I am the minister of Revolution; you are the minister of Conservation. We cannot walk together, but we can live together. I will not place any obstacle in your path."

Guizot, who needed supporters, feigned to believe him.

25

The Death of the Duc d'Orléans

"Well, chère Majestée, as you wish it absolutely, I will come tomorrow morning."

These words, spoken on 12th July 1842, were to resound in the ears of Marie Amélie to the hour of her death.

The royal family were spending a few days in their favourite retreat, the Château de Neuilly. That evening was perhaps the most sultry of an extraordinarily hot summer. As the Duc d'Orléans walked with his mother in the deliciously scented garden, he told her that, as he proposed to leave the next afternoon for the Camp at St. Omer, he had to receive a number of people in Paris the next morning, so he would take leave of her that night.

The Duchesse d'Orléans was taking the waters at Plombières, so after St. Omer he would rejoin his wife and then, together with their second son Chartres,[1] they would return to the Tuileries.

But Marie Amélie, selfish in her love for her children, especially for this, her eldest son, insisted that he should hurry through the audiences the next morning, and come back for luncheon to Neuilly. She could not bear to say goodbye that night. It was then that he promised to come in those fateful words.

The next morning, the 13th, the heat was greater than ever. The Duc, anxious to please his mother, hurried through his engagements, and gave orders for a carriage, with fast horses, to be ready just before noon.

Most of the horses had been sent away—some to the camp for his own use, others to Plombières for the Duchesse, and to Eu for the service of their elder son, the Comte de Paris.

[1] The Duc d'Orléans had two sons, the Comte de Paris born in 1838, and the Duc de Chartres born in 1840.

231

Monsieur de Cambès, his equerry, chose a low light phaeton with four wheels, and two young horses were harnessed. The head groom protested that they were not yet fully trained for the road, but Monsieur de Cambès told him that he was a fool, and the carriage, with its highly nervous team, was driven into the courtyard of the Tuileries.

The Duc did not like the look of the equipage. He looked at his watch, there was no time to change horses; he jumped in and off they fled to Neuilly.

The prince sat alone; behind him, on the dickey seat, a tiny groom, a "tiger," a mere child. All went well until the barrière de l'Etoile, when the horses became restive. At the Porte Maillot, the postilion took the wrong road and the Duc rose to give an order; at least, that is what the "tiger" said; he himself felt frightened and managed to slip down.

The horses went faster and faster. Had that been the Duc's order? No one ever knew. The little groom saw the Duc flung from the vehicle and lying unconscious on the pavement of the Avenue de la Grande Armée, a municipal guard bending over him.

The postilion at last mastered his horses and, seeing the carriage empty, turned back. He arrived just in time to witness the unfortunate prince being carried into a half-shop and half-shed kept by a very humble grocer.

It consisted of a stall by the roadside, and a tiny square room with a brick floor. From it, a low door led into a dark hole with no windows, only an ill-fitting board giving on to a heap of dung. It was in this room, if it can be called such, that the heir to the throne was laid, on a mouse-eaten straw mattress with a dilapidated armchair overturned to support its back. A broken-down stove stood quite close; on the wall were shelves on which lay greasy pots and pans; an ancient gun stood in the corner. Somebody, some time, had pinned on the wall two pictures, worth two sous, one representing Napoleon, the other Louis Philippe; both fly-stained. The whole place was smelly, gruesome.

A message reached Neuilly that the Duc had fallen and was slightly hurt. Marie Amélie, in her anxiety, started off on foot towards Paris, but was soon overtaken by the King with a carriage.

As they drew up outside the miserable building, the King rushed in, then immediately returned to reassure her; but when Marie Amélie penetrated into that awful hovel and saw her son, she had no illusions.

Several doctors were working, goblets had been borrowed from a tavern, and a blunt razor, with which they bled him. His limbs moved convulsively. The heat was excessive. Gradually, the rest of the family arrived, all crowding in, and even the little air which filtered through was stifled by the crowds massed on the pavement outside.

Hours passed, and the agony increased. The Curé of Neuilly arrived and, before the whole assistance, administered the last Sacrament. The Queen, in a loud voice, was imploring God that her son might have a moment's consciousness, in which to adore and crave mercy from his Redeemer. It had been her greatest sorrow that her son's faith was not as strong as she had wished.

The King stood near, tears pouring down his face, occasionally giving a gasp of despair. Six hours dragged by. The doctors, the Curé, could do nothing but wait for the inexorable visitor who would soon appear.

Suddenly, the Queen rose, pressed her lips on those of her son, and his last breath passed into her soul. She uttered a scream, then, once more bending over her beloved child, cried:

"My God! Forgive him his sins."

*   *   *

A courier was sent to the Duchesse d'Orléans at Plombières reporting "a slight indisposition"; nevertheless, she left at once and speeded through the night towards Paris. Her coach stopped for a relay of horses, and she was met by Dr. Chomel; his presence was enough; she knew he would never have left her husband if he was alive. So she learnt the awful tragedy.

The Duc de Nemours, always a close companion of his brother, was distracted. Sorrow, distress and horror were so universal that even the Opposition parties allowed sympathy to overcome their passions.

For Marie Amélie it was almost a death blow. The body of

233

the Duc was laid in the Chapel at Neuilly, and for eighteen days the King and Queen kept watch in turn beside the coffin.

At last, the state of Marie Amélie bordered on madness; it was realized that the body must be taken away from her. So the Ministers decided that the Duc would lie in state for two days at Nôtre Dame. Anything to break the insane grief. When the day arrived for the numerous officials to remove the body to the Cathedral, Louis Philippe took hold of the casket in which the heart of the young Duc was encased, and Marie Amélie clung to the coffin; force had to be used to drag them away.

Crowds streamed past in homage day and night; then, at last, the body of the Duc was laid to rest in the crypt at Dreux.

The King had affairs of state to divert his thoughts, but Marie Amélie sank deeper in despair. She kept repeating:

"Chère Majestée, as you wish it absolutely, I will come tomorrow morning."

She felt that her selfish love had destroyed him. For weeks this went on; everything was done to interest her in other things, but in vain.

One day, she went as usual to the crypt at Dreux with Madame Adélaïde. She prostrated herself on the marble steps before the coffin. Madame Adélaïde waited. The Queen never moved. The princess, worried by her stillness, approached and listened: she was breathing very calmly, but still she lay prostrate. At length she arose with a smile, and said, "Let us go." They left the church, Marie Amélie talking quite naturally. From that moment, she never alluded to her sorrow, but mentioned her son as if she had never mourned so bitterly.

Had a spiritual miracle taken place that morning? Perhaps the Queen had been vouchsafed an assurance that the sins of her son had been forgiven?

*   *   *

The Duchesse d'Orléans had never been a part of the family. She stood aside like a stranger. She may have felt the unspoken disapproval of the Queen, who had once said: "Hélène has not the spirit of the family."

Sc. Chapu

THE TOMB OF THE DUC AND DUCHESSE D'ORLÉANS AT DREUX

The Duchesse, being a Protestant, could not be buried in the Catholic church, so a small adjacent chapel was built, with an aperture to allow her hand to pass through

The Duchesse, overhearing, had replied: "Madame, I have the spirit of *my* family."

Her husband and small sons were her whole life; for the others she did not care.

The entire family were astonished, and rather hurt, that on hearing the dreadful news she had only fainted, and not succumbed, immediately. Hélène d'Orléans had a strong character, and at once she realized that she must bear up and protect her sons, as she naturally expected to be Regent for the Comte de Paris in the event of the King's death.

Yet at once, intrigues started over the future Regency. Thiers, head of the Opposition, asked to be received by the King.

On entering the study, the monarch said:

"Mon ami, I rely on your discretion not to divulge our conversation."

Guizot, who was in power, was not to know of the interview.

Louis Philippe, crying bitterly, thanked Thiers for his sympathy on the death of his heir. When he had mastered his emotion, he said:

"Well, what are you, as head of the Opposition, going to do? I tell you frankly, I do not want Hélène to be nominated as future Regent."

"Sire, I intend to put forward the name of the Duc de Nemours."

"That is what I wish," answered the King. "I know that Nemours is disliked, he has no charm, and does not even try to make himself popular; but he is a good young man, brave, and above all a Frenchman. Hélène is German, a woman, and she is so elusive that I am never quite certain of her. I do not ask you in what way you will act, only act. Nemours must be the future Regent, and the Duchesse d'Orléans only the mother of the future King."

It was not an easy task that Monsieur Thiers undertook. Much of the popularity of the late Duc had been transferred to the Duchesse in her hour of grief. As she drove in her crêpe-covered carriage, her small boys by her side, the heart of the people went out to her. They uncovered their heads and a murmur of sympathy reached the ears of the Duchesse as she acknowledged their homage, and the little Comte de Paris bowed and waved his hand. It never crossed her mind that her future Regency should even be questioned.

Then the testament of the Duc was read; in it he requested the King to entrust to the Duchesse the education of his sons. In her name, he gave solemn assurance that they would be brought up in the most orthodox principles of the Catholic Church; but he pronounced himself to be strongly opposed to any woman being appointed Regent, saying, "The Head of the French Nation should always be ready to mount his horse within a quarter of an hour."

The Duchesse d'Orléans was stunned, but bent her head in acquiescence. From this moment she withdrew into the Pavillon de Marsan and held herself more than ever aloof from her husband's family.

In her hours of loneliness, did she ever remember that other Duchesse who had lived and mourned in those very rooms? The Duchesse de Berri. Both had expected to become Queen of France. Both were left broken and alone.

The Duchesse de Berri had a lighter nature and in time she forgot her sorrow in the gaiety and excitement of life. Hélène d'Orléans never did; she lived for her children, she felt that she alone could guide the Comte de Paris and teach him to be a King. Nemours was a good creature, but his character was as yet unformed. He was loathed by the people, who thought him haughty, and that he was ever trying to hide behind another's back. Yet Louis Philippe had denied her authority, and Nemours had been appointed by the Chamber to instruct her son how to become a people's King.

The one person who had probed the true character of the Duchesse was Marie Amélie, her mother-in-law. She had never quite trusted this seemingly quiet, disinterested nature, and had said, "Hélène is much deeper than she allows anybody to think. She is unconsciously ambitious, and will go far to get what she wants."

The little Comte de Paris, the centre of all this, cared not at all. He played with his cousin, Prince Philippe of Würtemberg, son of Princesse Marie. One day Philippe ran to the Queen crying:

"Isn't it true, Grandmamma, that Paris has no Papa and I have no Mama?"

Thus reopening a wound which never healed.

* * *

Château d'Eu. 4th September 1843

Queen Victoria to the King of the Belgians:

My dearest Uncle,

I write to you from this dear place, where we are in the midst of this admirable and truly amiable family, and where we feel quite at home and as if we were one of them. Our reception by the dear King and Queen has been most kind; and by the people, really gratifying. Everything is very different to England, particularly the population. I am highly interested and amused.

Little Chica (Joinville's wife) is a charming, sprightly, lively creature, with immense brown eyes.[1]

So Louis Philippe had realized his dream; the Queen of England was sleeping under his roof. It had been a difficult and long task to achieve this great triumph.

But Queen Victoria felt that her visit to the French King would bring about an unofficial alliance between the two countries. Besides, in her heart, she was young; she had never been to this bewitching country, and to be somewhere else than at Windsor would be wonderful!

Lord Melbourne had nothing against the visit, but he warned the Queen that no political agreement should be made.

When Louis Philippe was informed that his invitation had been accepted, he became almost crazy with excitement. Queen Victoria proposed Eu as the rendezvous, Paris being too official and, at the moment, too unsafe.

The Château d'Eu was comfortable, but of course nothing like the Tuileries, and the King was anxious to make everything resplendent for his royal visitors.

For weeks the whole place was bustle and fuss; furniture

---

[1] *The Letters of Queen Victoria*, published by John Murray.

from the royal "garde-meubles" arrived in huge vans; priceless carpets were laid down; pictures, chairs, writing-tables, porcelain, all that had been used by the Sovereigns of France was brought forth: Marie Amélie flew about, Adélaïde gave orders, the sons and daughters-in-law scarcely saw each other, as the latter were kept busy mending delicate lace or embroidery. In fact, the whole place was pandemonium.

The day before the arrival, as the entire family stood in admiration, Marie Amélie alone felt that one thing was lacking —the easy manner of receiving a Queen.

On 2nd September 1843, the Queen of England stepped ashore at Tréport amidst scenes of extraordinary enthusiasm. She embraced the royal family, emotion overflowed; the crowd looking on worked themselves into such a state of hysteria that they nearly all wept.

They found the Queen "adorable" but small, and rather red in complexion; not pretty, yet very gracious and dignified. In contrast, Prince Albert was declared to be coldly polite, insipidly good-looking, lifeless, listless and bored.

The Queen, who had never been on the Continent before, was in a wild state of excitement, exclaiming over and over again her favourite phrase, "the dear King! the dear Queen!"

A grand entertainment in the Banqueting Hall, a *fête champêtre*, a review—Louis Philippe had done it all magnificently.

It was during this visit that Winterhalter was commanded to make a picture of the whole party: he painted the beautiful group which is reproduced in this book by gracious permission of Her Majesty Queen Elizabeth the Queen Mother.

There is one episode of the visit which delighted the French people.

Whilst Louis Philippe and Victoria were walking in the gardens of the château, they came to a wall ablaze with golden peaches. The Queen stopped: "How beautiful they are!"

At once, the King picked one and offered it to his companion. She, rather abashed, wondered how to peel it. The King drew a knife out of his pocket, saying:

"When one has been, like me, a poor devil, reduced to living on forty sous a day, one keeps a knife in one's pocket; I could

THE ROYAL CIRCLE AT THE CHÂTEAU D'EU

From the painting by Winterhalter at Kensington Palace. By gracious permission of
Her Majesty Queen Elizabeth, the Queen Mother

Standing: Prince de Salerne, Louis Philippe, Prince de Joinville, Prince Albert, Prince Auguste Louis de Saxe-Coburg-Gotha.
*Seated : Duchesse d'Orléans, Princesse de Salerne, Duchesse d'Aumale or Princesse de Joinville, Mme Adélaïde, Queen Victoria, Queen
Marie Amélie, Princesse Clémentine.*
*Children: Duc de Chartres, Comte de Paris, Comte d'Eu, Duc d'Alençon, Prince Auguste de Saxe-Coburg, Prince Philippe de Wurtemberg,
Prince Philippe de Saxe Coburg.*

[*These names are as given by King Ferdinand of Bulgaria—son of Princesse Clémentine—to Queen Amélie of Portugal*]

have lost the habit many years ago, but I preferred not to; one never knows what may happen." [1]

The King often spoke thus; he loved to appeal to people's pity.

The Queen's eyes filled with tears. She took his hand and said: "You must forget the past and rejoice in the present."

As he returned the delicious fruit to her Majesty, she greedily bit into it. He took out his lace handkerchief and held it under her chin. The Queen said:

"It is many years since I ate a peach in this manner."

On the 7th the Queen and Prince Consort sailed for England, Victoria enthusiastic and enchanted with France and everything French; Prince Albert wondering if the visit had been wise. Would the British people think that their Queen had lost prestige by dancing and mixing with these frivolous foreigners?

Yet Victoria, twelve years later, when staying at St. Cloud with the Emperor Napoleon III and the Empress Eugénie, wrote to her uncle, King Leopold of the Belgians:

"Everything is beautifully staged at Court. I must say we are both much struck with the difference between this and the poor dear King's time, when the noise, confusion and bustle were very great."

*   *   *

Louis Philippe was bitterly disappointed, after all his wonderful display, that he had not received the Garter in return; everything else had been perfect. The Queen had invited the Duc and Duchesse de Nemours to visit her in England before the end of the year, and she had written to the King of the Belgians:

"You must encourage the dear King and Queen to send over some of the dear family to us; ils seront reçus à bras ouverts." [2]

It was at this moment that a most mortifying thing happened. The Duc de Bordeaux, by then better known as the Comte de Chambord, now twenty-three years old, arrived in England, took a house in Belgrave Square, and issued a proclamation commanding his faithful supporters in France to pay their homage, in London, to him, Henri V, their lawful King.

[1] *Louis Philippe Bourgeois*, by Jules Bertaut.
[2] 17th October 1843

239

Chateaubriand, the famous author, was to lead the delegation.

At the Tuileries, the news provoked an uproar. Madame Adélaïde collapsed, but Louis Philippe, after calling on Heaven to witness his plight, suddenly thought of his son-in-law, King Leopold, the only person who could bring his influence to bear on his niece Queen Victoria. So he wrote to him:

"I hear with anxiety that the Duc de Bordeaux intends going to London. His intention is to proclaim himself King. It is of no great importance unless her Majesty the Queen should receive him, and so acknowledge his pretentions. Please do all that is in your power to prevent such an insult to me."

His message was understood. Queen Victoria had no wish to hurt the good King who had received her so graciously at Eu, and she decided that she would ignore the presence of the Duc in England.

She could ignore him, but she could not help hearing of what was taking place in Belgrave Square where, on 30th November, the rightful King of France, wearing the magnificent uniform of Lieutenant-General, across his chest the blue cordon of the Ordre du St. Esprit, and a profusion of foreign decorations, was acclaimed by the ancient France; and their cries of "*Vive Henri V*" re-echoed far beyond the leafy quietude of Belgrave Square.

Queen Victoria herself was deeply annoyed by this manifestation in the heart of her own city of London. Her sympathies were, for the moment, at least, firmly with the Orléans King, and it was most tactless of "this poor stupid boy", as she called Bordeaux, to court this ludicrous publicity, without even seeking her permission.

Another complication arose when, in March 1844, a certain Mr. Pritchard turned up in London, fuming against the French authorities because a French admiral had first imprisoned, and then expelled him from Tahiti, where for some twenty years he had been established as a Protestant missionary, British Consul, and anti-French firebrand.

Righteous opinion all over Great Britain seethed in sympathy with the victim, and French opinion crackled back. For a time, all the vicars of England, and all the retired admirals of France, clamoured for war. But after a few months the incident was forgotten, as quickly as it had flared up. It was too much trouble to go to war for Mr. Pritchard.

So, with clear skies once more, Louis Philippe crossed the Channel to visit the Queen at Windsor—the first French King to pay an official visit to the Sovereign of Great Britain.

On 5th October 1844, the Queen of the Belgians wrote to Queen Victoria:

> I have not much to say about my father's lodging habits and likings; my father is one of the beings most easy to please and satisfy. His eventful life has accustomed him to every-thing, and makes any arrangements acceptable to him.
>
> There is only one thing which he cannot easily do, it is to be ready very early.
>
> He means, notwithstanding, to try to come down to your breakfast; but you must insist upon his not doing so; it would disturb him in all his habits, and be bad for him, as he would certainly eat—a thing he is not used to do in the morning. He generally takes hardly what can be called a breakfast, and eats only twice a day. It would also be much better for him if he only appeared to luncheon and dinner.
>
> You must order for him bowls of chicken broth; it is the only thing he takes between his meals. He must be watched, that he should not catch cold, as he is imprudent.
>
> Now, about his room; a hard bed and a large table for his papers; he generally sleeps on a horsehair mattress with a plank of wood under it.[1]

Of all these recommendations, the bed question alone must have sent the Master of the Household off his head.

Excitement and curiosity grew as the day of the royal visit drew near, and on 8th October 1844, enthusiasm knew no bounds.

Prince Albert met Louis Philippe and the Duc de Mont-pensier at Portsmouth. The contrast between the bonhomie and exuberance of the King of the French, and the self-discipline of the Prince Consort, was noticed by all.

The King made a movement to embrace his "cher cousin",

[1] *The Letters of Queen Victoria.*

241

but the "cher cousin", always conscious of the correct gesture, drew back very slightly and, with a stiff bend of the body, shook hands. The King did not seem to perceive this; waving and smiling broadly, he delighted the crowd, who cheered loudly. The Duc de Montpensier, who walked behind, laughed outright in his youthful amusement.

At two o'clock the party arrived at Windsor. Queen Victoria's welcome almost smothered them. "The dear charming boy," she kept repeating as she looked at Montpensier; then, turning to her small son Bertie, "I hope you will grow up like him." From that moment, it appeared that "Bertie has immediately taken a passion for Montpensier."

Everybody was enchanted. The Queen wrote to her Uncle Leopold:

> The dear King's visit went off to perfection; I deeply regret its being passed.
>
> He was delighted, and was most enthusiastically and affectionately received whenever he showed himself.
>
> What an extraordinary man the King is! What a wonderful memory, how lively, how sagacious! He spoke openly to us all, and is determined that our affairs should go well.
>
> He wishes Tahiti, "au fond de la mer". The King praised my dearest Albert most highly and fully appreciated his great qualities and talents; and what gratifies me so *much*, treats him as his equal, calling him "mon frère", and saying to me that my husband was the same as me—which it is, and "Le Prince Albert, c'est pour moi Le Roi!" The King is very sad to go, but he is determined, he says, to see me every year.[1]

During this visit, he drove one morning to see a house which meant little to him at the time—Claremont, near Esher, once the home of the Princesse Charlotte and Prince Leopold of Saxe-Coburg. In four years' time it was to be his home, when, having lost the kingdom which had never been his by right, he would end his stormy life in its quiet seclusion.

But this lay hidden in the future. He was now a Knight of the Garter, and felt that at last he ranked as an equal amongst the Sovereigns of Europe.

[1] *The Letters of Queen Victoria.*

26

A Queen for Auction

Marie Amélie had at last managed to secure for one of her sons a member of her own family. The Duc d'Aumale became engaged to the Princess Caroline of Naples, daughter of the Duke of Salerno, Marie Amélie's favourite brother. She was pretty, very small, well proportioned, with finely cut features and a shapely head. The thing which marred her perfect beauty were two teeth which had been allowed to overlap.

For Louis Philippe, it was a triumph: more than once, he had offered his children in marriage to the House of Naples, and every time they had been refused.

He confided to Guizot: "At last the Sicilian dynasty have agreed to allow one of my children to enter their precious family.

"After all, who the devil do they think they are? I am just as well, if not better born than they—but there you are, they all hate me. They liked their sleepy old Bourbons because they did not fear them. But they cannot fathom me; if I disappeared, and France with me, nothing could please them more."

Adélaïde had had sleepless nights, waiting for the consent of Salerno; when it arrived, instead of taking a breathing space, she started at once on the one remaining prince, Montpensier. Her success in Naples encouraged her to try for still higher game—Queen Isabella of Spain.

Isabella II, Queen of Spain in her own right, was fifteen years old in 1845, and it had become necessary to find her a husband.

She was not unlike her cousin, the Duchesse de Berri; she had the same courageous *panache*, and the same sensuality and love of amusement.

When the marriage question came to the fore, the British Government immediately put forward the name of Prince

243

Leopold of Saxe-Coburg, but Louis Philippe could not accept this; there were enough Coburgs already, in England, Belgium and Portugal. He argued that the Spanish throne must be occupied by a Bourbon, as it had been for two centuries, and, very cautiously, he let fall a hint for Montpensier.

Britain did not deign to listen.

So Louis Philippe, unabashed, started on the Infanta Luisa, sister of Isabella and heir-presumptive to the throne, as a future wife for Montpensier.

Now, it was as though Isabella went up for sale by auction. The Duke of Cadiz, cousin of the Queen, offered to pay eight million francs to some Paris bankers if Louis Philippe would benevolently press his name forward as a possible husband. Knowing that the "gratitude" of Cadiz would be substantially expressed, Louis Philippe became his champion.

The Duke of Cadiz was not an engaging personality. He was a degenerate creature with mincing manners, sexless, affected, a dancing puppet.

His family called him "Paquita".

After much argument, Guizot and Lord Aberdeen settled the problem. Queen Isabella would marry the Duke of Cadiz, and the Duc de Montpensier would marry the Infanta, but only after the Queen had borne an heir to the throne of Spain.

Then three things happened. Lord Palmerston returned to the Foreign Office, and, breaking the arrangement entered into by Lord Aberdeen, instructed the British Ambassador in Madrid to press on the Coburg suit at once; but Guizot was quicker: he sent orders to the French Ambassador to arrange without delay the double marriage of the two sisters to the two Dukes, of Cadiz and Montpensier respectively.

At that moment, Queen Isabella declared to the astonished diplomats that she disliked and despised Paquita, and would have none of him. This was a complication which nobody had anticipated, and from this moment, Queen Isabella was subjected to a whole battery of pleading, reasoning and threatening. Every hour of every day the cruel persecution continued. Paquita figured perpetually in the foreground. Church and Ministry had joined forces—and yet nothing could bend the will of the fifteen-year-old Queen.

But a strange influence was at work in the depths of that shadowy palace. The world outside had never heard of Sister Patrocinio, a nun who bore the stigmata of the Crucifixion. Was she a saint, or was she an intriguer? Her influence prevailed, and Isabella married Cadiz. On the same day, the Duc de Montpensier became the husband of the Infanta Luisa.

Then Lord Palmerston's fury broke forth. His rage at being outwitted by that "unscrupulous liar Guizot" was unbounded. As for Louis Philippe, and the Bourbons in general—his contempt for them knew no bounds. He sent secret instructions to Lord Normanby, British Ambassador in Paris, that, while he was to avoid becoming involved in riots, he could give surreptitious support to any intrigues against the Government of Monsieur Guizot.

Queen Victoria lamented that her good friend Louis Philippe had proved unreliable, and had not hesitated to break his formal promise to her. In her heart she felt that now all relations with the French King must be at an end. Of course, she was outraged; but what must have hurt her most was that she could not pay a visit to that heavenly Paris, which she so longed to see.

The three letters which follow are, the letter which the Queen wrote to her uncle on the subject of the marriage, the apologetic and hypocritical letter of Marie Amélie announcing Montpensier's marriage, and Queen Victoria's reply.

Queen Victoria to the King of the Belgians. On board the *Victoria and Albert*, Falmouth Harbour.

7th September 1846

My Dearest Uncle,
   . . . The settlement of the Queen of Spain's marriage, coupled *with Monpensier's* is *infamous*, and we *must* remonstrate. Guizot has had the barefacedness to say to Lord Normanby, that, though originally they said that Montpensier should *only* marry the Infanta *when* the Queen was married and *had children*, that Leopold of Coburg being named as a candidate has changed all, and that they must settle it now! This is *too* bad, for we were so honest as *almost to prevent* Leo's marriage.
   . . . The King should know that *we* are extremely indignant,

and that this conduct is *not* the way to keep up the *entente* which *he* wishes!!

The Queen of the French to Queen Victoria.

Neuilly, 8th September 1846

Madame,

Trusting in the precious friendship of which Your Majesty has given us so many proofs, and in the kind interest which you have always manifested towards our children, I hasten to announce to you the conclusion of the marriage between our son Montpensier and the Infanta Luisa Fernanda. This family event fills us with joy, because we hope it will ensure the happiness of our darling son, and that we shall find in the Infanta another daughter as good and as amiable as her elders, who will add to the happiness of our home, the only true joy in this world, which you, Madame, appreciate so well.

I request in advance your friendship for our new child, confident that she will share all our sentiments of devotion and affection for you, for Prince Albert, and for all your dear family.

I am, Madame, Your Majesty's most devoted sister and friend,

MARIE AMÉLIE

Queen Victoria to the Queen of the French.

Osborne, 10th September 1846

Madame,

I have just received Your Majesty's letter of the 8th of this month, and I hasten to thank you for it.

You will perhaps remember what took place at Eu between the King and myself; you know, Madame, the importance which I have always attached to the maintenance of our Cordial Understanding, and the zeal with which I have worked for it; you have learned, I have no doubt, that we refused to arrange the marriage between the Queen of Spain and our cousin Leopold, with the only aim of not drawing away from a line of conduct agreeable to your King, although we did not consider this line as the best.

You can therefore understand that the sudden announcement of this *double marriage* could only cause us surprise, and a deep regret.

I beg your forgiveness to speak of politics at this moment, but I like to tell myself that I have always been *sincere* with you.

Requesting you to present my compliments to the King, I am, Madame, your Majesty's most devoted sister and friend,

VICTORIA R.[1]

*   *   *

Madame de Boigne, in her memoirs, describes the first time she saw the young Duchesse de Montpensier. It took place at St. Cloud, as she sat in a corner of one of the drawing-rooms, waiting for the Queen.

Suddenly the door opened and a very young girl entered, jumping and playing the castagnettes; she ran up to a tall mirror, and danced and sang, posing before it.

It was charming; she was not doing it just to admire herself in the mirror, but to amuse herself happily.

When the Queen entered, she ran to her, as a child would do, and put her arms round her saying, "Madre mia, te quiero mucho." [2]

Then, when she perceived the Comtesse, she was astonished, but not abashed. The Queen and Madame de Boigne left the room together, and the little Duchesse resumed her song and dance.

When Montpensier arrived from Madrid with his young Spanish Infanta, all the Society of Paris went mad over him. Fête after fête was given in their honour, but the one which outshone all the others was the dazzling gala offered by the Spanish Ambassador.

It recalled all the splendour of Spain; the greatest dancers were brought from Madrid, the guitars, the cymbals, the rhythm of the "castagnettes", and the tapping feet, were intoxicating, and the Duc, it seemed, was the centre of it all.

Suddenly, he turned to Joinville and said, "Why? Why? Why?"

[1] The three letters are reproduced from *The Letters of Queen Victoria*.
[2] "Mother of mine, I love you very much."

Joinville replied, "Only because you have married an Infanta of Spain."

The true reason of all this rejoicing throughout the country was neither Montpensier nor his Duchesse.

It was a secret delight to know that their marriage had annoyed Great Britain. France had so often been humiliated by that country that the knowledge that now they had stung the British Lion was glorious.

*　　*　　*

On 16th June 1847, the Duc de Montpensier gave a fête which he had determined should surpass in magnificence even that of the Spanish Ambassador.

It took place in the Parc des Minimes amidst the woods of Vincennes. The night was ideal, the scene—Victor Hugo tells us—unbelievably enchanting.

Many of the famous tents which belonged to the Treasure of France had been erected. This alone cost 10,000 francs. Among the most sumptuous were one which had been captured from the Emperor of Morocco, and the tent of Abd-el-Kader, with red and yellow arabesques embroidered in silk.

But the most beautiful of all was the one which the Sultan Selim had presented to Napoleon. From the outside it resembled an ordinary tent, with several windows inserted in the canvas; inside it was a casket of gold brocade, on which were embroidered thousands of flowers, arabesques and ornaments. Gold and silver cords hung from the ceiling, the carpets were of the richest blue and red silk; all around priceless orchids and lilies had been planted.

It was in this oriental atmosphere that the Duc de Montpensier and his childlike bride received their guests. They looked so young, and so delighted with themselves, greeting each one with enthusiasm; after all, it was the first time they were entertaining by themselves.

The Ball took place in an immense marquee. The entire royal family were present, except the Duchesse d'Orléans—she still held herself aloof. Everywhere the trees shone with Chinese lanterns resembling huge oranges. Tables laden with delicacies stood between the trees. Music seemed to echo from every corner, accompanying the singers and the dancers of the quadrilles.

Amidst all this, the high Society of Paris, the intellectuals, the artists and the Diplomatic Corps circulated.

It was during that evening that Louis Philippe, swelling with pride at the magnificence of the scene, came up to Marie Amélie and said, "Are you satisfied? Montpensier has surpassed the English Court!"

The Queen looked at her husband and replied: "Perhaps it would have been better if he had not done so."

Although the fête had been unbelievably lovely, it left many with foreboding in their hearts.

For the fortnight which preceded it, all Paris from the highest to the lowest had talked of nothing else. From early morning on the day of the Ball, spectators had lined the streets from the Tuileries to the Barrière du Trône, to see the procession of carriages. Rarely had a fête caused so much comment.

Many of the guests, as they arrived, had disagreeable adventures to relate. One had been booed, another spat at, others had been bespattered with mud, or had received handfuls of dust and pebbles. Most had been the object of howls, yells, and insults. It was as if a cloud of hate had surrounded the passing guests.

In moments of real want and poverty such as that year 1847, when the disaster of floods had brought so many to the verge of destitution, such arrogant luxury stung the uninvited needy throng. "They extended their hands towards those glittering realities which would become shadows if they touched them." But they knew it not.

*　　　*　　　*

When Lord Palmerston had sent forth his cunning private instructions to the British Ambassador Lord Normanby, he could hardly have realized what a very little effort was needed to set the blaze alight.

France was tired of Louis Philippe, and at that moment, all the political parties outside the Government, those in favour of the monarchy, those against it, the most moderate Republicans, the most fanatical anarchists, Communists, socialists, all hating and distrusting each other, were united in this one thing—they were satiated with Monsieur Guizot; and beyond Guizot, Louis Philippe himself. Something approaching a cult was forming around the word Revolution.

Guizot knew all this, but swept aside any suggestion that all was not well.

Louis Philippe was growing old, and he intended to enjoy his riches. For sixteen years he had fought to keep his throne, and now, as Guizot rocked his difficulties to sleep, he relaxed.

Louis Philippe had ever been subject to fits of temper, but lately these had been growing more frequent and violent.

He had always monopolized the conversation; his vast knowledge and entertaining manner had been agreeable; but this monopoly had recently become so aggressive that his Ministers were alarmed.

Cabinet meetings often came to an end without anything having been discussed. The King had not ceased speaking, and no one could interrupt him. Was it a sign of mental agitation, or simply his assurance that he alone counted?

One day, the King, at one of these meetings, attacked his Ministers, saying he had had enough of them. They did not think of what he desired, but were all prostrate before "its Majesty the people".

A strange remark from Louis Philippe! Did he feel so secure upon the throne, for which he had so vulgarized himself, that he could now afford to shout at his Ministers for prostrating themselves before the people?

Monsieur Guizot, to calm the King, said that certainly he would make amends and behave differently. He smiled behind the King's back, but the other Ministers lowered their eyes and shrugged their shoulders.

If the Cabinet were perturbed, the royal family were still more so. The monarch's love for money had become a ruling passion with advancing years, and he resented parting even with what was not his own. Aumale had great difficulty in obtaining a small monthly allowance out of his huge fortune. Joinville had not been permitted to touch his wife's dowry. The King had grasped the fortune of his grandson, the Comte de Paris, and his mother, the Duchesse d'Orléans was not allowed to administer the finances of her son's household, or even her own. All the princes, except the Montpensiers, were in financial difficulties.

Another subject which had become a grudge among the brothers was that the Tuileries had been ransacked to adorn the apartments of the Duchesse de Montpensier, because, as heir-presumptive to the throne of Spain, nothing was too good for her. The other daughters-in-law, the Princesse de Joinville, the Duchesse de Nemours and the Duchesse d'Aumale, who had been almost banished to the attics, became enraged and deeply offended. After all, why this great preference for Spain?

Jealousy grew to such an extent that Louis Philippe, who up to now, out of economy, had not allowed Aumale to occupy his own residence of Chantilly, had to give way. All this distressed the Queen, and she prayed longer than ever.

Marie Amélie kept a strict watch over her young daughters-in-law. She would not allow them to go out alone, or receive visitors without her permission. The princesses had to spend long hours reading dull books aloud to each other, and some-times, to break the monotony, Marie Amélie would allow each in turn to accompany her on her weekly visits to some insti-tution for young children or old women. The only one who rebelled was the Princesse de Joinville, she who had been so free in Brazil, with her parakeets, and her nuts, and her intoxi-cating love songs, so far removed from the everlasting *Te Deums* of the Tuileries. Sometimes she would slip out and not tell.

There was one place in the Tuileries where Marie Amélie's word was not law: the establishment of the Duchesse d'Orléans in the Pavillon de Marsan. She was determined that her own life at least would be her own. Let her mother-in-law gasp with horror at the thought of heretical Protestant ministers under the same roof as her darling grandsons. Let Tante Adélaïde cry treason when she suspected that the Duchesse was receiving those whose loyalties were uncertain. Hélène d'Orléans did not care!

* * *

Now that the reign of Louis Philippe is almost at its end, let us pause for a while to review the change which has taken place during the last seventeen years.

It has always been fashionable in France to follow the English way of life, but at this time, Anglo-mania became almost a disease. Ladies went to their milliner or to their favourite patisserie with the *Quarterly Review* folded under their arm—it was rarely unfolded, for, when they were alone, like their English counterparts, they far preferred the latest novel of Alexandre Dumas. Servants lost their French names of "Baptiste" or "Gaston", to become "John" or "William". Racing, which had never been known in France before the reign of Louis Philippe, had now become the fashionable sport; a French Jockey Club had been founded by Lord Seymour.

Men abandoned their laces and velvets for good heavy English cloth. The fashionable colours were "vert fumet de Londres" and "gris brouillard de Londres".[1] But, whatever happened to the men, women never attempted to follow them in their craze for English taste. The ladies of France always did, and always shall, lead the world in dress.

These ladies now carried such names as Madame Molé, Madame Thiers, Madame Dosne, Madame Périer—wives of politicians, lawyers and bankers, who had superseded the Duchesses and Marquises of the Bourbon era. The aristocracy had diminished in significance, and the middle class had soared into importance. Finance became the outstanding theme, the god of life, the power of France.

Two new features entered the life of France at this period, very different from one another, one of supreme importance to the new conception of finance, the other seemingly trivial, yet heralding the overthrow of stateliness.

The first was the Baron James de Rothschild, that Nabob of finance. He became the providence of all that stood for finance, art and reason. Louis Philippe received Rothschild at the Tuileries, perhaps the first Jew to be admitted within its precincts. He built a sumptuous palace in the rue Laffitte, surrounded himself with the most grandiose luxury, entertained the highest in the land, yet never allowed himself to be dazzled by the glory of it all. Poets, artists, musicians, filled his drawing-room; his kitchen was reigned over by Monsieur Carême, Talleyrand's famous chef during the Congress of Vienna. He

---

[1] "Green smoke of London", and "grey fog of London".

would boast that, without his exquisite menus, Talleyrand would never have become a great personality, and perhaps he thought that he had also built the greatness of the "House of Rothschild".

The other innovation took place one evening at the Austrian Embassy. The young son of the Ambassador determined to astonish his father's guests with the new Bohemian dance, the polka.

He cleared the floor, ordered the orchestra to strike up the music, and, to the bewilderment of those around, he drew his partner into this frenzied gymnastic dance. At first, the guests' eyes opened wide—that such a thing should be permitted in an Embassy! Mothers turned towards their daughters, and whispered behind their fans, "don't look!" But in a few weeks, the polka became the great chic of the season.

It is strange that Louis Philippe, who had made the Palais Royal the centre of the arts, could never capture that atmosphere at the Tuileries. Sometimes, he would summon a few artists to appear before him, and often, in great secrecy, Chopin would escape the vigilance of George Sand, and play to the King and Queen.

Chopin was already ill, but those evenings at the Tuileries seemed to give him hope for the future. He would wrap himself in his own melodies, improvise and compose, and forget for a while the life he was made to lead by the woman who seemed to own his soul as well as his body. The love of George Sand, his mistress, was killing him.

Louis Philippe and Marie Amélie, surrounded by their family, sat in the dimly lit salon, almost breathless, lest any sound should rouse Chopin from his endless melodious dreams. Other artists were invited, but none equalled Chopin, that great Pole who evoked the patriotic soul of his beloved country and gave it life.

27

A Duchesse is Murdered

1847 was a year which brought trouble everywhere. The harvest had been bad, floods devastated immense areas, the potato pest assumed terrifying proportions, and the winter seemed threatening.

The great discontent against the King and his Ministers seems to date from then. In reality, no one could put a finger on a supreme grievance; nothing had dramatically changed during the seventeen years of the Orléans dynasty, but as one listened to the man in the street, it was one long complaint: the King did not care for his people any more, he was growing old and allowed himself to exist in luxury; Guizot and the Ministry were corrupt, scandals emerged with a breathless rapidity, the apathy of the politicians was intolerable.

All the boredom and discontent became centred on two problems. The first is best expressed in the words of the chemist Regnault, when he remarked: "How can I agree with a law which allows my grocer, my cobbler, to vote because they have money, and denies me the same right because I am poor?"

There were thousands who felt like Regnault. Only people who had certain means were allowed to vote. The Government refused to recognize that men of the lower classes had progressed, and that they intended, whether they were rich or needy, to assert their rights.

The second grievance was that many officials at Court or in the Ministries, had become deputies. The people justly said, how could these men govern the country otherwise than in the way the King wished, with the threat ever-present of losing their highly-paid positions?

Bribes passed from hand to hand, votes were bought and

sold. Even justice was sometimes for sale. Guizot himself said later, "They accused me of being corrupt. I was told to be corrupt. All France was corrupt."

*   *   *

How lovely the gardens of the Tuileries were, in the late spring of 1847. The numerous gardeners had excelled themselves in the variety of flowers, which seemed to greet Louis Philippe as he walked with Marie Amélie, pausing now and then to admire an exotic plant, or breathe the scent of an early rose.

He was explaining to the Queen all the innovations he intended for the following season. From the other side of the protective ditch which separated the people from their King, crowds watched the little princes, the Comte de Paris and his cousin the Prince of Würtemberg, sailing their small boats on the water of the fountain.

The Carrousel was alive with sparrows. Louis Philippe felt young again, Marie Amélie was almost happy. They did not know that this was the last time they would watch the yearly miracle of resurrection from the Tuileries.

They did not see a shadow, which gradually deepened, entering the orbit of France; could nothing be done to sweep it away?

The answer is—Nothing.

One tragedy after another was leading to the final débâcle of the Orléans monarchy. Never does one single word or action precipitate a great disaster, but a succession of events, large and small, moving and pushing each other along an inexorable road.

The final stage began with "l'affaire Teste et Cubières". In the month of May 1847, Monsieur Teste, President of the highest Court of Appeal, "La Cour de Cassation", and an ex-Minister, was arrested and charged with receiving a bribe of 94,000 francs from another ex-Minister, General Cubières, in return for a salt mining concession.

The trial revealed that the whole of Monsieur Teste's career abounded with corruption. He persisted in denying all, until the receipts of his bribes were produced, with his signature. At that moment, Teste collapsed.

A witness relates: "His face seemed to shrink, his eyes became glassy, the bile erupted, and we saw him seized with instantaneous jaundice."

He admitted all, and tried unsuccessfully to commit suicide with a little ivory and silver pistol, which misfired. The Court condemned him to civic degradation and three years' imprisonment, and General Cubières to degradation and a fine.

For the Government, the Army and the Law, it was a death blow. Louis Philippe's indignation was pitiful and, not knowing whom to accuse, he turned his wrath against Chancelier Pasquier, who had pronounced the condemnations. "You had not enough with one of my ex-Ministers; you needed two! I have spent seventeen years restoring law and order in France; and in one day—in one hour—you have destroyed all." [1]

"L'affaire Praslin" has become almost legendary. A few weeks after the Teste and Cubières scandal, another shook France, a murder in the *grand monde*.

The Duc de Choiseul-Praslin—as Victor Hugo, who was his colleague in the Chamber of Peers, tells us—"was an almost flaxen-haired man, pale, sallow in complexion; he had an ugly mouth and a distorted smile. He was neither fat nor thin, neither good-looking nor bad-looking, his hands showed no breeding; they were strong and coarse. Yet in Paris, he passed for a man whose adventures were numberless. He always seemed on the point of saying something which he never said."

In 1814, the Duc had married the only daughter of the Corsican Marshal Sebastiani, later, under Louis Philippe, Minister and Ambassador in London. Praslin was then nineteen years old, and Mademoiselle Sebastiani sixteen. They lived in the sumptuous Hôtel, 55 Faubourg St. Honoré.

The Duchesse was truly a Corsican, sensually in love with her husband, jealous to fanaticism, highly-strung, yet lazy and not willing to exert herself; a combination of the wild possessive nature of that island, and the *dolce far niente* of the south.

She knew that the Duc, although giving her nine children,

[1] *Louis Philippe*, by J. Lucas-Dubreton.

had often been unfaithful to her, but life was passable. Then, in 1841, a woman of twenty-eight entered their household as governess to the four younger children. She was a scheming woman. At once she realized the abnormal relations between the Duc and Duchesse—he calculating, enjoying the fortune which his marriage had brought him, trying to keep up appearances as he realized that, if he goaded his wife too far, her father might cut him off from her huge fortune—the Duchesse terrified of losing her husband, living in a state nearing madness, giving in to him, yet making his life a nightmare.

Mademoiselle Deluzy-Desportes determined to worm her way to power in that household, by appealing to the Duc in all matters, against the Duchesse.

From being a subordinate, she became mistress of the Duc, and of his house. He gave into her hands the entire control of the children: in a way it reminds one of the Comtesse de Genlis and Philippe Egalité, but the Comtesse was brilliantly clever and in a position to carry out her plans. Henriette Deluzy-Desportes was a middle-class woman of twenty-eight, at that time considered already elderly, of no great intelligence, but of a sentimental, ambitious nature.

The terrible scenes which ensued—the Duc determined to retain the governess, the Duchesse insisting on getting rid of her —ended in murder.

During the night of 18th August 1847, the household were awakened by the violent ringing of a bell; servants rushed to the bedroom of the Duchesse; it was locked. So they ran to the garden and forced an entrance to the room by the window. The smell of blood seized their throats; blood was everywhere, in pools and streams; it was still dark but, by the quivering light of a night-light, they perceived the Duchesse lying riddled with wounds, dead.

As they were standing aghast, the Duc appeared, paler than ever. He was wearing a dressing-gown, and on his head a black velvet cap. He threw himself on the body, and asked anxiously if the Duchesse had spoken.

"Oh, my God! What a tragedy! What will happen to my nine children. Who will inform the poor Marshal?"

At this moment the police entered; the head serjeant took in the scene at once. "This is the bungled work of an amateur, a man of the world."

There was no doubt who had been the murderer; the hand of the victim still held a tuft of hair—the Duc's.

The news spread from that room to every part of the world. The Duc was arrested. Louis Philippe hastened to Paris; this was no ordinary crime.

The whole of France waited for the verdict. But on the night of 21st August, a small empty phial which had contained arsenic was found on the Duc. He lived in agony for three days longer. It was suspected that the poison had been smuggled to him from a high source.

The mob were furious to think that a peer had been allowed to poison himself, and so escape the guillotine. To calm the people, a most extraordinary procedure took place. The Duc de Praslin, though dead, was condemned to death. But this did not appease the public; a member of the aristocracy had been protected from a felon's death.

Two scandals in two months. France was shaken.

*   *   *

While the temperature was rising throughout the country, at the Tuileries the pulse of life was slowing down.

One evening in 1847, the Duc de Nemours gave a fête at the Tuileries. After all, he, as future Regent, must figure before the public. Precisely at ten o'clock, as the guests stood waiting, the King and Queen entered through the great doors of the Hall, preceded by Chamberlains.

Marie Amélie, white haired, her curls arrayed in martial order around her temples, and wearing a white satin gown, on her head a silver turban, trimmed with gold fringes. Her gestures were tremulous, but she still looked a great lady. Beside her, Louis Philippe, aged, walking heavily, slightly bent, wearing an ill-fitting coat.

Someone murmured: "They are very tired; it is time they retired."

The King sat down wearily in an armchair, and while Mario and the famous Madame Grisi sang, he fell asleep. Then, from under a drapery on the wall, a small mouse crept out, ran up the side of the royal chair, stopping to nibble the upholstery, wriggling into the cushions and out again, brushing past the hair and neck of the sleeping monarch.[1]

The people, intent on the magnificent music, saw nothing; the King felt nothing; the mouse cared nothing. Only one person noticed it. This tableau seems the epitaph of the Orléans.

*   *   *

In the cabinet of Monsieur Thiers, in his house in the rue St. Georges, a few men met so regularly that they had come to call themselves "the Committee".

Since that day in 1841 when he had walked alone by the tomb of Napoleon, wondering what lay ahead, Monsieur Thiers had become the greatest personality in the intrigues that went on behind the scenes. His aim was power, and the only manner of obtaining it was to overthrow the present régime. Guizot—even the reigning monarch—all must bend or disappear, and he alone dictate.

The public rarely saw him, and never heard him. He let more stupid people, like Odillon Barrot and Ledru-Rollin, travel round the country, show themselves, and make speeches. But the few well-informed knew that these were only puppets, and that Thiers pulled the strings.

As they sat nightly, discussing the indefinable *malaise* which, like a spreading sore, was gripping the country, they sensed that the moment was ripe—but how to begin?

Then one evening, as they talked, Monsieur Pagnerre, one of the Committee, rushed into the room saying, "Mes amis! I have the key to the whole situation. Let us revive the banquets." [2]

There were a few moments of utter silence. Then Thiers stood up, struck the table, and exclaimed, "You have solved the problem!" Banquets would be an infallible way of attracting the people, through their stomachs. Then, when they were well satisfied within, it would be easy to convince them that they were much more unhappy than they thought, that to be unable to vote was an outrage to their human dignity, and that they

[1] *Louis Philippe*, by J. Lucas-Dubreton.
[2] These banquets consisted of huge repasts given freely to the people, during which inflammable speeches would be made.

would only discover what life really was if they disorganized France, and let Monsieur Thiers reorganize it for them.

So, while Louis Philippe slumbered in his armchair, undisturbed by tiny mice or politicians, Monsieur Thiers and his Committee were active. The rumour of a social banquet brought no ripple to the everyday existence of the Tuileries. Guizot mentioned it to the King, who simply said, "*bon appétit* to them".

The first banquet, given in Paris on 9th July 1847, was a stupendous affair. In the huge Hall of the Château Rouge, the 1,200 guests were crowded. The heat was appalling, the smell of humanity revolting, but nobody seemed to mind.

At the end, amidst the torn tricolor streamers, the buzzing flies, and the stained table-cloths, the orators rose to speak. The fine phrases boomed, interrupted constantly by the cheering of the audience, who were only barely lucid and hardly understood what it was all about.

The journalists scribbled away at their notes, and at the end, the "Marseillaise" was sung with great emotion. It was a strange scene, this multitude of humanity, all of different creeds and ideals—royalist embracing communist, firebrand arm-in-arm with moderate—a union of hate.

After this, banquets spread like a rash over France. Guizot began to take fright. In his memoirs, he relates how, one day, he approached the King and suggested very cautiously that perhaps it would be wise to grant the people a few insignificant concessions.

Louis Philippe felt tired, and it was such an effort even to see Guizot. But this day the Minister seemed persistent, so reluctantly the King had received him. Adélaïde was sitting near, and the King was in his dressing-gown.

Guizot decided that, for once, he would see the King alone.

"Sire, may I speak to your Majesty in private?"

Louis Philippe looked embarrassed, and sheepishly made a sign to his sister who, with a furious expression on her face, left the room, noisily banging the door.

"Sire, these banquets are disturbing. They seemed trifling at first, but now the reports are serious. I venture humbly to submit to your Majesty, the idea of granting just one or two small concessions; shall we say, to remove a few functionaries from the Chamber?"

"What is this you propose?" exclaimed the King with a movement of great impatience. "Are you—even you—going to abandon me, and the policy we have maintained together?"

"No, Sire! But it might be necessary for your Majesty to take such a step."

"Who knows whither that declining plane, on which they wish to place me, would lead? One is very near falling when one commences to descend: with your Cabinet I am sheltered from these wretched first steps."

"Perhaps not as much as I could wish, Sire."

In reality, under his disguise Louis Philippe was a true Bourbon. Like Louis XVI and Charles X, he had become blinded, and failed to grasp the life-line which might have saved him.

* * *

The face of Madame Adélaïde had become less smiling than ever. Age had brought asthma, complicated by an affection of the heart, and she was rarely well enough now to leave her apartments. It is difficult to know how much influence she retained over her brother at this time.

The King certainly visited her every day; these tête-à-têtes lasted sometimes one hour, sometimes three, and naturally, no record has remained of them.

Inactivity was torture for her. Since the first attempt on her brother's life, she had not left his side. She gave up all personal distraction, and followed him like a shadow. He alluded to her as his "better judgment", and to his wife as his "guardian angel".

Madame Adélaïde always sat with him during those long evenings, often far into the night. While the King signed document after document, his sister would read and alter them for him to alleviate his fatigue. All this told on her frail health and, little by little, as she sat by his side, her head would drop on her chest, and she slept.

On 30th December 1847, a reception took place at the Tuileries. Madame Adélaïde insisted on rising from her bed to attend it. Did she feel that her end was near and that, for the last time, she would show herself as she had ever done, next to her brother? She looked terribly drawn, and yet the family, as all royal families do, resented any allusion to her ill-health.

That night, just before three o'clock, news was brought to the King that his sister was dying. At once, doctors and the Curé of St. Roch were summoned. When they arrived, the room was crammed with relations and attendants.

Suddenly, Louis Philippe gave an order for all to leave; he wished to remain alone. He watched in silent prayer. At the supreme moment, he rose from his knees and drew towards the couch. Then, taking the hand of the dying woman, he murmured a farewell to the one who had inspired his every action in life. She knew nothing: her soul had fled, and he remained alone, now master of his actions.

It has often been said that, had Madame Adélaïde lived, the Revolution of 1848 would not have taken place. But who can tell whether, in that epoch of transition, one single woman could have stayed an avalanche?

A few minutes later, each member of the family passed reverently before the body of Madame Adélaïde.

Then, without more ado, the Duc de Montpensier opened the drawer of her writing table and drew out a large envelope with the word TESTAMENT. Amidst their grief, a wave of excitement passed round the room. Aunt Adélaïde was so wealthy. They longed to open it, but etiquette must be followed.

So, into the drawing-room of the dead princess, the King summoned the Duc de Nemours, the Prince de Joinville, Monsieur Guizot, President of the Council, Marshal Gérard, Marshal Sebastiani, and Monsieur Dupin, a member of the Conseil Privé.

In tense silence, the seals of the envelope were broken, Monsieur Guizot received the sheaf of papers from the hands of the King, and began to read.

Princesse Adélaïde had left to her favourite nephew, the Prince de Joinville, almost her entire fortune, except the castle of Randan which went to the Duc de Montpensier. But she left to her brother, the King, the enjoyment of all her revenues and the administration of all her fortune, during his lifetime.

This was too much. Joinville, always the most rebellious of the brothers, pushed back his chair abruptly and strode to the window, hardly able to control his fury.

How long would this bondage last? Would none of them ever be free of the strangling purse-strings of their miserly father?

Montpensier, who had been fidgeting with a pen, suddenly threw it down, got up and joined his brother.

The King watched his two sons. Well, let them be furious. He would keep Adélaïde's fortune. So he rose and left the room.

Thus passed the year 1847.

28

"Will Paris be King, Grandpapa?"

On the first morning of 1848, the bells were ringing merrily from every church in Europe. All people, from monarch to peasant, were rejoicing in the New Year.

Over the breakfast table, Queen Victoria consulted Prince Albert as to whether she should write a letter of sympathy to the King of the French, on the death of his sister. Since the Spanish marriage, no message had passed between them, and the Queen was still resentful.

That year, which was to bring so much disaster, was opening with the usual presents, compliments, small hopes, fears and preoccupations.

At the Tuileries, the déjeuner was a jumble of emotions. Grief, hate and indifference surrounded the table. The Comte de Paris and his brother the Duc de Chartres sat near their mother, longing for the meal to be over, in the hope that their grandparents would give them their New Year's presents.

No one seemed to take any notice of the two little boys. Louis Philippe cast furtive glances at Joinville, but the latter never looked at his father. At length, the King could stand no more. Without waiting for the traditional dish of *échaudés*, he stood up and, banging his fist on the table, shouted:

"I have had enough of this disloyal attitude. I shall abandon all. I shall retire to Eu with my good Queen, and we shall see how the country will manage without me."

Nobody answered except the little Duc de Chartres:

"Will Paris be King then, Grandpapa?"

*   *   *

In the Tuileries, a storm raged over Adélaïde's fortune. On their side, the Government were working individually for themselves. Throughout the land, people's heads were whirling with phrases heard at the banquets. These had proved so effective that even those who had inspired them were growing anxious.

Thiers, in his heart, did not actually want a revolution, only to bring about the fall of Guizot; and when he saw the effect which the banquets produced, he became afraid of the storm which he had aroused.

He summoned his Committee: the whole night they fought, extremists against moderates, those who insisted on going on, and those who wanted to stop. As dawn filtered through the curtains, they reached a compromise. They would give one last banquet, as a grand finale to the campaign. The place would be the Champs Elysées, and the date 22nd February 1848.

So, after eighteen years, we come to another three days.

*　　　*　　　*

21st February 1848

A steady, endless torrent of rain fell over Paris, washing the streets, flooding the gutters.

In the office of the Prefect of Police, Monsieur Delessert, the Prefect, and his friend the Comte de Rambuteau, Prefect of the Seine, were sitting waiting. Would the Cabinet decide to prohibit tomorrow's banquet, or allow it to take place? The two men were anxious. They knew that Paris was restless, but so far they had failed to convince Monsieur Guizot of this.

The clock struck eleven as a messenger splashed through the mud to the entrance of the Prefecture, carrying a sealed envelope—the decision of the Ministers.

Two hours later Paris was placarded with posters, announcing that the banquet, or any form of public meeting, was prohibited on the next day.

As the people stood reading the proclamation, many shook their heads, and some were heard to murmur, "Maintenant, il y aura du grabuge." There will be hell to pay.

Thiers and his Committee, having learned that on the morrow 27,000 troops of the Paris Garrison were to line the streets, from the Tuileries, along the Champs Elysées, to the Barrière de l'Etoile, were dismayed. If they proceeded with the banquet, it meant bloodshed. So once again, they met at the house in the rue St. Georges. All the afternoon the debate raged. At last the decision was made. The banquet would not take place.

It was very late when Monsieur Duchatel, Minister of the Interior, learnt the news, but immediately he went to the King.

Louis Philippe was sitting before a huge fire playing patience, the Queen, in a low chair, helping him. They were peaceful and undisturbed.

"My dear Monsieur Duchatel, what brings you at this hour? Is it good or bad news?"

"Good news, Sire! They have called off the banquet. I humbly suggest to your Majesty that the troops should remain in barracks tomorrow, as their presence might irritate the people."

The King rose from his chair. "But of course. I had thought of that myself."

Then he returned to his patience, thankful that this tiresome question was finally settled. For him, this meant the end of all troubles.

That night, at the Opéra, a very different opinion was being expressed. In the interval, in the foyer, the beauty and the intellect of Paris were whispering of nothing else. It would not be a riot, they said—it would be a revolution. Tomorrow, perhaps, or the day after.

That same evening, a dinner had taken place at the Princesse de Lieven's residence in the Hôtel Talleyrand. Those present included the British Ambassador, Lord Normanby, the Prefect of the Seine, the Comte de Rambuteau, the Prefect of Police, Monsieur Delessert, and of course her faithful Monsieur Guizot. Their well-known liaison had lasted so long, that Society now accepted it as a matter of course.

The princess had invited her guests to try to discover the true state of affairs, but Guizot was too used to her intrigues to disclose all the secrets of his trade; the others were novices compared to him.

When dinner was over, and the guests were standing about the drawing-room sipping liqueurs and talking, the princess approached the two Prefects, who were in earnest conversation in the far end of the room.

"Messieurs, I am anxious about the present events in this country. You can trust me!"

"Princess, do you really want to know the truth? It may alarm you, but no more than it alarms us."

They then told her that the Army was at sixes and sevens, the Garde Nationale was unpredictable, and that all the afternoon, police had been employed against crowds of students and workmen demonstrating in the boulevards.

Their account so frightened the princess that she called to Monsieur Guizot, who was talking to the British Ambassador.

"Come, cher ami, listen to what these gentlemen are telling me."

Guizot listened, and then replied, "Is it for this, Princesse, that you have interrupted my conversation with Lord Normanby? These gentlemen are in a panic over a trifle, unworthy of robbing them, or you, of a single minute's sleep."

He then gave them one of his patronizing, self-satisfied smiles, turned on his heel, and went back to the sofa where Lord Normanby was sitting.[1]

22nd February 1848

At the Tuileries, at six o'clock in the morning, the servants, half-awake, were going through the long vista of reception rooms, drawing back the heavy curtains and peering out into the gloom of the streets.

It was still dark, and there was little sound except the patter of the steadily falling rain, which had continued for the past two days without cessation.

In one of the rooms there was a light: Louis Philippe had left his bed, and was lighting his fire. Even now, he had not lost this habit. He also looked out and, hearing the downpour, said to Marie Amélie, "The weather is on our side. Those *coquins* hate water. They will not bother about their banquet today!"

At eleven o'clock, Monsieur Jayr, Minister of Public Works, entered his carriage with his secretary to drive to the Tuileries.

[1] *Mémoires* of the Comtesse de Boigne. Librairie Plon.

As they splashed towards the quai de la Seine, the secretary remarked: "This rain will have more effect than the whole garrison of Paris."

"I wonder," came the reply.

Their carriage turned on to the quai, and there before them was the answer. Groups of men and women trudged by, their hair and clothes sodden with the rain, all moving towards the Place de la Concorde.

At the Concorde, the Place was already crowded, and from the side streets, as far as the eye could see, more converged towards the rendezvous. They seemed excited, and were shouting some indistinct words.

The coachman turned. "It will not be easy, Monsieur le Ministre. Shall I go on?"

"Yes," answered Monsieur Jayr. Soon they were in the midst of it: the mob milled around the vehicle. "Down with Guizot!" "Down with the Ministers!" Jayr leant back into the far corner of the carriage, out of sight.

Half an hour later, they reached the palace. He hurried into the King's presence. The monarch came towards him with a smile of satisfaction, his hand outstretched.

"Eh bien! Mon cher, you come to congratulate me. You must acknowledge that I have handled this little matter perfectly . . . You know, of course, that *they* have given up their banquet. *They* saw at the last minute that the stakes were rather high. When I think that so many of our friends wanted me to give in!"

"Sire, your Majesty has not been informed of what is happening on the Place de la Concorde? There are hundreds there, screaming against your Ministers, and more are on their way every minute."

"Naturally," answered the King, "there is some disappointment; that was to be expected. But it will pass. I will mention it to Guizot."

That afternoon, the gunsmiths' shops in the city were ransacked. No one intervened. The King still knew nothing, the rain still fell.

At five o'clock, dusk had fallen, but the Champs Elysées

seemed alive with soaked and shivering humanity. Suddenly there was a shout. "Let's have a fire."

In a few moments, a flame leapt up. People were seen running from every quarter, bringing chairs, tables, pulling down small booths—anything made of wood, to add to the flames. The acrid stench of damp smoke entered their throats and pricked their eyes, but still they shouted, danced, and sang the "Parisienne".

At length they drifted away, and the Champs Elysées was empty once more. The fête of the populace was over, and the scene shifts to the Faubourg St. Germain, where Society was crowding to the salon of the Princesse de Ligne and the Ball of the Duchesse d'Etissac.

All were speculating, "Is it over? or is it only just beginning?"

In the salon of the Comte de Sainte Aulaire, Monsieur Guizot, conceited and all-knowing as always, reassured his hostess in a loud voice so as to be heard by everybody. "No surprise is possible, chère Comtesse; every precaution has been taken. Troops are surrounding the few noisy groups. You can sleep quite calmly in your beautiful surroundings."

Outside, one by one, the noises of the streets died away. The only sound, an occasional crash: some stragglers returning from the Champs Elysées had thrown a brick at a passing patrol. A small scuffle, a sound of running feet; then again, silence. About one o'clock in the morning, the troops returned to their barracks, the police went to bed, and the rain droned on undisturbed.

23rd February 1848

Three o'clock in the morning. A few gendarmes were patrolling the streets, tired, bored and wet. They thought of their warm beds, of the still warmer wife—some wondered perhaps if the warm wife was alone! But there it is, they must keep going until they are relieved.

There was not a soul on the boulevards, the shutters of the houses were closed, not even a flicker of light came through. Paris seemed exhausted.

But in the side streets, although it was so early, the doors of houses were opening, and figures, well wrapped up, appeared, other people passed, and seemed to be handing them something, guns or pistols perhaps. And then they followed on.

At six o'clock, the Prefect of Police was awakened and informed of the mysterious movements. He sent word to the Minister of the Interior, who decided to summon the Garde Nationale. So once again the drums of the "Rappel" beat through the muddy streets of the capital.

At the Tuileries, it was such an ordinary morning—like yesterday, like every other morning for so many years. But it was to be the last.

The King seemed so calm; his several visitors were astonished by his attitude. Horace Vernet was among them, and when the King asked him to leave for Blois as soon as possible to begin a portrait of Abd-el-Kader, the painter could not refrain from saying:

"Would it not be better to wait a little, Sire?"

"What nonsense," answered the monarch, "all this is only a very small bonfire, it will die out in smoke." [1]

Exactly one hour after Louis Philippe had spoken these words, General de Rumigny burst in unannounced, almost beside himself:

"Sire, the twelve Colonels of the Garde Nationale ask to be received."

Louis Philippe rose from his chair, and said, "Let them enter."

The Colonels filed in and stood at attention, and the Colonel of the Third Legion spoke:

"Sire, we can no longer answer for the safety of the streets. I was on duty with my Legion near the Place des Victoires. A menacing crowd were assembled. A squadron of your Majesty's Cuirassiers emerged from a side street, and prepared to charge the mob.

"At that moment, before I could give an order, my men rushed forward between the people and the Army, and crossed their bayonets to bar the way.

"The news of my Legion's mutiny spread through Paris, and nearly all the other legions of the Garde Nationale have followed their example.

[1] *Mémoires* of the Comtesse de Boigne. Librairie Plon.

"Now we humbly beg your Majesty to relieve us of our command."

The King stared at them. The Colonel's words had hardly been understood. Then slowly they seemed to enter his consciousness. He waved his hands in an uncertain gesture, he staggered to the window, he retraced his steps, sat down, and his head fell on his chest; he stammered some disjointed phrases, and the word "impossible" was heard, and then "Adélaïde"; tears came to his eyes, and he wept.

Half an hour later, Monsieur Duchatel, Minister of the Interior, was announced.

"Sire, it is a Revolution; they are wrenching the cobbles from the streets and erecting barricades; everywhere, one can hear nothing but 'à bas Guizot'. The situation is becoming graver every minute; we must take energetic measures."

At this moment, a door opened and the Queen entered, followed by the Duc de Montpensier. It was then that Marie Amélie showed a nature which had never been suspected. She looked at the King, and saw that she was the only person who could make a decision.

She turned to Duchatel and, in a firm voice which astonished all present, she spoke to him.

"The Ministers are devoted to the King and to France. This is the moment for them to show their devotion. I invite them to resign."

Louis Philippe looked at her, then at the speechless Minister, then again at her. At last he said, "Fetch Monsieur Guizot."

At two-thirty the same afternoon, Guizot entered the Tuileries by a back door, and was immediately ushered into the presence of the King. The Queen, the Duc de Montpensier, and the Duc de Nemours were around Louis Philippe.

As the King saw his Minister, tears rose to his eyes. He held out his hands:

"Oh Guizot, have we come to this? Only by separating myself from you, I am told, can I save the monarchy. In reality, I should prefer to abdicate."

Marie Amélie intervened quickly:

"You cannot say that, Sire. You belong to France; you do not belong to yourself."

"That is true," said the King. "I am more unhappy than a Minister. I cannot even resign."

Then Louis Philippe bowed his head and said no more: Montpensier stepped forward and spoke a few words of regret. After eight years, Guizot was finished, and Monsieur Molé was summoned, to form a new Cabinet.

The news swept through the antechambers, down the corridors, through the kitchens and the hallways, till it reached the gates. It was sung through the streets, "Guizot is down! Guizot is finished!" Within an hour, all Paris knew, and the capital was resounding with a kind of furious joy, more frightening than the rage of the morning.

Barricades were abandoned, bonfires were lit, *farandoles* were formed, strangers dancing hand in hand from quarter to quarter, crying the good news to those who knew it already.

Dusk fell, lighted lanterns were placed on balconies and window ledges. On the boulevards, the gas lamps streamed down sheaves of light, music poured from the cafés, bands of people went about yelling the "Marseillaise", and calling to the unlit houses to bring out their lanterns. The city seemed bewitched, beautiful and hideous all at once.

Then the catastrophe.

Darkness had fallen, it was nine-thirty in the evening. The 14th Regiment of the Line, under the command of Colonel Courant, blocked half of the rue Cambon where stood the Ministry of Foreign Affairs, residence of Monsieur Guizot. They could see a distant glare moving towards them from the Place de la Concorde; there were cries of "Light up your houses—light up or we shoot!" Hurriedly, candles, night-lights, anything with a flame, appeared at the windows of the rue Cambon.

The glare became a blaze as a cheering, screaming mob emerged carrying torches. The Ministry showed not a single light. The shutters were closed and nothing could be seen from the outside.

Now the rabble came face to face with the Regiment guarding the Ministry. There was a shout.

"Stop!"

The mob halted. The Colonel advanced alone on his horse, and asked in a stern voice: "What do you want?"

A man sprang forward: he had a black beard, huge arms, and in his powerful fist he held a torch. He seemed the moving spirit of the gang. He roared at the officer: "We want the Ministry to light up."

The Colonel turned to the crowd: "I am here to guard the Ministry. Nothing else concerns me."

The leader retorted: "Make it concern you, then. We give them five minutes to light up."

The officer gave no sign of having heard. One minute passed. Two minutes. The soldiers stood motionless. The crowd gazed fixedly at the windows. Three minutes—four—five. Nothing.

"Now we *shall* pass!"

The Colonel made no movement.

The bearded man drew nearer and sneeringly said:

"Swine, I will light up your moustache!"

Saying this, he pushed his torch into the Colonel's face; the latter jerked back his head.

Standing near was a serjeant named Giacomoni. He was a true Corsican, violent, loyal and capable of risking his life for his superior officer. At this moment he only saw the Colonel's face, white in the flame. He raised his gun and aimed. A Captain leapt on him crying "Are you mad?" and knocked up the muzzle of the gun. Giacomoni retorted, "They want to kill my Colonel; I must defend him."

Around them, confusion was growing. The people massed on the sidewalk were calling out senselessly: "They will pass! They won't pass! Down with Guizot! Let's go home! Long live the Army! Light up your houses!" Like the rustling of leaves at the approach of a hurricane.

The Colonel looked steadily at the mob. "You shall *not* pass."

Then the creature, convulsed with rage, gripped his torch and hurled it at the officer's face; the horse reared; the Colonel gave a sharp order: "Cross bayonets!" Giacomoni fired; the bearded leader fell; the mob surged forward.

There was a burst of firing.

Fifty-two of the crowd lay in the road, dead or wounded. The mob pushed on; the soldiers were so bewildered that they began to shoot at one another. One could scarcely hear the cries of pain of those who lay in the road, trampled to death in the demented stampede as the rioters fled in every direction, some jumping over barriers, others throwing themselves flat on the ground, others running in circles, not finding their way. The soldiers themselves started rushing for their lives along the side streets.

Their Colonel, standing in his stirrups, tried to rally them: "Quatorzième de Ligne, you dishonour yourselves!" But none looked back, even for a moment.[1]

Then the real agitators got to work. A family of emigrants was passing, pushing a cart towards the Gare de l'Ouest; they were thrust aside, their goods hurled from the cart, and sixteen corpses piled onto it. A procession formed round it, and, lighted by torches, toured the city with cries of "Vengeance! They are murdering our brothers." It was an abomination, these corpses heaped on one another, in pools of blood, their bodies rocking from side to side, as they were wheeled over the unpaved road.

As the macabre cortège proceeded, chanting its awful litany, those who had already returned to their houses, exhausted, stumbled out again. Suddenly the tocsin sounded; the ring-leaders had penetrated into the belfries.

Soon the cobbles were being torn up, more gunsmiths were pillaged, and before morning broke, the whole city was one network of barricades.

[1] *Souvenirs d'un Demi-Siècle*, by Maxime du Camp.

29

"*Abdicate! Abdicate!*"

The night of 23rd February 1848

The Tuileries was strangely silent; few servants were to be seen; it was whispered that some had joined the yelling groups on the barricades.

Louis Philippe paced his study, anxiously waiting for news of Monsieur Molé. It was almost eleven-thirty, and the King wondered why he was taking so long to form a Cabinet.

Marie Amélie, watching his rising anxiety, tried to reassure him. "Certainly Molé will succeed, but it must be difficult in this uproar to move about; and many of the men he intends to ask to join his Cabinet live far apart."

The gloomy atmosphere was oppressive. The candles burned low in their sockets; some bending, as if they too felt the strain. The Queen turned up the wick of the oil lamps. She rang for new candles, but no one answered her call.

At this moment, General de Rumigny announced, "Monsieur Molé."

The King went towards him.

"Well?" The monarch's voice was slightly shaky.

"Sire, I have failed to form a Cabinet."

Had he even tried? But the question did not enter the King's mind; he clutched Molé's hand.

"Mon ami, what then?"

For a moment, the three stood still, the King bewildered, Molé embarrassed. They could hear, far in the distance, the confused rumble of shouting beyond the gates of the Tuileries. Suddenly, the Queen walked across the room and threw open one of the large windows.

The darkness rolled into the room, lit only by the distant waving torches, and with it a terrific clamour for "Vengeance!"

275

Then, above the din, came the cry, distinct and savage, "Down with Louis Philippe—murderer of the people!"

The Queen closed the window, drawing close the heavy curtains, and turned to face the King.

"Send for Thiers."

.The King heard her words. He was still standing, still holding Molé's hand. He dropped it, walked to his desk, and, without a word, wrote a note. As he sealed the message, he turned to Molé.

"We have come to this!" He had summoned Thiers.

Molé, taking this for a dismissal, bowed to the King, saying: "Sire, this is no time for politicians, but for armed force."

Louis Philippe sat on at his desk, still holding the pen which had summoned Thiers—the man who had said, only a short time ago, "The worst would be the old man's abdication. Would that be such a tragedy?"

*　　*　　*

Once more, Marie Amélie rang. She wanted coffee to revive her husband; he had a long night before him.

Again, no one answered. At last, a man in plain clothes appeared, one of the underservants; the King had never seen him before. When questioned, he said that only a few had remained loyal; most of the others had fled, taking with them their liveries, and helping themselves to anything they fancied as they passed out of the château.

It was two o'clock in the morning; the King and Queen, sitting opposite each other by a dead fire, had fallen into a fitful doze. A knock on the door made them start, and Rumigny announced Monsieur Thiers. The King struggled to his feet.

"Monsieur, I have sent for you to ask you to save the monarchy." It was a curious request, to one who for years had not ceased to destroy it.

Thiers looked at the King with a contemptuous half-smile: "On one condition, Sire—that I choose my own Ministers, Odillon Barrot, Duvergier, Remusat."

The King knew that all these were his enemies, but he merely made a gesture: "I agree to all, and accept you and your baggage; but you will have Marshal Bugeaud as Commander-in-Chief."

Bugeaud was the one man who could be relied on to suppress a rising.

"Remember, Sire, that he is hated! He has used such brutal methods when quelling previous riots. It will madden the people and inspire terror."

"That is what they need—Terror!"

Thiers left to begin his difficult task, and Louis Philippe, worn out, staggered to his bedroom.

So, for the last time, the old couple lay side by side in the Tuileries.

24th February 1848

Under the low clouds, the streets of Paris seemed like a battlefield. Along the line of boulevards which runs from the Madeleine to the Chaussée d'Antin (then rue du Mont Blanc), the trees had been uprooted; the gaily painted sentinel boxes, benches, railings, everything had been battered to pieces or removed to pile on the barricades, leaving only desolate wreckage everywhere.

The everyday world had evaporated, to be replaced by one made up of brutal gestures, ugly repulsive faces, loathsome voices, issuing from evil-smelling throats.

Marshal Bugeaud deployed his troops to repress what was now visibly a Revolution.

The order was, not to provoke, but to crush mercilessly, all armed resistance.

The announcement of the Marshal's nomination as Commander-in-Chief had provoked a new tidal wave of anger amongst the population. Everywhere the cry was, "The King is having us murdered! Louis Philippe the traitor! Louis Philippe the strangler!"

*   *   *

At the house of Monsieur Thiers, nobody had slept. In the study, since his return from the Tuileries, the Minister had sat with his confederates, arguing, planning, questioning. His hair was untidy, his face grey with fatigue, but still he talked. From outside, the din reached him, now loud, now faint, but always there.

He hardly noticed it.

At six o'clock in the morning, Thiers and Odillon Barrot went to the stables, mounted their horses, and set off to tour the barricades. Thiers was so sure that, when he appeared, curses would change to enthusiasm, and the whole city would rejoice and acclaim him as the conciliator.

But, as they rode from street to street, uttering promises and soothing words, endeavouring to calm the tumult, to his consternation they were only answered by stronger cries of "No peace!" and "Down with the cheats and the liars!"

Thiers now realized that things had grown beyond his control. His name meant nothing.

Odillon Barrot, on the other hand, had been greeted by a few cheers, some had stretched out their hands to him, others had cried, "Hail, father of the people!"

Thiers determined to see the King. He reached a side door of the Tuileries, followed by the now beaming Odillon, sure of his triumph. A frightened servant opened the door, and shut it quickly behind them. There was nobody to announce them, so they walked unescorted to the private apartments of the King.

The monarch was still sleeping. The King's valet Thuret met them to ask if they could wait a little, as his Majesty had looked so dreadfully ill when he had helped him to bed. How strange, in the mighty Tuileries, only a valet left to speak to the governing body of France. But the Ministers declared that they must see the King at once. So, reluctantly, the man left them and went to awaken his master.

In a few minutes, Louis Philippe appeared, in his nightshirt, a nightcap on his head. Even Thiers felt a moment of compassion; the King had suddenly become a very old man.

"I have come to ask your Majesty to accept my resignation. I am already out of date." Then Thiers pointed to Odillon: "He might succeed."

278

"Try, Monsieur Barrot; it is all the same to me. Form your Cabinet."

Saying this, the King left the room.

Whether the Minister was Guizot, Thiers, or Barrot, no longer mattered to the advancing throng on the boulevards. A senseless instinct urged them towards the Tuileries, to drive out this King, who stood for all they hated. The one man they dreaded was Bugeaud; he alone had the courage to mow them down, and restore peace.

The Marshal had given orders that his officers should address the people, and try persuasion. But no words seemed to reach their fanatic brains.

Then, when the Marshal was losing all patience, a hurried message came from the King:

"Withdraw your troops."

Bugeaud, astonished, galloped to the Tuileries. In the Hall of the General Staff he found the Duc de Nemours, his Aides de Camp, and Monsieur Thiers; the latter had taken the lead and was directing events at the palace.

"The King has decided to withdraw all troops from Paris," he said.

The old soldier looked aghast.

"Do you realize that if this is done, the monarchy is damned, and we with it?"

"The King refuses to allow blood to be shed."

The Marshal retorted: "His Majesty is throwing the country to the dogs."

At that moment, the Duc de Nemours approached Bugeaud and murmured a few words in his ear. Without hesitating, the Marshal turned to his Aide de Camp:

"Send forth an order to all Commanders: 'Cease fire everywhere, and withdraw all troops to the Carrousel.' "

So, from every corner of the city, columns of men began to march slowly towards the Carrousel. They had been loyal, and now they were abandoned. They marched, sagging, weary, demoralized.

Crowds pressed round them as they tramped along, shouting, "You are our brothers; join us."

279

Some soldiers, disgusted, cried, "They won't let us use our bullets. Well, here they are!" and they threw their ammunition into the midst of the mob.

And, answering a surprised citizen, "Oui, mon bourgeois, we have been dropped, so we are dropping everything!"

Many never reached the Carrousel. The rioters surged through the breaking ranks, dragging individual soldiers away to the nearest café, where the men, abandoned by their King, drank themselves into a stupor, in their utter misery.

On the Place de la Concorde, there was a small guardhouse occupied by thirty-five men of the Garde Municipale.[1] They knew that they were the most hated troops in the capital. So, when they saw the mob, they barricaded themselves in, and prepared to fight for their lives.

Suddenly, a brick crashed through the small window, and a woman was seen to run forward and hurl a lighted torch through the aperture into the midst of the doomed men. The smoke soon forced them out, then the carnage began. People fought their way into the smoking guardroom, others came out half asphyxiated; blood splashed on the walls and ran to the floor. One could hear the cracking of crushed bone, as chests were battered and skulls split. The thirty-five men were hacked to pieces.

Several detachments of Cavalry stood by, inactive, obedient to the orders of the King. One Captain, horror-stricken, rushed to General Bedeau, in command of the Cavalry, and implored him, "For God's sake, sir, let us charge this vermin!"

Bedeau hesitated, his face white and distorted, but he had his orders. He answered briefly, "Go back to your place."

And so thirty-five men died, because the King did not want bloodshed.

*   *   *

All that morning, Louis Philippe sat in his Cabinet by the fire. People came in and went out, but he did not even see them. His eyes were closed, yet he did not sleep. One of his ex-Ministers asked him: "What does your Majesty intend doing?"

"Nothing. I am defeated."

[1] Military Police of Paris.

280

Then Marie Amélie came to him. "Mon cher ami, there is one hope. Go to review the men who are guarding the Tuileries, who are still true to us, and perhaps their enthusiasm may bring the others back."

At that moment, the Duc de Montpensier entered the room, and endorsed his mother's suggestion.

"What's the good? I'm finished."

"Never say that word. Do your duty to the end."

Shortly afterwards, the King appeared, dressed in the uniform of a Lieutenant-General, and slowly descended the Grand Staircase. Did he remember that it was in the uniform of a Lieutenant-General that he had performed his first ceremony eighteen years ago? And now, today, in that same dress, he would perform his last.

He mounted a horse and rode towards the men, followed by his sons.

At first he was greeted by shouts of "*Vive le Roi!*" But suddenly a voice arose, "Down with the monarchy!" Another voice took up the cry, then another.

Louis Philippe turned his horse, and rode back to the Tuileries.

Although Paris was in a state of Revolution, the daily routine of the Court continued. At ten-thirty in the morning, lunch-time, the doors were flung open by the few officials that remained, and the King, leading his family, entered the dining-room.

Little was said; still less was eaten. Shooting and screams could be heard in the distance, but still the life of the Court must go on.

Then, above the hubbub, a curious rhythm emerged; the orders "En arrière . . . en avant . . .",[1] followed by a thud, repeated again and again. The mob were attacking the gates with an improvised battering ram.

At that moment, unannounced, Emile de Girardin, a well known journalist, ran into the room. The King looked astonished; Girardin was not a familiar figure at the Court.

"Sire, they are breaking into the gardens. Every minute counts. Your Majesty must not lose an instant, or your life, Sire, may be in danger."

[1] "Back . . . forward . . ."

Louis Philippe looked at him. "What do you propose, young man?"

"Abdication, Sire."

The word had been uttered. Louis Philippe did not move. Marie Amélie leapt up with a scream.

"No!" she cried. "No! You shall not abdicate! Better to die here."

The King stood motionless; then Montpensier came forward and seized his father's arm. He almost pushed him out of the room, towards his Cabinet. There, awaiting him, were his old Marshals—Soult, Gerard, Sebastiani. The King looked at them solemnly.

"Can we defend the country?"

They did not answer. The monarch understood, and he murmured, almost to himself, "Abdicate".

Again those old soldiers stood silent. Marie Amélie swept into the room, followed by a medley of individuals—some they had never seen before—all pushing their way in. Outside the clamour drew nearer.

Montpensier touched his father's hand. "Mon père, abdicate, quick; don't you hear—they are forcing the doors. In a few minutes they will be upon us!"

For the last time, Louis Philippe turned to his old companions, the Marshals of France: but they would not meet his gaze.

So he walked to his desk—the famous desk which had belonged to Napoleon—and took up his pen.

"Faster!" urged a voice, "or it will be too late!"

"Faster! Have you forgotten how to write?" cried another.

Montpensier spoke again. "For God's sake hurry; we shall all be murdered."

"I have always written slowly; this is no time to change my habits," answered the King. Then he began to write:

I abdicate this crown, which the will of the nation called upon me to wear, in favour of my grandson, the Comte de Paris. May he succeed in the great task which falls to him this day.

LOUIS PHILIPPE

Girardin tore the paper out of the King's hand and cried: "At last I've got it."

Marie Amélie looked at him with scorn as she responded: "Yes, you have it, but remember—you will regret it!"

Girardin shrugged his shoulders and rushed out to show the document to the crowd.

Hélène d'Orléans was leaning against the wall. The King raised his head.

"Hélène, it is your right to remain here to maintain your son's crown."

30

The Terrifying Flight

"Sire, you must leave."

The words were all around him. Feverishly, the King tore off his gold-braided coat and picked up his general's hat, handing them to a man standing by.

"Bring me a round hat and a frock-coat."

They were brought. In a few moments the King of the French was transformed into a shabby citizen. The battering on the doors of the château itself grew louder. The King called to his valet: "Quick—my keys!"

Someone screamed, "There is no time for keys." The King replied, "I will not leave without my keys."

The valet ran in; he had found them. Louis Philippe stuffed some papers into a portfolio. He kept on repeating: "They will take all I possess."

Around him, those who feared, and those who triumphed—all alike were distraught with terror. The princes shouted, "Quick! Quick!" The King fumbled. Alone among them all, the Queen stood proud and calm.

At last they were ready. The King advanced towards the Queen and, with a slight bow, offered her his arm. And so, walking heavily, they started.

They had only gone a few paces down the long gallery, when screams of triumph rang out in the deserted corridors; a sound of rushing feet, as a human torrent poured into the palace. "They're in!"

Instinctively, the old people hastened their steps, stumbling through the endless salons, breathing in gasps. The King's heart seemed almost bursting, as the Queen dragged him along, the noise growing closer each instant.

At last they reached a narrow stair, and beyond it the little door leading through the garden to the Place de la Concorde. Outside, Louis Philippe knew that two carriages which he had ordered would be waiting. He unlocked the door and stood, gazing dizzily at the emptiness of the Place. Debris, formless, lying stupidly around; to the right, the ruins of the little guard-house still smoking. No sign of the carriages, but the body of a coachman in royal livery lay sprawling in the puddles on the gravel.

In the midst of all this desolation, the only living thing a little cab with one horse standing in the centre of the Place, the old coachman dozing, infinitely patient, on his box; it was unreal.

They perceived their salvation, they walked to the little cab. In it four women were seated, each with a child on her knee— the Duchesse de Nemours, the Duchesse de Joinville, and two ladies of the Court with the King's grandchildren.

Louis Philippe said one word. "Out!" Cowed, the women obeyed, and stood helplessly on the pavement.

The King hurriedly entered the little vehicle, followed by Marie Amélie. "Go!" he cried.

The coachman cracked his whip, and the horse trotted off.

Hastily, Louis Philippe leaned forward to draw the curtains of that little carriage; then, removing his hat and toupet of false hair, he pulled out of his pocket a black silk bonnet which he proceeded to put on, drawing it down to his eyes.

He turned to Marie Amélie; she stared. "You are now a hundred years old."

Taking the back streets to avoid the angry crowds, they made their way to Versailles; here the driver refused to go any further, and demanded his money. He had not recognized them. The King put his hand in his pocket, to find that, despite the huge fortune he had accumulated, he had come away with only fifteen francs. The porter of the Palace lent them two hundred francs, and the little cab which had saved their lives drove away.

The King immediately gave orders for two coaches to be prepared, one coach for the Queen and himself, and a large omnibus for those of the family who had managed to follow them.

He was in a fever to push on—anywhere, any way, to get

further from that satanic Paris. The other members of the family were told by the King, "Find your own way, but do not follow me. You are not important, but I must escape."

Marie Amélie insisted that they should go via Dreux; she felt that she must pray once more near the tombs of her beloved; in her heart she knew that it would be for the last time. Louis Philippe kept saying, "Ma chère amie, all this will pass. We shall soon be back in our dear Tuileries." But the Queen knew better.

At five o'clock, they saw the lights of Dreux. The château evoked so many loving memories of the days before 1830: the Chapel, which enshrined her beloved ones; the surroundings, which epitomized the traditions of the House of Orléans.

Louis Philippe, tired and broken though he was, insisted on visiting the vast interior to inspect the alterations he had undertaken. It looked bare, damp, forlorn; yet to the fugitive it seemed a haven of refuge. At last he lay down to rest.

Marie Amélie, carrying a lighted candle, went to the crypt. Alone in that musty gloom, she knelt to pray. The hours passed. At last the time came to say farewell to those she had loved. As she mounted the steps, the flickering spark of the candle went out.

The early dawn of 25th February did not awaken the exhausted King. For the first time for what seemed a century, his sleep was enveloped in silence. Even the rain had ceased. Louis Philippe slept at last, tranquil in the belief that his grandson, the Comte de Paris, reigned King of the French, that the capital had been restored to order, and that today he would, with Marie Amélie, drive to Eu to rest after these days of nightmare.

A voice, calling insistently, brought him back to life.

"Sire! Awaken, Sire. The Sous-Préfet is here with alarming news!" It was the faithful Rumigny who had rejoined them the previous evening at Versailles.

Louis Philippe sat up in bed. "I will see him now."

A minute later, Monsieur Maréchal, the Sous-Préfet of Dreux, entered the room. He looked distressed.

The King beckoned to him to approach the bed. As he did so, the Sous-Préfet could scarcely refrain from an exclamation.

THE TOMB OF KING LOUIS PHILIPPE AND QUEEN MARIE AMÉLIE
AT DREUX

It was still daylight when they jolted to a stop and Monsieur Maréchal opened the carriage door. Before them spread the town of Evreux; a short way off, behind some trees, they could glimpse the slate turrets of a little château. "This is not a friendly town, Sire, it would be wiser to wait till dark before we go through it."

The Sous-Préfet enquired from a passing peasant to whom the small estate belonged.

"Monsieur Dorvilliers," was the reply. Was this again an answer to Marie Amélie's prayer? Monsieur Dorvilliers was the administrator of one of the royal forests.

Monsieur Maréchal walked up the gravel drive in search of the owner. Instead, he met the farmer, Renard, who agreed to give shelter and warmth to an old lady and gentleman called Monsieur and Madame Lebrun who were both very tired. The farmer regretted that his master was away for the day at Evreux.

So Marie Amélie and Louis Philippe sat down in the farmhouse kitchen. The floor was of beaten earth; there was a huge feather bed in one corner, so high that steps were needed to climb on to it; there was a black open fireplace, and on the wall a crucifix with a holy palm threaded over it.

In the centre of the room stood a long wooden table, around it a few rush stools. Renard laid before them a steaming onion soup, garlic sausage, a loaf of black bread, and a jug of strong cider. In this simple milieu they gradually regained a certain feeling of confidence and repose.

An hour later, the door opened and Monsieur Dorvilliers walked in. He stood for a moment, then exclaimed: "The King!"

Renard stared. Louis Philippe rose slightly and, looking intently at Dorvilliers: "You are mistaken, Monsieur: my name is Lebrun and this is Madame Lebrun."

"Sire, your Majesty need have no fear in this house."

There was a general sigh of relief. Louis Philippe made a sign to Dorvilliers and the farmer to sit at the table, whilst Rumigny explained their plans. When he had finished, Renard spoke.

"I wish to serve his Majesty. The King wants to go to Honfleur. I will take him there. I guarantee to get his Majesty through, but he must separate from the Queen. Together, they would be recognized. I will drive; the King will sit beside me in my cabriolet. The Queen and Monsieur le Général can take the other road in the coach. I must warn you, it is a long journey; the night is cold and it is still possible your Majesties may be recognized."

The King seemed quite indifferent to his fate, he was so tired. He merely said, "Do as you think best."

Night had fallen. Renard took a lantern and led the King to the stables. The horses were already harnessed. Pushed on one side by Renard, pulled on the other by Thuret, the monarch was hoisted into the groaning vehicle. He took his leave of the Queen, of Rumigny, of Dorvilliers, and lastly of Monsieur Maréchal. The latter was carrying two heavy sacks which he laid at the King's feet. They contained 12,000 francs.

Renard drove, with the King on his left and Thuret on his right. They crossed Evreux, not without trepidation. At the last houses of the town, near the church of St. Taurin, a group of people halted them. A man seized one of the horses by the bridle and shouted, "Hey, you! They're saying the King is making off this way." Another pushed a lantern under the King's nose. Finally, a man in some kind of uniform cried out, "It's only old Renard! I know him, citizens!" Then he whispered to Thuret, "I recognize your other companion; go quick!"

Renard whipped up his horses, and they left Evreux.

They drove all through the night, only stopping at long intervals in tavern yards, where Renard would feed the horses, and address the King in a familiar manner so that no one could suspect the King's presence. Louis Philippe pulled the black bonnet still lower on to his nose, and remained profoundly silent.

The cold was intense, a blizzard was blowing from the sea, and, as they drew nearer the coast, it became almost unbearable. The hood of the cart threatened to fly off. Now and then Thuret glanced anxiously at the King. He wondered if his master was still alive: no movement could be discerned in that huddled shape.

Towards early morning, they reached Honfleur, and Monsieur de Perthuis' house. The horses were quite done; they had covered fifty-five miles in twelve hours.

Thuret got down and rang a bell. No answer. He waited, and rang again. Still no answer, and every door tightly locked, with no sign of life anywhere, save for the wind lashing the branches of the trees.

Then, from the end of the garden, came a man holding a lantern: he told them that he was the gardener, and that Monsieur de Perthuis had sent him word that relations of his might require the house for a few days. Nothing was ready, but he would light a fire and bring some food.

Louis Philippe was almost frozen and could not move. With difficulty they helped him out of the cart, as Racine, the gardener, unlocked the door. A smell of dampness assailed them. The house consisted of four rooms, two downstairs and two attics.

The King sat before the smoky flame which Thuret managed to produce. He had no idea what the future held, how he would get to England, whether he would even reach that country. His thoughts during these hours of waiting must have been distressing: he was stealing away from his Kingship, as he had acceded to it, in fear and humiliation.

Outside, the noise of wind and rain was alarming. Meanwhile, Trouville was astir: the news of the King's flight had spread, and it was rumoured that he intended to embark there for England.

Marie Amélie and Rumigny had not arrived. Could they have been recognized? Louis Philippe kept looking at his watch, as hour by hour his anxiety increased. When, at last, the Queen came, her nerve seemed to have deserted her. She had gone through so much. They had been obliged to change their route several times, and had been stopped, questioned, searched, and now she only asked to sleep. So a narrow canvas bed was made up in the little attic room, and she slept.

But Rumigny could not rest; his mind kept searching for a means by which the King could escape. That evening he left for Trouville.

The Port of Havre

During this time, in every country in Europe the same question was being asked. Where was the King? He seemed to have vanished from the earth: was he even alive?

Queen Louise of the Belgians was almost distracted; she wrote to Queen Victoria:

> *28th February 1848*
> What an awful, overwhelming, unexpected and inexplicable catastrophe. . . . Our anguish has been indescribable; we have been thirty-six hours without any news, not knowing if my parents and the family are alive or not, and what has been their fate. . . . It was the Almighty's will, we must submit. He had decreed our loss the day he removed my beloved brother [Duc d'Orléans] from this world. Had he lived, all this would have turned otherwise. It has also been a misfortune that Joinville and Aumale were both away. They were both popular, which poor dear never-to-be-sufficiently respected Nemours was not. . . . Oh, how I long to know what has become of them. . . . Poor dear Joinville had foreseen and foretold almost all that has happened. . . . Alas, nobody would believe him.

The King of Prussia also wrote to Queen Victoria.

> *27th February 1848*
> The fate of the poor old King, of the Duchesse d'Orléans, of the whole honourable and amiable family, cuts me to the heart, for up to this time we do not know what has become of any of them. We owe Louis Philippe eighteen happy years of peace; no noble heart must forget that. And yet—who would

not recognize the avenging hand of the King of Kings in all this?

Queen Victoria to the King of the Belgians.

1st March 1848

Every hour seems to bring fresh news and events. . . . Victoire [Duchesse de Nemours] and her children and Montpensier are in Jersey, and are expected to arrive tomorrow. About the King and Queen, we still know nothing. . . .

All our poor relations have gone through is worthy only of a dreadful romance, and poor Clem[entine] behaves beautifully, courageously . . . but she can get no sleep, poor thing —and hears the horrid cries, and sees those fiend-like faces before her! . . .[1]

*　　*　　*

In a narrow room of that tiny house, Louis Philippe waited for the return of Rumigny from Trouville. Of the clamour and fear which he had unleashed in all Europe, he knew nothing.

Two days passed, then Rumigny returned. He had met a sea-captain named Barbey, who had arranged with the master of a fishing smack to take "Monsieur Lebrun" to England for 3,000 francs.

The sea was demented, and it was unthinkable that a boat should attempt to leave the harbour that night; but the sea-captain had put his brother's house in Trouville at their disposal, so that Monsieur Lebrun could seize the first opportunity to embark.

"I have visited the house myself," continued Rumigny. "It is situated in a quiet alley, away from the hustle of the town, and I believe I can guarantee the loyalty of the brothers Barbey. They are both convinced that Monsieur Lebrun is a person in danger, but they do not know that it is the King.

"Your Majesty must leave tonight. Only under cover of darkness have we a chance of entering Trouville unobserved.

"I start back immediately for Trouville, to make the final arrangements. You, Sire, will follow me by coach, and meet

---

[1] These three letters are reproduced from *The Letters of Queen Victoria.*

Captain Barbey and myself at the Parc aux Huitres outside the town at one-thirty in the morning. From there we can walk to the house."

The time came to leave. Louis Philippe drew Marie Amélie into the little room, and kissed her goodbye. For them it was a hard parting. Would they ever meet again?

Rumigny and Barbey were waiting near the Parc aux Huitres. At one-thirty they heard the carriage approaching. The two men came into the road with a lantern, and gave the signal. Racine the gardener, who was driving, stopped. Two shadows climbed out—Louis Philippe and Thuret. The carriage immediately turned back towards Honfleur, and Louis Philippe, surrounded by his small escort, started towards Trouville.

Silently, they gained the short alley. The house stood out, with its white-painted frontage shining beneath the lantern at the corner of the lane. It was a two-storeyed narrow house; the party approaching it looked like conspirators.

They must have been expected; the little door was quickly opened by a young woman, and the King found himself in a passage. For greater safety, he was asked to mount the narrow staircase into the upper room.

All the daylight hours of 29th February were passed by the monarch in that room, listening to the storm beating against the window panes. He could scarcely hear himself speak as the wind came roaring down the small alley, and even the wooden shutters could not muffle the frightening noise. Rumigny, Thuret, the brothers Barbey, came in and out, and, to the anxious question in his eyes, their answer was ever "It is getting worse!"

The next morning (1st March), although the wind and rain still beat against the house, there were signs that the storm was abating. Captain Barbey arrived to announce that he had arranged for Monsieur Lebrun to embark that night at seven o'clock precisely.

The King could not resist saying, "Monsieur Barbey, the King of the French will ever be grateful for your great kindness

and friendship." Thus Barbey learned the real identity of
Monsieur Lebrun.

At six o'clock, the King had donned again his old overcoat,
his black bonnet, and his spectacles. The certainty that his
ordeal was nearly over had revived him. He smiled, joked,
and tried to comfort poor Thuret, who was terrified and kept
moaning, "I shall never see my family again. I cannot even
swim!"

The King listened; someone was running up the stairs. He
turned to Thuret: "Quick! They have come to take us to the
ship."

The door opened, and Barbey burst in. "Sire, we are betrayed: the people have learned that high personages are hiding
in this house. So far they do not suspect that it is your Majesty.
They imagine that it is Monsieur Guizot and other Ministers.

"The Commissaire of Police is coming to search this place.
Your Majesty must leave at once."

"This does not prevent my embarking tonight," exclaimed
the King.

"It does, Sire, the coast is closely watched. But there is not
a second to be lost. I am here to accompany your Majesty to
the house of my friend, Monsieur Billard, which for the moment
is free from suspicion."

Rumigny interrupted, "Sire, this may be a trap."

The King looked enquiringly at Barbey, who retorted: "I
can only assure your Majesty that you have no more devoted
servant than I. But believe me, Sire, we must leave at once. I
only hope we are not too late. Monsieur Guittier is downstairs,
waiting to escort your Majesty. He was until lately Mayor of
Trouville, and I can answer for his loyalty."

This decided the King. Followed by Rumigny and Thuret,
Barbey leading the way, Louis Philippe hurried down the
narrow stairs, Rumigny loading his pistol as he went. A man
was standing in the doorway of the kitchen. Rumigny instantly
raised his weapon, but Barbey said quickly, "This is Monsieur
Guittier," and cautiously the party left the house.

Barbey insisted on complete silence; no lantern or light could
be carried, but he knew the way blindfold.

The lane, as yet, was quite empty. Louis Philippe gave his arm to Guittier, and Rumigny held a tail of the King's coat with one hand, whilst the other gripped the pistol in his pocket.

Then came Barbey, and the valet Thuret carrying a bundle containing woollen socks, handkerchiefs, and a white wool shawl with a pink edging which the Queen had worked for her husband.

The darkness, wind and rain made the King stumble. He wept; he mumbled without ceasing, about his children. He was being led he knew not where. God! When would all this end?

At last, drenched again, Louis Philippe and his companions reached Monsieur Billard's house. It was in total darkness. The door was ajar. Guittier, who was leading, pushed it open, and they groped their way down the corridor. Rumigny had placed himself behind Guittier, and was holding his pistol between the latter's shoulder-blades. In this manner, they penetrated into the salon, and at last a candle was brought by the owner of the house, Dr. Billard.

It was a moving moment. The King sat in the only armchair of a provincial doctor's consulting room. A few men were assembled round him, so honoured by his presence, ready to risk their lives for him, waiting for his orders—and he had none to give.

Monsieur Guittier invited him to go upstairs, to a room where he could pass the night. Blankets had been nailed across the window, so that no sign of life could be perceived from the street.

After a moment, the King noticed that the owner of the house had disappeared. He asked, "Where is the good doctor?"

"Sire, he is sitting in a café, crowded with the more excitable elements of the town. He is ostensibly reading a newspaper and sipping a glass of Calvados, so unconcerned, that no one could imagine that at this moment he is sheltering the King."

An hour later, Billard returned to his house. He came up to Guittier and spoke quietly: "The King must leave Trouville immediately. All Trouville knows that important fugitives are trying to embark for England. The King could not possibly leave this house in daylight without being recognized. His only chance of safety is to return to Honfleur now."

At midnight, with infinite precautions, the King, Rumigny, Guittier, Billard, and the faithful Thuret, walked out of the house. The rain had ceased, but the wind was still blowing hard. The population, notwithstanding their curiosity, seemed to have gone home. The Place Bellevue was deserted.

In order not to arouse suspicion, two carriages were waiting some way out of the town. Louis Philippe lagged with fatigue: the journey this time seemed twice as long. Two days ago, it had been filled with hope, and now it was filled with a feeling of failure and defeat.

In the early morning, they reached Honfleur. The King stopped the carriage, thanked Monsieur Guittier, and bade him rest in the town, while he would walk to the Pavillon.[1]

The Queen was dressing when he arrived: she heard his voice from her bedroom, and she ran down the stairs only half-clothed, laughing and crying at the same time, crazy with relief and joy.

Later, she told Rumigny that the last three days had held some of the greatest suffering in her life. "Almost," she added, "as deep as that of 1830, when my husband became King."

She added, "You, General, who have followed our destiny through all these years, tell me—are these terrifying trials which overwhelm us, the avenging hand of God?"

Rumigny had no reply.

On 2nd March, about eleven in the morning, a loud thump at the door shook the small house. Trembling, the valet Thuret went to open. A stranger stood before him.

"The British Consul at le Havre, Mr. Featherstonhaugh, has instructed me to find the King, and to bring him a message. Can his Majesty receive me?"

---

[1] Louis Guittier describes the events at Trouville in a pamphlet entitled "Récit de l'arrivée, du séjour, et du départ de S.M. le Roi Louis Philippe à Trouville-sur-Mer", published with the *Souvenirs* of General de Rumigny.

The King saw the agent for half an hour, while he listened to the Consul's plan.

It was proposed that their Majesties should gain the port of le Havre, on the other side of the Seine estuary, where he had chartered the British steamer the *Express*, in the hope that it would convey them that night to England.

It was a bold plan, as it meant that they must cross the estuary by the public ferry, where they might be recognized, and the ports of Honfleur and le Havre were teeming with gendarmes.

Their Majesties must take stringent precautions; first, they must travel separately: during the whole journey, the King, the Queen, and the members of their suite must on no account recognize each other.

His Majesty would travel as a Mr. Smith, uncle of Mr. Featherstonhaugh. He would be provided with a passport, and with a cap and check tweed ulster, in which he would look like a travelling Englishman. He would be escorted by Mr. Jones, the Vice-Consul.

Marie Amélie, as Mrs. Smith, would be in the care of a Monsieur Bresson. Thuret, Rumigny, and Mademoiselle Müser the maid, would go on board the ferry separately, mixed with the crowd. At the landing of le Havre the Consul would meet them, and contrive to get them to the ship.

While Louis Philippe listened to these arrangements, the Consul was making preparations at le Havre. He "confided" to the worst gossips of the town that the King and Queen had sailed from Tréport in a fishing smack on the previous evening. He also ordered two of his clerks to go to the quay of le Havre, pick a quarrel, and stage a fight, to draw the attention of the gendarmes at the critical moment.

Finally, he instructed Captain Paul of the *Express* to get up steam at eight o'clock, ready to cast off and sail as soon as Mr. and Mrs. Smith arrived on board.

The success of the plan depended upon not a slip being made.

The ferry boat from Honfleur docked at the quayside of le Havre at seven-thirty in the evening of 2nd March 1848. Standing among the evening idlers, Mr. Featherstonhaugh was watching the swarm of passengers landing with their bags, pigs, poultry and all the chattels bought at Honfleur market that day.

Amongst them was a portly Englishman holding a white handkerchief, the agreed sign. The Consul stepped forward to meet him, calling out: "My dear Uncle, I am delighted to see you!"

The portly gentleman answered: "My dear George, I am glad you are here."

Perhaps the voice was unnaturally loud.

A little way behind, several people followed: they all seemed strangers to one another. The Consul took his uncle's arm and, walking thus, they crossed the quay. Unfortunately, the uncle would talk in loud tones; several people turned their heads and stared. An oldish lady followed them; she kept covering her face with her handkerchief. People pitied her, she was crying. They thought, "she is leaving a dear one". They were right; she was leaving all.

A woman porter, leaning against some packages, was watching the bizarre Englishman with the sonorous voice. Where had she seen him before? Suddenly, she clapped her hand to her forehead, and ran to warn a port official.

"Look!"—she pointed at the figures mounting the gang-plank of the *Express*—"It is the King!!"

Wasting no time, the official hurried over to the ship and leapt on board as the little group of passengers were disappearing below.

"I demand to search this ship!" he panted.

"Certainly," said Captain Paul, "but you will have to go with us to England, as it is now eight o'clock, and we are casting off at once."

The official had only time to jump ashore.[1]

A few seconds later, through the open door of their cabin, the King and Marie Amélie heard the command:

"Let go!"

As the ship slowly moved away from the quayside, Louis Philippe walked to the doorway, and stood facing the land of

[1] The escape is described by Mr. Featherstonhaugh himself, in a letter to Lord Palmerston published in *The Letters of Queen Victoria*.

France. He raised his hand in a gesture: was it the same gesture which Charles X had made eighteen years ago?

A farewell sign of the Cross!

On the quay, the frustrated official asked Mr. Featherston-haugh: "Who were those people?"

"My uncle and aunt."

"Ah, Monsieur le Consul—what have you done!"

"What you would have done in my place."

As one looks back to 1830, and remembers the royal pageantry which accompanied Charles X to the coast; neither threats nor force could hasten his dignified progress. At Cherbourg he still commanded the situation, and insisted that no Tricolor flags or emblems should be visible.

And that last scene of all, when, as he stood on the deck of the ship, his troops presenting arms, he gave the order, "Raise the anchor!"

In vivid contrast, Louis Philippe, like a hunted rat fled in disguise, hiding in dark corners, fearing discovery, and at last forced to leave his Kingdom as "Mister Smith".

Envoi

The Duc de Nemours to Queen Victoria.

Claremont, 26th August 1850

Madame my dear Cousin,

The hand of God has brought us deep sorrow. The King our Father is no more. After having received yesterday with peace and resignation the benefit of religion, he passed away this morning at eight o'clock, surrounded by us all. You who knew him, my dear Cousin, will realize all that we are losing, you will understand the inexpressible grief with which we are overwhelmed. You partake in it, I feel sure!

The Queen is broken, notwithstanding her great courage, and only finds relief in solitude, in which she can give vent to her sorrow.

Will you kindly inform Albert of our great loss, and receive here, my dear Cousin, the homage of respect and attachment of your affectionate Cousin,

LOUIS D'ORLÉANS

Queen Victoria to Viscount Palmerston.

Osborne, 26th August 1850

The Queen wishes Lord Palmerston to give directions for a Court mourning according to those which are usual for an abdicated King. She likewise wishes that every assistance should be given, and every attention shown to the afflicted Royal Family who have been so severely tried during the last two years, on the melancholy occasion of the poor King of the French's death.

The Queen starts for Scotland tomorrow.

Thus expired, in his seventy-seventh year, a man who had been a royal prince, a Jacobin, a vagabond, a teacher of mathematics, a King, and finally a fugitive.

Coppins Cottage
21st January 1957

Bibliography

Duchesse d'Abrantès: *Mémoires.*
Th. Anne: *Journal de Saint-Cloud à Cherbourg.* 2 vols.
France and its King, Court and Government, by an American (anonymous).
R. Arnaud: *Adélaïde d'Orléans.*
S. Berard: *Souvenirs Historiques de la Révolution de 1830.*
J. Bertaut: *Louis Philippe Bourgeois.*
L. Blanc: *Histoire de Dix Ans.*
Comtesse de Boigne: *Mémoires.* 4 vols. Librairie Plon.
M. A. Boullée: *Etudes Biographiques sur Louis Philippe.*
Duc de Broglie: *Souvenirs.*
R. Burnand: *La Vie Quotidienne en France en 1830.*
M. du Camp: *Souvenirs d'un Demi-Siècle.*
H. Castille: *Les Hommes et les Mœurs sous le Règne de Louis Philippe.*
F. R. de Chateaubriand: *Mémoires d'Outre-Tombe.*
Wm. Connely: *Count d'Orsay.*
Duff Cooper: *Talleyrand.*
Creevey, selected and re-edited by John Gore.
A. Cremieux: *La Révolution de Fevrier 1848.*
Crowe: *Louis Philippe et Charles X.*
Duchesse de Dino: *Chronique.* 3 vols.
Dosne (Mme): *Mémoires.* 2 vols.
A. Dumas: *Mémoires.*
C. C. Dyson: *Marie Amélie.*
Elliott (Mrs.): *Journals of My Life During the French Revolution.*
P. d'Espezel: *Le Palais Royal.*
R. Field: *All This and Heaven Too.*
Marquis de Flers: *Le Roi Louis Philippe. Vie Anecdotique.*
Cuvillier Fleury: *Grands Hommes.*
    Journal. 4 vols.
R. Fulford: *George IV.*
C. Gavin: *Louis Philippe, King of the French.*
Comtesse de Genlis: *Mémoires.*
P. de la Gorce: *Charles X.*
    Louis Philippe.
F. de Groisellier: *La Chute de Louis Philippe.*
P. Gruyer: *Jeunesse de Louis Philippe.*
L. Guittier: *Récit de l'arrivée, du séjour, et du départ de S.M. le Roi Louis Philippe
    à Trouville-sur-Mer.*
F. Guizot: *France under Louis Philippe.*
    Last Days of Louis Philippe.

Mémoires de la Reine Hortense, edited by Prince Napoleon.

Victor Hugo: *Choses Vues.*

Lady Jackson: *The Court of the Tuileries.* 2 vols.

J. C. Jeafferson: *The Queen of Naples and Lord Nelson.*
Lady Hamilton and Lord Nelson.

Prince de Joinville: *Vieux Souvenirs.*

Knight (Miss): Autobiography. 2 vols.

A. de Lamartine: *Histoire de la Révolution de 1848.*

Duc de Lauzun: *Vie.*

E. Lavisse: *Histoire de France Contemporaine.*

G. Lenôtre: *The Tuileries.*

Princess Lieven: *Private Letters.*

D. Loth: *Lafayette.*

Louis Philippe: *Journal.*
Correspondance, Mémoires et Discours Inédits.

J. Lucas-Dubreton: *Louis Philippe.*
Charles X.

Baron de Maricourt: *Madame de Souza et sa Famille.*

Maréchal Marmont: *Mémoires.*

L. Ménard: *Prologue d'une Révolution.*

P. Merimée: *Lettres à la Comtesse de Montijo.*

L. Michaud: *Biographie de Louis Philippe.*

A. Nougarède: *La Vérité sur la Révolution de Fevrier.*

V. de Nouvion: *Histoire du Règne de Louis Philippe.*

Journal de Marie Amélie, Duchesse d'Orléans, edited by S.A.R. Madame la
Duchesse de Vendôme. 3 vols. Librairie Plon.

E. Pelletan: *Histoire des Trois Journées de Fevrier 1848.*

Comtesse Potocka: *Mémoires.*

A. Pravel: *Vie de S.A.R. Madame la Duchesse de Berri.*

Princesse Antoine Radziwill: *Souvenirs.*

M. Recouly: *Louis Philippe, Roi des Français.*

de Rémusat (Mme): *Mémoires.*

Général Comte de Rumigny: *Souvenirs,* edited by R. M. Gouraud
d'Ablancourt.

George Sand: *Histoire de ma Vie.*

Prince de Talleyrand: *Mémoires.*

A. de Tocqueville: *Œuvres et Correspondance.*

Trognon: *La Vie de Marie Amélie.*

H.M. Queen Victoria: *Letters.*

Vigée Lebrun: *Souvenirs.* 3 vols.

C. Yriarté: *Les Princes d'Orléans.*

Index